Still Foolin' 'Em

Still Foolin' 'Em

Where I've Been, Where I'm Going, and Where the Hell Are My Keys?

BILLY CRYSTAL

St. Martin's Griffin New York

Photograph credits:

p. 97: Courtesy of Broadway Video Enterprises and NBC Studios, Inc. p. 102: Courtesy of MGM Media Licensing © 1986 Metro-Goldwyn-Mayer Studios Inc., All Rights Reserved. p. 107: NBC / NBC Universal / Getty Images. p. 110: Courtesy of Peter Montagna. p. 111: Jeff Kravitz / Getty Images. p. 140: Ken Regan / Camera 5. p. 151: *City Slickers* – Licensed By: Warner Bros. Entertainment Inc. p. 153: *City Slickers* – Licensed By: Warner Bros. Entertainment Inc. p. 155: © Academy of Motion Picture Arts and Sciences. p. 159: *Mr. Saturday Night* – Licensed By: Warner Bros. Entertainment Inc. p. 171: *Analyze This* – Licensed By: Warner Bros. Entertainment Inc. p. 178: © Academy of Motion Picture Arts and Sciences. p. 190: Getty Images. p. 192: © Berliner Photography. p. 239: J. Meric / Getty Image Sport / Getty Images.

www.stmartins.com

Designed by Meryl Sussman Levavi

The Library of Congress has cataloged the Henry Holt edition as follows:

Crystal, Billy.
Still foolin' 'em : where I've been, where I'm going, and where the hell are my keys? / Billy Crystal. — First edition.
    p. cm.
ISBN 978-0-8050-9820-4 (hardcover)
ISBN 978-0-8050-9823-5 (e-book)
1. Crystal, Billy.   2. Comedians—United States—Biography.   3. Aging.
I. Title.   II. Title: Still fooling them.
PN2287.C686A3 2013
792.702'8092—dc23
[B]   2013012238

ISBN 978-1-250-05184-4 (trade paperback)

St. Martin's Griffin books may be purchased for educational, business, or promotional use. For information on bulk purchases, please contact Macmillan Corporate and Premium Sales Department at 1-800-221-7945, extension 5442, or write specialmarkets@macmillan.com.

First published by Henry Holt and Company, LLC

First St. Martin's Griffin Edition: October 2014

10   9   8   7   6   5   4   3   2   1

For Janice

Contents

Still Foolin' 'Em

65 Is Not 60

March 14, 2013, my sixty-fifth birthday. I got up that morning, padded over to the bathroom, threw some water on my face, looked in the mirror, and my uncle Al was staring back at me. My scream brought Janice, my wife of forty-two years, running in. I kept yelling, "HOLY SHIT! What the fuck happened to me?" Somehow, overnight it seemed, I had turned from a hip, cool baby boomer into a Diane Arbus photograph. I looked at Janice for an encouraging word, for a hug, for an "It's okay, Billy, you look great. It's an old mirror." All she did was glance down at my robe, which had opened up, and ask: "When did your pubic hair turn gray?"

It's hard to believe. Not the part about the pubic hair or that my package now looks like Einstein with Barry Scheck's nose. It's the part about how it's really happening. And fast. As a kid, I was drawn to the dark side of things. I knew at a young age that no one gets out of this alive, but it seemed that I had time. Back in 1961, when I was thirteen, I would think, *In 1978 I'll be thirty. Great, that's so far away.* Then when I was thirty I thought, *In 1998 I'll be fifty and that's so far away.* Now that I'm sixty-five I think, *In the year 2038 I'll be . . . mostly dead.* Or as Miracle Max in *The Princess Bride* would say, "Slightly alive."

There's some comfort in knowing that there are so many of us boomers in the same boat. Truth is, very soon, the entire country is pretty much going to smell the same, from Los Angeles to Maine. We are all in this together and are all having the same thought: I FUCKING HATE THIS! There are seventy-seven million of us in this age group, and with all our diversity, we have one thing in common: OUR PARENTS WERE RIGHT! It all happened so fast.

During the past year I saw my dermatologist more than I saw my grandkids. Things started to grow on me where they shouldn't. My ass looks like the bottom of a boat. I don't shower anymore; I'm sandblasted twice a week. I'm always at the dermatologist's. He keeps picking at me; I'm like his own personal honey-baked ham.

Don't get me wrong, I'm not here to bitch and moan. . . . Wait, I am, but I'm trying to answer the really fundamental questions of life: Where are we as baby boomers? Where are we going? Where have we been? Did anything we do really matter? If there's an afterlife, do they have digital cable? What's next for us? Do the Yankees have enough pitching? Why does God make everything small that should be big and everything big that should be small? Like my nuts, why are they now HUGE? Every time I sit on the toilet, I make tea with my balls. Thank you, God, put that and the Nazis on your greatest hits album.

The whole idea of sixty-five is scary, because I'm now closer to (gulp) seventy than I am to sixty, but to me, fear has always been a motivator. America's kids are plump and out of shape, but not me. Have you been to Disneyland lately? It's not a small world after all. It's a big, fat, sweaty-ass-crack world. I, on the other hand, eat organic food, I juice, I work out, and I take comfort in the fact that my sixty-five is not my grandparents' sixty-five.

When my grandfather was sixty-five he looked eighty . . . and he smelled ninety.

....

We all have a different image of what old is, and if you were exposed to senior citizens at a young age, as I was, and they told you, "One day you'll look like this," it can color your soul with terror. For me, old is my grandfather, coming to visit in his Bermuda shorts hiked up to his tits, and wearing black socks and sandals, and when he would sit down you could see what looked like a small dog in his pants surrounded by a bag of pears. Terrifying. I never wanted to look like that, so I push myself.

At sixty-five I can do the same things I could do at thirty-five, if I could only remember what those things were. At sixty-five things do change . . . quickly.

For one thing, your libido slows down. You don't kid yourself and look at twenty-five-year-olds anymore. Actually, I do, but they're out of focus, and by the time I get my glasses on, they're gone. When you're sixty-five, you're surprised by what now turns you on. You look at Dame Edna and think, *You know what, maybe.*

At sixty-five, when you go out to eat and tell the family that dinner is on you, you mean it literally. It's on your chin, on your shirt, on your pants. You're usually wearing more than you ate. At sixty-five, you've already had ten colonoscopies. My colon has been photographed more than the fucking *Titanic.* And it's horrible, because we fear the colonoscopy, we're terrified of it. For me, I never enter a door marked EXIT. It's the fear of the procedure with the camera and the whole nine yards going up there. It's going to be painful, but as they say, it's not the camera that hurts, it's the crew. For those who haven't had it, let me explain what a colonoscopy is. Basically, you're driving north on a southbound highway . . . if you catch my drift . . . and the drift comes after the procedure. I'm telling you, they fill you with hot air. I was literally a hybrid car, I was half gas. You're like a walking whoopee cushion.

The key to having a happy time as you develop chicken hands is you just have to stay upbeat and optimistic, even as you're trying to make your comb-over not look like Rudy Giuliani circa 1999. Stay positive! I hate seeing guys give up when they turn sixty-five. Just go to the mall. There are the wives, with the husbands trailing behind them. Poor guys, they have no shoulders. They look like paramecia in suburban coats. They're just following their wives around the shopping mall, getting excited only when they can have a new front door key made at the locksmith kiosk. They drift around the mall, drifting, drifting, drifting. It's like the march of the very depressed penguins; they're walking—it's not even a walk, it's a waddle, it's a shuffle, it's a wuffle. They just wander around the mall with their wives leading them, and they're holding the wife's coat in one hand and her pocketbook with the other. And you know what's in her pocketbook?

Their balls.

At sixty-five, you're always a little cold. Even the new thicket of hair on your back doesn't help. You start to think, *Global warming isn't such a bad thing.* Global warming isn't the only inconvenient truth. The real inconvenient truth is that I now pee in Morse code. Am I painting a pretty picture?

Which gets me to my most important point, the one thing I want you to take from this book, because it can change your life. It's this: that if you're feeling what I'm feeling, don't worry because . . . wait, I forgot what I was going to say, what was I talking about . . . give me a minute. Shit! Damn it, I hate when this happens. Oh well, I'll remember sometime before the book is done. . . . Hey, where are my keys?

I Worry

One thing is constant for me. Every night I go to sleep at eleven. I wake up refreshed, ready to go, full of energy, look at the clock, and it's one-ten A.M.

Hi, I'm Billy and I'm an insomniac. Right now, I've been up since 1948. It actually started back when I was born: First seven days, perfect. I was doing great, sleeping in, clocking twenty hours a night. Then day 8, they woke me up and somebody with a black hat and a beard cut off the tip of my penis. I've been up ever since.

Insomnia, from the Greek word meaning "I can't fucking sleep!" Ah, sleep . . . to sleep, perchance to dream—ay, there's the rub. I tried rubbing it. Nothing. My penis looked at me and said, "Are you trying to start a fire?" So now I'm awake and I feel like a fool. Guys, at our age, masturbating is the worst type of high school reunion. You're with your first love, who looks older and smaller, there's no real excitement, and ultimately you're sorry you came.

"Did you sleep well, did you sleep?" I tell people I sleep like a baby: I'm up every two hours. And it's so lonely when you can't sleep and your spouse can. Sometimes when I wake up, I fake nightmares, just so I have someone to talk to. "Don't—no, no, put the gun down, no!"

"Honey, you okay?"

"Yeah, I'm okay, it was just a bad dream. You want to play cards?"

I feel bad about waking Janice up, but it's better than watching her sleep in that middle-aged way with the occasional snore. Men hate when women snore. It's a double standard: we men fart, cough up things and spit them in the street, we pick our noses while we drive and, if we're alone, wipe it on the bottom part of the seat, we pee in the shower and on the golf course. Come on, guys, admit it: we all pee in the shower because it feels so good, but if a woman snores, we're ready to get a lawyer. We're Vikings at the social tea of life.

So I've tried everything to fall asleep. I tried the glass of red wine before bed for a few months. I still couldn't sleep, and I ended up in Betty Ford. Then I got one of those sound effects machines that creates the experience of being on the beach. My model is called Coney Island. It has waves, weeping Mets fans, and gunfire. They say it works because the sound of rushing water makes you want to go to sleep. It made me want to pee. Now I have another problem.

Getting up quietly in the middle of the night is a challenge. I'm groggy and walk to the john with all the grace of Buzz Aldrin doing the tango on *Dancing with the Stars*. Once I get to the bathroom, I don't want to stand up and pee because God hasn't messed with my stream today and the noise will wake everybody up as I yell, "That's what I'm talking about!" So I decide to sit down, and I fall in because some schmuck (who would be me) forgot to put the seat down.

You know why we can't sleep? It's because we think. The brain doesn't shut off; there's a little factory going all night. We never think about good things, only the bad things we've done.

The regrets. When you can't sleep, every night is Yom Kippur. "Why did I say that to that schmuck? Okay, he was a schmuck, but why did I say that? After all, he is the pope."

So I try to calm down by eating. They say turkey makes you drowsy because it has tryptophan. If it works so well, how come you never see a turkey nod off? I have a turkey sandwich and a warm glass of milk—and once you have milk, you gotta have a cookie. Now I still can't sleep and my cholesterol is at 800.

I'm so upset, I try to watch some TV. That late at night, it's all commercials aimed at my age group. First one I see is for a sleeping aid called Rozerem. That's the one where they say "your dreams miss you" and they show Abe Lincoln talking to a beaver.

They said it's the first sleep aid with no potential for dependence. Really? If I'm taking a drug that makes me dream about Lincoln talking to a beaver, I'm taking that five times a day.

Next comes the onslaught. Every ad is for beer, big fat hamburgers, Rogaine, and Viagra. They think we're all one fat bald guy who can't get it up.

But at least the new impotency ads are aimed at women. Now they show a really hot woman in her forties; she has that happy, contented look we've all forgotten, like she's just made love for hours. And then the guy comes into the bedroom, the guy who had the problem. He looks like a middle-aged model (or Mitt Romney), he's got perfect hair, a great smile, a sweater tied around his neck, and at the end of the ad he and the wife are on a little boat that has the biggest mast you've ever seen in your life. I'm not stupid; I get it.

Then there's that Cialis ad where they say you take it and it lasts for thirty-six hours. You can have sex anytime in that thirty-six-hour window. That's way too much pressure for me. We're a fast-paced society: we want things now, we have instant Internet, instant messages, we want instant sex, not thirty-six-hour Cialis. Thirty-six hours is more than my whole history of sex. Cialis is a bad pill for us Jews. "Irving, take this pill, it's good for thirty-six hours." He says, "That's over the whole year, right? Can I redeem hours if I don't use them? Can I trade them in for that set of dishes?"

But at least the Cialis ads are done well. The original Viagra ads were terrible. They were all athletes, prominent people revealing that they suffer from ED. The idea is if it can happen to them, it can happen to anybody. Even Mike Ditka and Bob Dole did impotence commercials. I applaud them for admitting this personal problem, but honestly, the thought of them with erections is enough to make *me* impotent.

Whatever the affliction, they make the commercials look so beautiful. These people have real problems and in thirty seconds it's all solved, there are butterflies and bike rides and people walking their puppies, whatever they have is cured, their prostates are shrinking, their bones aren't brittle, their hairlines are back, and I'm filled with hope. Then right at the end of the commercial that voice comes on and quickly says . . .

"May cause lack of appetite, dizziness, nervousness, psychotic episodes, blurred vision, stuttering, skipping and jumping, Tourette's syndrome, barking at the moon, bile backup, speaking in tongues, anal leakage, diarrhea, and impotence." And I'm thinking, *Okay, who cares? I have to get some sleep!*

I get sick of all the commercials, so I change the channel. Now I'm watching high-speed car chases at three A.M. That'll put you right out. Might as well have a double espresso. In Los Angeles, car chases do bigger ratings than *CSI*. They're the original reality TV. I'm watching a car going the wrong way on the freeway, then it's going ninety through a school zone, it hits a fence, the suspect is out of the car now, running, the TV camera is in the chopper overhead as the perp, now in a dramatic spotlight, runs through backyards and jumps fences. Personally, I think it's the best work Lindsay Lohan has ever done.

So I go back to bed. I toss and turn and turn and toss and just can't get comfortable. Then finally I find the right position, the pillow is nice and cool, and I fall asleep. Five minutes later, the alarm goes off: time to start the day.

Now I get up and I'm cranky. I'm Jeffrey Dahmer and there's nothing in the fridge. I'm overtired. *Overtired.* The excuse every mother gives for a nasty kid. "Why did he light the garage on fire?" "He's . . . overtired." "Why did he do that, Mrs. Hitler?" "He vas overtired, just a little cranky, he didn't sleep vell in the 1920s."

I'm up all night because I worry; I worry about everything. Like the fact that I'm not fucking asleep.

- I worry about the axis of evil: Syria, North Korea, and Wall Street CEOs.
- I worry that if I'm ever arrested and go to prison, I'll like anal rape.
- I worry that one day my kids will look down at me and say to each other, "I changed him last time, it's your turn."
- I worry that Scientologists may be right.
- I worry that I'm writing this chapter via texting while driv—
- I worry that the paramedics will not speak English and won't be able to read the words PLEASE RESUSCITATE I have tattooed on my chest.
- I worry that I am not worried about my grandkids being stuck with the national debt.
- I worry that playing Angry Birds for thirty hours a week may not qualify as aerobics.
- I worry that I'll die while too many of the people I hate are still alive.

But the one thing I don't worry about is dying in my sleep. Because I never sleep! When the angel of death comes to my bedside and puts his hand out for me, I'm going to look him right in the eye and say, "Get the fuck out of here." Then Janice will tell him, "Don't listen to Billy—he's overtired, he's a little cranky."

Sex

've always thought that the key to a good sex life is variety. That's why God gave me two hands.

Humans love sex, we need sex, it's how we connect, it reminds us we're alive, it's the third most basic human need, after food and good movie popcorn, but over time the need changes, as does the act itself.

If you're twenty-five, you're probably reading this chapter in between your third and fourth go-arounds of the night. If you're forty-five, statistically you had sex sometime in the last three nights and will have it again another 5.8 times this month . . . but if you're sixty-five . . . HEY, WAKE UP . . . if you're sixty-five, certain conditions need to be just right in order to do the nasty. She can't be having a hot flash, he can't have had too much asparagus, dinner had to be light and over by four-thirty, and there can't be a new episode of *Homeland* on that night. Also, your cell phone has to be on Vibrate, not so you don't hear it, but it adds a nice sensation if you sit on it just right.

When you're young, all you ever think about is the next time you're going to have sex; when you get older, you can't remember the last time you had sex.

Let's eavesdrop on a couple I will call Him and Her. They were twenty-five in 1973; now they're sixty-five.

1973

HIM: I love when you do that.

HER: You mean tighten it like this?

HIM: Oh my God, how do you do that?

HER: Punji, my yoga instructor . . . he taught me.

2013

HIM: Wow, you're so wet down there.

HER: Oh sorry—I coughed before.

1973

HER: What do you want to fuck to?

HIM: Marvin Gaye.

2013

HER: Move a little bit to the right and turn up the sound on the TV.

HIM: I can't hear you, the TV is on. . . . Oops, I'm done.

1973

HIM: Look at you, you're so beautiful.

HER: Awwwww.

2013

HIM: I can't believe these tits.

HER: Stop looking in the mirror and come to bed.

1973

> HIM: God, I'm hard.
> HER: God, you're hard.

2013

> HER: Did you take your Viagra?
> HIM: What?
> HER: God, you're hard of hearing.
> HIM: You lost an earring?

1973

> HIM: Why are your eyes open?
> HER: Because I love to watch you make love to me.

2013

> HIM: What are you looking at?
> HER: The drapes don't match the paint.

1973

> HER: Let's stay home and make love.
> HIM: I love rainy days.

2013

> HER: Let's make love . . .
> HIM: My hip hurts, it's going to rain.

1973

> HER: Wow, that must be eight inches.
> HIM: Wait until I get excited.

2013

> HER: Wow, that's so hard . . .
> HIM: The doctor said it's benign.

1973

> HER: I love to feel your heartbeat through your shirt.
> HIM: Every beat is for you.

2013

> HER: Maybe it's your pacemaker.
>
> HIM: Call 911, I'm having palpitations.

1973

> HIM: Now, now!
>
> HER: I'm there, I'm there!

2013

> HER: Now, now!
>
> HIM: Be patient—Larry at the barbershop says it takes thirty minutes to work because first the blood has to accumulate in the shaft.

1973

> HIM (whispering): Tell me what you want me to do.
>
> HER (sotto voce): Put your finger in there.
>
> HIM: Wow, I've never done that.
>
> HER: It's wonderful.

2013

> HIM: Tell me what you want me to do.
>
> HER: Get me my vibrator and go for a walk.

1973

> HIM: Wear something sexy to bed.
>
> HER: How about just a smile?

2013

> HIM: Have you seen my sweatpants?
>
> HER: They're in the drawer. And wear some socks, your toenails cut my leg.

1973

> HIM: Let's do something we've never done before.
>
> HER: Turn me over, baby.

2013

   Him: Can we try something new?
   Her: Oy.

Oy. A universal word that sums up how you feel when you hit sixty-five. Many people have said "Oy." I think it was Custer's last word when he saw all those Sioux Indians on the hill. Oy: it was what King Kong mumbled when he saw those planes buzzing him on the Empire State Building—until the studio cut it out because they thought it made him sound too Jewish. Oy: it was what Osama bin Laden said when he saw the Navy SEAL at the bottom of the stairs. Oy: it is what life is like at sixty-five . . . and as I approached my sixty-fifth birthday, I couldn't help but think, *How the hell did I get here?*

Growing Up Crystal

"You know how angry kids will sometimes say, 'I didn't ask to be born'? Well, you did," my mother used to tell me. "Your brothers took hours to arrive—not you. Thirty minutes, tops. Around my eighth month you started kicking a lot and I thought I could hear you saying, 'Let's go, I'm breaking your water.'"

On March 14, 1948, at 7:36 A.M., I arrived at Doctors Hospital in Manhattan, overlooking Gracie Mansion and the East River. I am the youngest of Jack and Helen's three boys. My brother Richard, known as Rip, is two years older than I, and Joel, my big brother— literally: he's six foot two—is six years older. We lived on Davidson Avenue in the Bronx until the lure of the suburbs seduced my parents, who had a dream to own a house with a lawn the size of a toupee. My folks followed my grandparents, who were perpetually not well and whose doctor had advised that the salty sea air of Long Beach, Long Island, a lovely, quaint beach town, would do

Long Beach, 1953.

wonders for them. Not true: they were always sick, and anything metal they owned, including my grandfather's hip, rusted quickly.

My grandmother Susie Gabler was a large woman of Russian heritage, weighing in at over two hundred pounds, and my grandpa Julius was a diminutive, cranky Austrian who had twin albino brothers. Tiny little pink Jewish elves we called the lab rats. Very rare, they would fetch a grand sum on eBay today. They usually wore woolly three-piece suits, and when they stood together they looked like salt and pepper shakers. Grandma, who loved to laugh, was the dominant force in the family and actually is credited on Wikipedia with inventing guilt. For instance, once she asked my mom to take her to a doctor's appointment, and when Mom said she couldn't, Grandma responded, "I bought your house for you." She also put the fear of God in me, literally. If any of us did something she felt was wrong, she'd tell us, "God will punish you." One time when I was about six, she told me not to skip. I did anyhow and fell, and she said, "See, God punished you." Terrifying. Grandpa was slowed by arthritis and crankitis. He and

I understood each other. He was in pain a lot, and I was pissed that I was short. Yes, I had a case of little guy's disease for a while. It ended about a week ago, when I finally understood that my big "spurt" had already happened.

Nonetheless, Growing Up Crystal was a great time. My dad was the manager of a popular record store in New York City, called the Commodore Music Shop, which was owned by Grandpa Julius and his sons Milt and Danny. Milt had transformed the place from a hardware store into the center of jazz in Manhattan when he got rid of the light bulbs and whisk brooms Grandpa was ped-dling and created Commodore Records, the first independent jazz label of its time, and sold hot jazz records that he produced him-self. When Milt left to become an executive at Decca Records, my

Sixth grade at East School. On to junior high.

dad took over as manager and became the go-to guy for jazz enthusiasts. He also produced jazz concerts on the weekends at a place called the Central Plaza, on Second Avenue in Manhattan. Dad turned all of us on to jazz, and its great stars were family friends. It was also Dad who saw how much I loved being funny and would let me stay up on school nights to watch the great comedians of the fifties on television. It was Dad who brought home comedy albums from the store so I could listen and learn. And it was my mom and dad whom I most loved to make laugh.

My mom was our rock. Dad worked six days a week at two jobs, so much of our time was spent with her. She was a funny and graceful woman who could sing and tap-dance and was always the life of the party. In her twenties, she worked at Macy's, where she was in the store's theater group, and she was often the voice of Minnie Mouse in the Thanksgiving Day Parade.

Uncle Milt was the celebrity of the family. A force in the music industry, he produced more than thirty records that sold over a million copies each, including "Rock Around the Clock." He worked with stars such as Sammy Davis Jr., Bing Crosby, and Nat King Cole. But it was my uncle Berns, my dad's brother, who was the actual "star" to us. A large, unself-conscious Saint Bernard of a man, he just loved to be funny and was always the center of attention. He also would get us to perform with him—and we loved to perform. My brothers and I would do skits for our extended family, usually memorizing a bit we'd seen on Steve Allen's show or Ernie Kovacs's brilliant program. Joel was fast and razor sharp; Rip was the singer, was all personality; and I was simply nuts: the Jerry Lewis of the three of us. I couldn't wait for the living room to fill up with relatives so I could get up on the coffee table and imitate them. When we'd go to a relative's home for a holiday visit, my mom would make sure to pack our props and anything else my brothers and I needed for our "act." She was our test audience, our out-of-town tryout before we brought it into the big room.

During school shows, I drove my classmates crazy, wandering off the script and improvising if a funny thought occurred to me.

I wasn't the loudmouth, class-clown type of guy. I was never one of those kids who was always "on," but I loved attention. I guess when you're the little brother with two charismatic older brothers, it's a natural craving. I also had other cravings. It was in the wings of a third-grade play that I not only kissed a girl for the first time but had my first erection. I knew that what I was doing was wrong, which probably made it more exciting. I was scared and confused about what was happening in my pants. Then I thought, *Oh no! Is God punishing me by stiffening me?* I made a mental note that in the future when I get an erection, not to think about my grandma. At my twentieth high school reunion I saw the recipient of that first exchange of fluids, and she introduced me to Lois, her mannish and unsmiling "partner." I took my first aside and asked, "Was the kiss that bad?"

....

I've written and talked about my hometown a great deal, but for new readers I must once again say that Long Beach was the perfect place to grow up, with its pristine white sand beaches and the pounding Atlantic on one side and the serene Reynolds Channel on the other. We took our bikes everywhere, and the two miles of boardwalk offered a paradise of games of chance like skee-ball and automated poker, a Ferris wheel, a batting cage, and miniature golf. There was an abandoned three-story concrete lookout tower that had been used in World War II to search the sea for enemy submarines. As teenagers, we'd sneak in and smoke a cigarette, grab a stolen kiss, or make water balloons out of condoms and drop them on unsuspecting passersby.

The Laurel Theater was an old-fashioned movie palace with red velvet seats and a balcony where petting was permitted. On Saturdays I'd go to the matinee and watch the Three Stooges and Green Hornet shorts that preceded the main attraction. Besides the ball fields, this was my escape. Walking into that darkened theater was akin to walking into Yankee Stadium—which I did for the first time on May 30, 1956. Dad took Joel, Rip, and me to our first game. Louis Armstrong had given Dad his box for the game and even arranged for us to get our program signed by the greatest star in baseball, Mickey Mantle. Mantle hit the most spectacular home run in Yankee history that afternoon, coming within inches of being the first ball hit completely out of the park. From that day on, all I really wanted to be was a Yankee. A Yankee who was also a comedian. Someday both dreams would come true.

Our house at 549 East Park was small, with two bedrooms and a den. It was a two-family dwelling, with another family living in the apartment above us. The main drag of town, Park Avenue, had a mall running down the center, with traffic on each side heading east and west. We played football and baseball on that bumpy, uneven grass strip; we figured that if you could field a ground ball on it, you could play anywhere. The Crystal boys were always out there. Often I organized tackle football games with my junior high friends, and cars would pull over to watch us. When they installed streetlights, we were able to hold night games. I loved when it snowed heavily; once the flurries began to fall, the phone calls started: "The mall, eight o'clock." Soon we had a dozen kids playing football under the lights, reflected by the beautiful falling snow. Mom would heat up a big pot of milk on the stove, and at halftime everyone came in for hot chocolate. The boiling milk lent its name to our games, Mutchkes. "Mutchkes" was what she called the gunky skin that rose to the top of the boiling milk. When Mom would skim it off and throw it in the sink, we'd all yell, "MUTCHKES!" After a while, when a snowstorm started, all we'd have to do was call one another, say "Mutchkes," and hang up. Then we'd all meet on the mall at eight.

Our house was around the corner from my elementary school, known simply as East School. Chuck Polin, the head of physical education, took my crazy energy and channeled it into tumbling. He taught me that form was crucial. Even as a fourth or fifth grader, I understood how my body should move, and I worked hard to be graceful. He would open the gym before and after school, and Rip and I started to excel in athletics. Mr. Polin would also hold "gym nights" and invite parents to watch the kids do the floor exercise routines he'd taught us. From a running start, I was able to dive over five or six kids lying on their backs shoulder to shoulder on a mat. Each time a new kid would take his place, the audience would cheer and someone—usually my mom—would yell, "Go get 'em!" It was exciting and, frankly, I loved performing in front of the crowd. *Performing.* The key word of my life.

••••

I was also a band geek. I played clarinet in the band and the marching band. I'd wanted to play trumpet or drums, but Rip had said, "Pick the clarinet and we can play duets together." I looked up to him so much that I agreed, stupidly thinking that you had to have two of the same instruments to play a duet. The cool musicians who would stop by our house taught us some Dixieland licks. Pee Wee Russell, a gentle, slight man, played clarinet with a haunting, breathy tone; he is still considered one of the great

1959, my first tuxedo.

soloists. He advised me to always "tease it out," saying that young players tend to blow too hard. When I was ten, I actually got to sit in on "When the Saints Go Marching In" with a group of Dixieland stars. I loved it, and for a time I acted like I was a jazz man. I wore a beret and sunglasses and borrowed money from my father.

I had a high-pitched voice until I was ten and my tonsils were removed—suddenly I was Pavarotti. It took two weeks for my throat to heal, and during my time away from school, my class was taught the basics of algebra. When I came back I was lost. Everyone was so far ahead, and I just didn't grasp the concepts. I never really recovered from that. To this day, the only math I can do is figuring out someone's batting average. Especially if they are 0 for 300.

I do remember puberty, though I'm not sure I actually went through it. I didn't get awkward, I didn't get a mustache, not many pimples, no hair on my chest or legs, which led me to believe I was part Navajo. I stayed small until I was twelve, and right before my Bar Mitzvah planning started, we went to Dr. Griboff, the family physician (and also Don Rickles's cousin, which is not why we chose him). With Rip and Joel having already reached "normal" size and beyond, my mom worried that I was not growing properly. So Griboff X-rayed my growth plates and we waited nervously in his office for the results. When he sat down behind his desk, he said the words that sealed my Yankee fate: "Maybe five-eight."

How the hell did this happen? Joel was over six feet, Rip five-ten, and the only thing keeping me from being a lab mouse was pink eyes. I was devastated. "We need to stimulate your growth hormones," the doctor said. So he gave me these pills that were supposed to make me hungry, the theory being "eat more, grow more." Well, I ate more, didn't grow more. I just got fat, bursting through the series of Robert Hall suits that were to be my Bar Mitzvah ensemble. I gained nineteen pounds in two months and grew one inch. I was in real danger of going from the quick little second baseman to the chubby kid catcher. I ate everything on everyone's plates. "What's yours is mine" was my motto. Rip nicknamed me "Are you gonna finish that?" I just couldn't stop eating, and they had to take me off the pills because I'd turned into a little white shark. So when the big day of the Bar Mitzvah rolled around, so did I.

My synagogue was a Reform temple, which means the service was half in Hebrew and half in Latin. Not only was I the last one in my family to get Bar Mitzvahed, I was the last one in my Hebrew school class, which means I had seen at least twenty services and knew what was coming. The Bar Mitzvah boy is basically the rabbi for the day. He conducts the service, leads the congregation in prayer, and finally he gets the chance to read from the Torah itself, which is the most dramatic moment in the show—I mean service.

After that reading, there is a moment in every service that is truly emotional. In our temple, the lights dimmed, heavenly organ music played, the ark containing the Torah was closed, and then the rabbi called the Bar Mitzvah boy over. As the music reached a crescendo, the rabbi, the most learned and trusted man in the Jewish community, would lean over, whisper some sacred, poignant, and holy words to the chosen one, and then seconds later the thirteen-year-old "man" would burst into tears. As the music swelled, he would leave the rabbi, come off the stage and into the audience, and hug his mother and grandparents; then he'd bound back onstage, like a Tony Award winner (which I am—wait, did that slip?), hug his father (women weren't allowed on the stage), and return to his seat, wiping the tears from his cheeks. It was the dramatic conclusion to the service, and soon we would all be eating stuffed cabbage and greeting relatives, who would spit Swedish meatballs on the boy's mohair suit as they handed him a Jewish War Bond that cost eighteen dollars.

After my friends' Bar Mitzvahs, I would ask them what the rabbi had said, to try to find out what magical insight from 5,721 years of suffering had been given to them on that day, but no one would divulge a word. They would either say, "We can't tell you" or "You'll find out when it's your turn." Even Joel and Rip, my very own brothers, refused to tell me.

Finally, March 25, 1961, arrived. My moment. I had never been better. Even though I was standing on an apple crate so I could be seen—a very sturdy apple crate, as I was still wider than I was tall. I did a tight twenty to open, had the crowd standing, sitting, reading responsively, nodding, smiling; I led them in silent prayer, did my blessings, even chanted a few, gave a really strong speech that advocated a ban on fossil fuels and equality in marriage. Then I was called to the ark, read from the ancient Torah, and the big stuff was done. After the Torah was dressed and put back in the ark, the rabbi motioned me over. The music started, and my heart began pounding: *This is it!* I was about to drink from the cup of knowledge. Wearing his home uniform of a black cloth robe and a puffy satin yarmulke, he put his learned, aging hands on my shoulders, leaned in close, and with that herring-and-pickle breath of his, whispered the words I was sure had come from God's lips to my ears:

"Count to ten, go into the audience, kiss your mother and grandparents, and come back onstage."

What? Five thousand years of anguish and suffering and having the tip of my penis cut off in my grandmother's living room and all I get to guide me through life is "Count to ten and kiss your relatives"?

I started to cry. "That's it?" I whispered.

"Yes, and I expect you to be in confirmation class Monday and don't discuss this with anyone," he replied, with a look in his eye that said, *Tell anyone, and I'll cut the* rest *of your penis off.*

Given how I felt about my penis, I haven't said a word to anybody. Until now.

....

Junior high was a disaster. The four elementary schools in Long Beach all emptied into the junior high. My class had more than five hundred students in it. I was out of my comfort zone. Plus, Rip was such a star that a lot of his teachers put pressure on me to be as good as he was, and I didn't think that was possible.

I'm still not sure what happened. I was a smart kid, good grades, test scores, the whole bit, but I let things distract me. By "things," I mean the two things on the front of girls. I went on a small rampage. This girl, that girl, on the phone, meeting them at the Laurel Theater, my first make-out sessions, copping my first feels—all of that stopped me from keeping my eye on the ball. Actually, my eyes were always on my balls, as that became a hobby as well. Once I knew God wasn't stiffening me, I was home. So as my erections went up, my grades went down, my self-esteem went down, and I floundered. If they gave grades for masturbating you'd be reading a book by another Einstein. I settled into life as a C+, B− student. As I started high school I couldn't stop thinking about two things: baseball and performing. Oh, right, and tits, so three things. Maybe that was puberty after all.

Performing stand-up in the high school variety revue called *The Swing Show* that spring was a turning point. My first big crowd had almost a thousand people in the audience. I rewrote a routine from a Jonathan Winters album. He was my favorite at the time. It was a takeoff on the Frankenstein movie, with the scientist building this giant monster, and at the end of the routine he calls UCLA and tells the coach his basketball player is ready. In my version, I was the scientist and turned the monster into a basketball player for my high school. I was a fourteen-year-old sophomore, and I didn't think it was stealing. I just did it word for word in front of an audience. I executed it perfectly, and it just killed. Well, of course it did—it was Jonathan's material. Dad was there, and taking a bow and seeing him smile up at me from his seat is something I will never forget, because I only got to see that once. He died suddenly the next fall, and my childhood came to a screeching halt. I never felt young again.

The night he died, we argued. My first girlfriend had dumped me, and I was moping around. He was frustrated with me, I got fresh, and that was the last time we spoke. I thought I had something to do with his death, which was a huge burden. I drifted through my junior year of high school. With Joel and Rip away at college, it was just my grieving mom and me alone in the house. I never felt I could have a weak moment in front of her, which, frankly, was exhausting, and I held in a lot more pain than I was able to bear. Making the high school basketball team gave me a place to go after school, and though I didn't play much, I loved and needed the camaraderie of my teammates. I had a good varsity baseball season, hitting just over .300, and did another strong performance in *The Swing Show,* but I was missing my dad and dealing with my mom.

I felt a little stronger during my senior year of high school, though the haze of sadness still blurred my vision. Mom had pulled herself together somewhat and had gotten a job, which, at the age of fifty, was a major accomplishment; she was determined to make sure we all graduated from college. I got the lead in the school show and won the intramural wrestling championship and, along with it, my nickname. I was all of 122 pounds. The title match in front of a raucous crowd in our packed gym was scoreless into the third and final period, when my opponent deliberately gouged me in the eye. Furious, I reversed him for a point, then got my shoulder into his stomach and drove him off the mat and threw him into the scoreboard—a portable blackboard, which fell over and shattered. My great friend David Sherman stood up and yelled, "You brute!" The crowd started chanting, "Brute! Brute! Brute!" From then on, Brute was my nickname. When I checked into a basketball game and got out on the floor, the fans chanted, "Brute! Brute! Brute!" At five foot seven with a buzz cut, I was hardly typecast for that moniker, and you have to wonder what my opponents were thinking.

During my last season of high school baseball, I was the captain of the team, hit .346, and even belted my first home run. Against a Calhoun High School pitcher who was later drafted by the Houston Astros, I took a high inside fastball and turned on it. It sailed over the fence at the 325-foot sign in left center field. As I approached first base and saw it clear the wall, I yelled, "Oh, baby!" When I rounded third, my coach, Gene Farry, was waiting

As Little Orphan Annie—Long Beach High *Swing Show.*

for me. He shook my hand and whispered, "Don't say that again." He was right, but I was just so damned happy.

That May, my buddy Neil Chusid introduced me to a young man named Lew Alcindor. Neil and Lew were classmates at Power Memorial Academy, in Manhattan. At over seven feet tall, Lew was the number one high school basketball player in the country and was on his way to UCLA; changing his name to Kareem Abdul-Jabbar, he became one of the NBA's all-time greats. We got to be friends, and Lew came over quite a lot and loved our family's connections to the world of jazz and its African American musicians.

One beautiful spring day, Lew, Neil, and I decided to play some hoops at the local basketball courts in Long Beach. We walked on the boardwalk toward the center of town. Lew was wearing a UCLA T-shirt, a panama hat, and round red John Lennon sunglasses. He looked at me and said, "You're not cool enough—wear these." He gave me his red sunglasses and Neil the hat. We arrived at the famous courts at Central School. Larry Brown, now a Hall of Fame basketball coach, had made these courts his home when he'd attended Long Beach High. College and high school players from all over came to Central School on Saturdays to play against one another. The games were in full swing as the three of us sauntered onto the courts: five-foot-eight Neil in his wide-brimmed hat, trying to look "bad"; five-foot-seven me with my red glasses, trying to walk like I was six-five; and the most famous seven-foot-two high school athlete in America. The players just stared at us as I uttered, "We have next." We didn't lose a game until we got hungry and Lew said, "That's enough—thanks, guys." Neil put on his hat, I put on my red sunglasses, and we walked out the way we had come in.

In June I was handed my diploma. After an anxious summer saying good-bye to my friends and family and all I had ever known, I got on a plane and headed to Marshall University, in Huntington, West Virginia.

Sitting alone on the plane as it flew south was a strange feeling. Not unlike how I feel at sixty-five. How did this happen so soon? I had never been away to camp, had rarely even slept over at a friend's house, and now I was on my way to my first year of college. After a harrowing landing at the Huntington airport (the runway was just over the lip of a mountain), I arrived at the Hotel Prichard, which would be my dormitory. The school had taken two floors of the hotel because of a lack of dorm space. My roommate wasn't in yet and our bunk beds weren't even assembled, so that first night I slept on a mattress on the floor. After my collect call home to say I had made it, words I barely got out because of the lump in my throat, I walked into town to look around and get a bite to eat at the White Pantry, a nearby burger joint. I was wearing a T-shirt, and my Star of David necklace peeked over it. I ordered a cheeseburger, and the counterman said they were closed, which they weren't; the place was packed. He pointed to the sign on the wall that said, WE RESERVE THE RIGHT TO REFUSE SERVICE TO ANYONE. He then motioned to my Star of David, and I stood up and walked out.

....

High school graduation, June 1965.
I think this was taken by Lew Alcindor.

I got a job as a DJ on WMUL, the campus radio station, and had two shows: one of my own, called *Just Jazz,* and another called *Nightlife,* which I did with a partner named Tom Tanner. We'd be on late at night in Huntington, and after a while people started listening. It was a way for me to perform and be funny, and it was just like I was home doing bits on our tape recorder with my brothers.

I was hoping to be the second baseman for the Thundering Herd, but the school had canceled the freshman baseball program, so that dream would have to wait until my sophomore year. I was very shy, didn't really date anybody, and even taught a Sunday school theater class at the local synagogue. My roommate, Mike Hughes, was a great guy; we were a solid pair even though he was in his mid-twenties and I was only seventeen. We made up some phony proof of age so I could get a beer now and then. One day, I was talking to some of the guys in the dorm about Lew Alcindor, and they doubted that I knew him. I bet a bunch of them five bucks each. So I wrote a letter to Lew care of UCLA,

"You are listening to *Just Jazz* here on WMUL—the voice
of Marshall University. I'm Billy Crystal."

and in a short time I got a letter back, which earned me a lot of
dorm cred and seventy-five dollars.

Then I told Mike that I could sneeze at will. I have a chemical
reaction to dark chocolate that can cause me to sneeze uncontrol-
lably. Up until then, my record was fifty sneezes before my nose
bled. Mike thought this could be great fun. So he got a group of
guys together in the rec room and they all threw five bucks into
a hat, and I ate a large bar of dark chocolate. I sat in the middle
of the jammed room with everybody starring at me. Within five
minutes, someone in the crowd said, "Hey, his ears are getting
red," which to me meant "Gentleman, start your engines." The bet
was fifty sneezes or better. *Achoo!* came the first. "One," said
Mike, who was holding the pot. *Achoo!* "Two," said Mike. As the

count grew, so did the amount of people in the room, all calling out the number as I sneezed away. I passed thirty-five easily, and guys threw more money into the hat. Forty-eight, forty-nine, fifty sneezes! Still not done but exhausted, somehow I worked my way up to sixty-four before a trickle of blood hit my upper lip. I made $225 and a few new friends.

I came home that summer and went to work as a counselor for my old teacher Chuck Polin at a day camp he ran at the Malibu Beach Club. One day while I was playing catch on the beach with a friend, this girl walked by. I followed her, and we started talking and then dating. I was in love, and I knew that if I went back to Marshall we'd never make it. Long-distance relationships rarely work out. I didn't want to let that happen. I transferred to Nassau Community College, only twenty minutes from Long Beach.

It's the best decision I ever made.

Count to Ten

As we face the challenges of getting older, some people want the comfort of knowing that there is a God watching out for them. People say it is a given that as you get older, you turn to religion. Personally, the aging friends I know have turned to the Holy Trinity: Advil, bourbon, and Prozac. Finding a relationship with God (if you believe in one) is littered with speed bumps. Now, I'd love to believe that there is a God watching out for us, but I can't. How would he explain things? "God, why did you take my father when I was fifteen?" "Did I? Oh, yeah, I was getting a root canal that day . . . my bad."

"What about Vietnam? World War II, Hiroshima, the tsunami in the Philippines?"

"Uh, migraine, I had a migraine. Plus, Vietnam's not my fault—even I can't control the CIA."

"Hurricane Sandy?"

"It was supposed to miss the East Coast by two hundred miles. I left the word 'miss' out of my e-mail to Mother Nature."

Can we have all these awful moments in our lives and believe that God had a hand in them? Think about it: when some ballplayers hit a home run and step on home plate, they immediately point to the sky, yet when they make an error or strike out, they don't point anywhere. Didn't the same God watch over them? Most people who are religious can be divided into four groups: the fanatics (the ones who want to kill everyone who is not them); the true believers (those who accept on faith that what science and common sense tell them is a bit far-fetched; I can't specify who fits this category, but let's just say that I'm not quite ready to go with the idea that seventy-five million years ago Xenu brought billions of his people to Earth, stacked them around volcanoes, and killed them using nuclear weapons); the spiritual (those who use their Good Book and teachings as a way to connect with something deeper than themselves); and the cultural (those who identify less with God and more with which deli has the best corned beef).

But as we age and feel that our time is dwindling, we need something because we're terrified. Terrified that this is it. Hoping that this God who has screwed up over and over will come to us and make it all better. We're Charlie Brown and we want to believe, we need to believe, that this one time Lucy won't yank the football away. The problem is that just as we want to become closer to God and have something to put our faith in, our life experiences have taught us to be disillusioned with organized religion. Especially if you are a former altar boy.

All religions have disillusioned followers. My personal disillusionment began at my "Count to ten" moment at my Bar Mitzvah. To add insult to injury, they kept telling me this was the day I would become a man, and that didn't happen until I was seventeen.

Don't get me wrong—I think all the basic tenets of my religion are great: fairness, education, respect, kindness. But let's face it:

My favorite photo: March 25, 1961, my Bar Mitzvah
reception. Jazz great Henry "Red" Allen performed.
He was a guest who got up and jammed. Not
many Bar Mitzvahs turn into jam sessions.

our holidays can't help but add to the disillusionment, because they
lag far behind. Take New Year's celebrations.

With the Chinese New Year, there are dragons, parades, fire-
crackers. With New Year's in America, there are big parties, the
ball drops in Times Square, you get drunk, tell someone you love
them, and throw up on their shoes. With the Jewish New Year, we
fast, we can't turn on the lights, we confess our sins. Happy New
Year! What a party! A bunch of guilty, hungry people sitting in the
dark.

Yom Kippur is when we atone for all our sins of the past year. It's like Catholic confession except we do it all in one day and the rabbi doesn't try to cornhole us. These services are always packed. Often we move to a bigger venue to accommodate the crowds. Tickets are expensive. It's like play-off seats for season ticket holders. Nothing is included in your basic package. Regular Friday and Saturday morning services are not well attended, but the chance to go to the big dance and spill your guts about the bags of Oreos you shouldn't have eaten or your flirtation with the pool boy brings the masses.

On Yom Kippur most Jews try to fast, so it's a very long service filled with sadness and guilt and the rumbles of growling stomachs. At one point there is a silent prayer, during which you basically get a few minutes of solitude to silently say to God how you fucked up all year, and that even though all he asks is that you fast for one day, somehow you gave in and ate a little nosh on the way over to keep your strength up. Even worse, it was a Sausage McMuffin. (If only there were a Yom Kippur app that could read the minds of all those hungry, tortured souls: "I bought retail," "I masturbated to that weather girl who wears the tight skirts," "I ate pork rinds," "I voted Republican.") When the service is ending, the shofar (a ram's horn) is blown, signaling the beginning of the New Year, and the masses go to someone's house for deviled eggs, bagels, and lox, and then to the nearest Chinese restaurant. This is called "breaking the fast," and it would be an incredible bonding experience if we hadn't all been sneaking food all day.

The next big Jewish holiday is Christmas. Everybody loves Christmas. Especially the Jews. Jews adopt Christmas and other people's holidays because they're more fun than ours. It's not an equal playing field. On TV, for instance, you never see *Have a Nice Hanukkah, Charlie Brown* or *The Grinch Who Returned His Presents for the Cash*. And the music? "Bagels roasting on an open fire" just doesn't cut it.

Christians have warm, festive gatherings where the family

comes over, they open their gifts, and they share a huge meal.
Gentiles' lives are a Hallmark TV special where the final scene is
the whole clan singing "I'm Dreaming of a White Christmas" by
a roaring fire. You can't help but feel jealous. There's a reason
Rockwell never painted a Jewish family dinner. We never look
happy! We need a makeover. For every Schlomo who loves his
holidays, there are fifty other Jews who wish their name was Tim.
That's why so many of my friends have huge, beautifully decorated Christmas trees surrounded by piles of gifts. We drink warm
cider and eat red smoked salmon blinis with green caviar on top,
in Christmas colors. We even sing carols. We do this just to fit in.
We bust our ass for Christmas, yet at Hanukkah we forget to light
the candles by the third night. Hanukkah isn't a sexy holiday. At
that time of the year, I feel that I should be wearing a Jewish star
on my sweater. The country is only 2 percent Jewish, marked
down from 3 percent, and I just don't feel a part of it for the holiday season.

The only Jewish holiday that's any fun is Purim, where we eat
cookies stuffed with prunes. And you know why: to clean out the
matzoh that's been wedged in my ass since Passover.

Passover: there's another holiday that isn't all it is cracked up
to be.

It's a holiday when we celebrate . . . suffering. There's a surprise.

What makes it even worse is that Passover occurs at the same
time as Easter. Again we can't compete. Two thousand years ago
Jesus is crucified, three days later he walks out of a cave and they
celebrate with chocolate bunnies and marshmallow Peeps and
beautifully decorated eggs. I guess these were things Jesus loved
as a child.

Passover commemorates the Exodus from Egypt. A fantastic
tale. Moses frees the slaves who were building the pyramids, we're
lost in the desert for forty years, cross the parted Red Sea, get to
the Holy Land, and we celebrate by eating cardboard and a fish
called gefilte that is so lacking in flavor you have to cover it with

horseradish and bitter herbs. Not one fucking chocolate bunny. We do have eggs, except they're hard-boiled and served in salted water. My mouth is watering as I type this.

Every year at the lengthy Seder service, we ask the four questions. Why is this night different from all other nights? And it's not: it's ten-thirty and we still haven't eaten! Two hours in and we're still suffering and still lost for forty years. How is that possible? Forty years? I never figured it out until I drove with my grandparents.

"Make a left."

"No, it's a right."

"What did the guy say?"

"I don't know, I thought you were listening."

"I'm not the driver, the driver should listen."

So, we wandered in the desert for forty years. And when we did get to the Promised Land, we claimed the only place in the Middle East that doesn't have a drop of oil under it. So much for Jews being the chosen people. You can almost see God and his staff laughing at the water cooler.

But the bottom line is, I want to reconnect with God, I want something to hold on to because I want to believe there is something better, something after this. And I hope there is. After all my disillusionment, I want to believe. I'm just afraid that after I die, I'll get to the pearly gates and God will say to me, "Billy Crystal."

"Yes, God."

"Come here," he'll say.

I'll make my way over.

All the people of my life who have gone before me will be assembled, watching.

God will lean in close, put his almighty hands on my shoulders, and with an angelic look he'll whisper, "Count to ten, turn around, kiss your parents and grandparents, and come back onstage . . . and never discuss what I just told you."

My Twenties

Three years after I met her, Janice Goldfinger (she heard all the jokes) and I were parked in the driveway of her family's house. As we finished listening to "Cherish" by the Association in her secondhand Chevy Impala, Janice said, "So we should get married." It wasn't the big, down-on-one-knee romantic event I'd been starting to contemplate, but as I've come to know over all these years, when Janice wants to do something, she does it. So basically, she asked me. As soon as she said it, I said, "Of course we should, I love you." I was twenty-one; she was twenty.

As I was about to go into her house and ask her father for her hand and the rest of her, here's what my scorecard looked like: It was 1969 and Vietnam was raging, I still had a semester to go at NYU, and I really didn't know what I was going to do when I graduated. Otherwise, things were perfect. The one thing I did

know was that I wanted to spend my life with Janice. I didn't
have any money for a ring, so my mom graciously gave us her
own cherished engagement ring, and we put the small diamond
into a new setting and I gave it to Janice under the statue of
George M. Cohan in Times Square. Corny? You bet. It still wasn't
that "Oh my God" moment, but to this day every time we pass the
statue we smile and hold hands, and we feel a lot better about
ourselves than the people who got engaged under the statue of
Joe Paterno at Penn State.

I was a film and television directing major at NYU's School of
the Arts (it had not yet been "Tisched"). Not sure why I didn't
audition for the acting program. Maybe I thought if the acting
thing didn't work out, at least I'd have something solid to fall back
on. I'd come to NYU after two great years at Nassau Community
College, where the theater program had been my home. I acted
in plays and musicals, and I directed as well. I did stock in the
summers, and this put an end to my baseball career.

In the film program at NYU, my fellow students were kids
like Oliver Stone and Christopher Guest, and one of my film
professors was a bearded, long-haired young genius named Marty
Scorsese. An intense guy, he taught a production class and a history of film class. His passion for making movies was strong, and
even though I felt nervous around him, his love of the history of
cinema inspired me. I made a few student films that weren't
very good (Marty confirmed that). Though I loved learning the
principles of directing, I needed to be onstage. I had done summer stock and was also the house manager for *You're a Good
Man, Charlie Brown,* a musical that ran in the East Village. I
tore tickets, directed people to their seats in the tiny theater,
sold drinks and souvenirs at intermission, and knew everyone's
parts. I could have gone on for any actor in the musical, including Lucy.

I was barely earning enough to share a tiny eighty-dollar-a-
month apartment in the East Village with David Sherman, one of

my oldest and dearest friends, dating back to junior high. He's now a doctor and we live near each other in Los Angeles. Back then, he was in medical school and I was in film school, and we would switch and do each other's homework. This meant he would go see a movie, and I would illegally dispense drugs to his patients.

We lived at 325 East Fifth Street, next door to the police station that would later be the home of *Kojak*. There was a red-haired detective at the precinct—I'll call him Sergeant Dinkus—and he was always busting music great Miles Davis. Oftentimes, Davis's red Ferrari would be towed and sitting in front of the precinct, and Sergeant Dinkus would be lecturing the pissed-off jazz man. "Don't come down here looking for trouble!" he'd say. Miles would say, "I wasn't looking for trouble—I'm just looking to buy some heroin."

"Down here" meant the East Village, the center of the sixties' cultural revolution. Plenty of today's balding boomers were then long-haired, peace-loving hippies who believed that we shouldn't be the world's police dog—including me, with my bushy "Jew 'fro." It was the perfect time to be young and angry. We hated LBJ, and then we really hated Richard Nixon. We despised the war, because it meant we could be drafted right away to fight for something we didn't believe in. The disaster of Vietnam fell on the heels of the violence of the civil rights movement and Martin Luther King Jr.'s and Bobby Kennedy's assassinations. National Guard units patrolled college campuses, students were killed at Kent State, and the Democratic convention in Chicago was chaotic. The country was divided between a mass of angry, idealistic people who felt that the government was blowing it and those who didn't. Other than that, it was a fun time.

The Lower East Side of New York had an electric energy. Head shops and restaurants were everywhere, and the Fillmore East was around the corner. It was the best music venue in the city, home to Hendrix, Zappa, Janis Joplin, and Dylan. It had also originally been a theater, and I'd seen my first movie there, *Shane*, when I was five. Next to the theater was the Central Plaza, a catering hall for weddings and big events and, for fifteen years, the place where my dad had produced jazz concerts. We grew up going there, and it was now an NYU building housing dance and theater studios. One of the studios was in the very ballroom Dad had used for his weekly jazz events. Alongside the Plaza was Ratner's restaurant, which had been a well-known spot in New York for years, but the young people that now packed the streets had given it a new life. When you're as stoned as everyone was in that neighborhood, a dairy restaurant with great whipped cream desserts is an oasis. David and I went there a lot. David had a heavy beard that he could grow as fast as Nixon. One day after a few hits on a joint, he shaved one side of his face, dividing it right down the middle. A little high, we sat down in Ratner's, and the waiter came over and asked David what he would like. The clean-shaven side, which was facing the waiter, ordered something, and then David turned his head and the bearded side ordered something else. David then got into an argument with himself, constantly turning his head. It was truly funny, but after a few hits, it was hilarious. Ever try to keep a straight face in front of someone who hasn't laughed since the Great Depression? The waiter simply stared at David. Ratner's waiters were mostly older Jewish men, weary messengers of matzoh-ball soup who had seen everything—everything but the straggly group of tripping, incense-smelling, "peace now" folks, many of them bearing a disturbing resemblance to Jesus Christ. Their table-side encounters sounded like this:

"VATZ IT GONNA BE?" asked the waiter; I'll call him Murray.

"Man, I'll have the LIZARDS THAT ARE COMING OUT OF YOUR EARS!" screeched the lost soul whose LSD-glazed eyes looked like slices of blood oranges.

Never losing his cool, Murray answered, "Oh, the special."

I had two great friends, Al Finelli and David Hawthorne, from Nassau Community College. They were funny and talented actors, and we had a great chemistry together and were always improvising sketches. We talked about forming a three-man comedy group someday, but it didn't seem possible because of the uncertain future we were all facing.

As my graduation from NYU approached, I was terrified. On December 1, 1969, the first draft lottery was televised. It was the ultimate reality game show: 366 Ping-Pong balls with the days of the year printed on them rolling around in a device usually used for Bingo night at the senior center.

One by one the balls were pulled (as mine were as I watched) and the fate of thousands of young men was decided. We'd been told that guys with the first 195 birth dates chosen were definitely going to be drafted and more than likely would soon be on their way to Nam. I was in a night class at NYU, and we all watched the dates numbered 100 to 199 on television. I wasn't in that group, but I didn't know about the first ninety-nine. I ran home and called my mother. "Mom, are you watching the lottery?"

"No, dear, there's a two-hour *Bonanza* on. Hoss got bit by a snake . . ."

Great. Finally, on TV, I saw that I wasn't in the first ninety-nine, so I lit a joint. Then I wasn't in the 200-to-249 group, so I lit another; then 250 to 299, another; 300 to 349, and I was giggling. Finally March 14 came up, number 354! I went to Ratner's and had a big piece of cake, and a side order of the lizards that were coming out of the waiter's ears.

....

I called Janice first, of course. It seemed we were free and clear of the army and that scary war. Before the draft, I had been interviewing at some Long Island high schools for possible teaching jobs, which would mean a deferment, but in my heart I knew teaching wasn't what I really wanted to do. Now, with the draft out of the way, I called Dave and Al and we formed a comedy group first known as We the People and then 3's Company and started to work on the Coffee House Circuit. These were nightclubs on college campuses, mostly on the East Coast. We traveled all over New England and New York and Pennsylvania, spending three nights or sometimes a week performing at a school, meanwhile living in a dorm. We made $350 tops, which was split three ways for a week's engagement. So I'm talking big money: $117 a man divided by three days is $39 a day, but in 2013 money, that's at least $40. At the same time, I was substitute teaching at Long Beach Junior High, which I had attended. It was strange to have lunch in the faculty dining room with teachers who had taught me. I could never call them by their first names.

In June 1970, Janice and I were married. After a large, beautiful wedding, we left for a five-day honeymoon disaster in Puerto Rico. By "disaster" I mean that Janice got terribly sunburned ("Don't touch me, it hurts") and I caught on fire in a restaurant. The waiter was showing me the flaming lobster dish I'd ordered, and without my knowledge, the flaming sauce dribbled onto my suit sleeve. I'm telling the waiter how great the lobster looks and he's

June 4, 1970. I did.

suddenly throwing water on my left arm and ripping off my burning jacket. If that wasn't bad enough, the shirt I had on was too big for me, so we'd shortened the sleeves with safety pins and rubber bands. With my jacket scorched, I ended up sitting there looking like a little boy wearing his father's shirt, next to my lollipop-red bride, who was in constant pain. ("It hurts to sit down.") Now, that's romantic.

We spent most of our honeymoon running lines for the play *Rosencrantz and Guildenstern Are Dead,* which I was opening in shortly after we returned. I played Rosencrantz, and Janice played everyone else. Over the course of our marriage, she has played, among others, Sally (before Meg Ryan did), Curly from *City Slickers,* and even Hamlet. Though she's not an actress, she gave Ken Branagh (who played Hamlet in the 1996 movie; I was the gravedigger) a run for the money. Seeing the mother of my kids, in a nightgown, say, "Alas, poor Yorik, I knew him well" is something I'll never forget.

As Janice and I settled into our married life, the comedy trio continued to perform, but we couldn't break through. I loved Dave and Al, but inside I knew I was really a stand-up comedian. I started to think about how to go out on my own, which seemed very daunting. The group finally caught a big break when we were signed by David Frost to make an appearance on a network special called *That Was the Year That Was.*

It was hosted by Jack Burns and Avery Schreiber, a popular comedy team at the time. Our sketch documented the making of the first marijuana commercial. (It was our best piece.) I played a stiff Ted Baxter kind of actor who gets progressively smashed as he does take after take, smoking "the product." We taped the show, and the audience loved it. We knew that appearing on a network program could really help get us going, so on the night of the broadcast we had a party to celebrate our television debut. What we didn't know was that the network wouldn't air the sketch because it was about pot. Our agent couldn't reach us, so there we were, first all excited, then freaked out as the show went on and on and no 3's Company. Finally, Jack and Avery said good night, the credits rolled, and there we were, waving and smiling, standing next to the hosts. They were able to cut us out of everything but the closing credits. The phone started to ring. It was the relatives: "Very good waving," "You looked good, Billy, I like the way you wave."

Things continued in this vein, the three of us always taking chances that never panned out. After a while, it gets lonely at the middle. My anxiety got worse and worse. Then Janice got pregnant. I have to admit, I was kind of shocked when she told me. It happened so fast. The Crescent should be this fertile. We weren't set up financially for a child. Janice had a good job, which she would have to stop at some point, and the substitute teaching brought a cool forty-five bucks a day into my Swiss bank account. The most money I had ever made with the group in one year was $4,200. After a few years like this, we were audited because I had well over $12,000 in travel expenses. Janice did our taxes at the time, and when the auditor sternly asked her, "Why is he in this business?" Janice simply said, "It's in his blood."

Now I was to become a father, before I could legitimately call myself a comedian. The responsibility of adding a new person to the world—not to mention our tiny apartment—was overwhelming. Still, I felt sure it was coming time for me to leave the group and go out on my own.

As the pregnancy progressed, we took Lamaze classes and, being the suburban hippies we were, decided to try natural childbirth. The relaxation exercises and the breathing techniques worked great in the class, and once Janice started having contractions . . . "THIS FUCKING HURTS! GIVE ME THE FUCKING SHOT!" I'm still not sure why I screamed like that; Janice was the one in labor. Actually, there were no drugs used of any kind . . . by Janice. I, on the other hand, was totally smashed.

Being the youngest of three brothers, and the uncle of a one-year-old nephew, I was sure we were going to have a boy. When the doctor, who had grown fond of us during the pregnancy, came out of the delivery room (in those days husbands weren't allowed in), he turned to me and asked, "What do you think it is?"

"Boy," I said with full confidence.

"No, schmuck, it's a girl." It hit me right between the eyes. Not the schmuck part, the girl part. How do you do girls? When I held beautiful eight-pound, four-ounce Jennifer Amie for the first time, she looked so calm and peaceful and safe, and my first thought was "I'll have to pay for the whole wedding." Then came fear. I was afraid that I couldn't be everything I would need to be. Would I be patient, would I be smart enough, was I emotionally prepared to handle a child? How would I make a living? I was barely able to handle myself, but a baby?

Babies are the toughest take-home exam of your life. I got off to a bad start when my gag mechanism freaked out at the first whiff of baby poop. When I put Jenny on the changing table for the first time and removed the diaper, I was staring at a few ounces of Dinty Moore beef stew. Instantly I started choking, my eyes watering.

"Oh, this is gonna be great," Janice laughed from bed as I hovered over the changing table, gagging.

Over the next few months, I learned how to relax, and once I could dispose of the scuba gear, I came to understand what it's like to love someone more than yourself. At the six-month mark, Janice went back to work, and I became a "motherfather." It was a difficult decision for Janice to be apart from Jenny, but she and I were a team and something significant had happened. The group had been seen by Buddy Morra, who was Robert Klein's manager and worked with the best managerial group in show business. Jack Rollins and Charlie Joffe were the aristocracy of comedy managers. They handled Woody Allen and Dick Cavett, among others, and also produced Woody's films.

So Buddy and his partner, Larry Brezner, took us on and got us a few jobs. After a while, though, Buddy and Larry pulled me aside and said they didn't think the group was going to bust through, but if I wanted to go it alone as a stand-up, they would be there for me. That was all I needed to hear. My anxiety had progressed to "eleven" when I got a call from a friend who needed a comedian for a ZBT fraternity party at NYU—did I know anyone? I lied to him, saying that I had been working on my own, and for twenty-five dollars, he hired me. I hung up the phone, thinking, *What did I just do?* Then I threw together a few ideas and rehearsed in front of Jenny, who, even at eighteen months old, was a tough critic. A few days later, when I nervously walked into the fraternity house, there were Buddy and Larry and Jack Rollins himself! I was supposed to do twenty minutes (which I didn't have), and I ended up doing an hour or so. I just exploded. I don't remember much of what I did to this day, but Buddy and Larry were thrilled. I was euphoric, and also guilt-ridden. I felt like I had cheated on my pals. Finally, I broke it to Dave and Al, and I went out on my own and never looked back.

••••

I threw myself into my stand-up. Everything was new; anything was possible. I had an amazing wife, a beautiful little girl, and finally now a real goal. Balancing my beginning career as a comedian and tending to the constant care of Jenny until Janice came home from work, around five P.M., was exhausting. We did that for two years and change. It was the most important part of my life, and it forever bonded me with this incredible pooping tax deduction. I was the only man in the play group; I was the only father at the playground. I was the only father with a baby in the shopping cart at the supermarket.

The Mr. Mom job became even more difficult after I broke away from the group. Creating an act from scratch is very hard, and I faced particular challenges. I wasn't a strong one-liner joke writer; my pieces were more like conceptual ideas that I developed, for the most part, by improvising while onstage. They needed fleshing out and honing in front of an audience, not a child in a high chair. We lived an hour outside Manhattan and its comedy clubs. I would leave around nine at night in the hopes of getting on at Rick Newman's Catch a Rising Star by one A.M or so; then I'd drive back to Long Beach. I'd arrive home around three and be up with Jenny around six-thirty A.M. I'd try to keep her entertained all day while also dealing with the household chores, and then Janice would come home and I'd hand Jenny off and get ready for my set that night. Sometimes, I would write; other times, a quick nap was the best preparation, though that was difficult.

....

In the middle of this hectic time, my brother Rip was about to move to California. He was at a crossroads in his life and career. He had been acting and singing in touring musicals and had decided that L.A. was where he needed to be. I hated to see him go. He was the more adventurous of the two of us, and a few nights before he was to leave, he asked me if I'd like to do organic mescaline with him. This doesn't mean he bought it at Whole Foods. This was the real deal, so to speak. He had done this hallucinogen a few times and enjoyed it, and he thought we could have a good time together. At the time I was just an occasional pot smoker, but I thought, *Hey, it's my big brother, I love him and I don't know when I'll see him again.* Plus, *If he says it's cool, it's cool.* We "dropped" just before sunset on a beautiful night in Long Beach. Nothing happened for a half hour or so, and then we just started giggling a lot for no reason. Long, laughing jags where nobody said anything. Rip suggested we play Frisbee on the mall in front of the house. "We won't be able to see it," I said, since it was getting dark out.

"Oh yes you will," Rip countered with a sly wink.

The DayGlo Frisbee looked like a flying saucer as it sailed through the night sky. We shrieked "WOW!" and "OOOOOH!" like inmates at an asylum when there's pudding for dessert. We then retreated to my tiny apartment upstairs in the house we

grew up in. My hair was enormous back then (picture Gene Sha-
lit's on steroids), and for some reason I just started brushing it and
combing it into different shapes, each "do" looking more absurd
than the one before. I can't describe our laughter other than to
say if Bigfoot laughs, it probably sounds like we did. Sometimes
we got intensely quiet while I pushed the comb through my thick
curls as if I was performing a delicate surgery. The finished product would elicit a whispered "Amazing" out of my stoned brother.
Then I took my wool sweater and turned off the lights and started
to shake it. Sparks flew out of it. "DID YOU SEE THAT?" Rip
screamed. "IT'S LIKE FIREWORKS. THIS IS IMPORTANT! WE
CAN MAKE A FORTUNE!"

"Rip," I reasoned, "it's static electricity."

"THAT'S THE PERFECT NAME FOR IT!" he screamed. After a
few more minutes of celebrating this scientific breakthrough, we
ate everything in the refrigerator, including Jenny's baby food.
Then, with a look in his eyes not seen since *Reefer Madness*, Rip
slowly whispered, "Let's go look at the baby." The baby, of course,
was six-month-old Jenny sleeping soundly in our bedroom. The
door to the room was maybe eight feet or so from us, but somehow it took us twenty minutes to get there. We tiptoed carefully
because we were afraid we could fall off the edge of the floor.
When the giggling idiots got to the bedroom, Janice opened the
door and, clearly pissed off, closed it behind her. She looked different to me.

Actually, I thought she was one of the rottweilers from *The
Omen* talking to us in a demonic Darth Vader–like voice.

"Get away from the child! Do not go in there. Look at you two
idiots. Billy, what did you do to your hair? Get away! Get away!"
She went back into the bedroom and Rip and I tried to calm
down, but now we were bummed. We were at that point when
you want to come down but you can't. We sat quietly for a
while, and the next day we were still sitting there. Rip took this
picture.

Never again.

Never again. That was the last time I took a drug my doctor didn't prescribe.

A few months later we moved into a bargain apartment on the first floor of a high-rise building. It was right over the entrance to the garage, meaning that every time a car drove in, the automatic door would open and shake the entire apartment. It was like living on a fault line. Nobody would rent it—nobody, of course, but us. After months of being rattled awake every night, I devised a plan: when I left for the city, I would stand on the roof of my VW Bug and unplug the electric eye of the door so it remained open, letting Jenny and Janice sleep soundly. Right here is the first time I have confessed to this, and if the super is still alive, hey, you got me.

I put an act together and improved quickly. It's so much easier to work when you're happy and when you have someone like Buddy to believe in you. Ideas were flowing, audiences were liking my stuff, and I was making great new friends like Jay Leno, Richard Lewis, Richard Belzer—all of us young comics on our way up. My early act was composed of "pieces." I did a routine about Nixon that was a parody of *The Exorcist,* the priest finally getting the devil child to release the infamous tapes. I did Tom Carvel, the ice cream king, drooling in the vanilla; a piece about a perverted Mister Rogers who would take off not only his sweater but everything else; and the highlight, an "interview" where I imitated Howard Cosell and Muhammad Ali.

Ali was my hero now. I'd always been a big boxing fan, from the time at Kutsher's Hotel in the Catskills, when we'd watched Floyd Patterson, then the heavyweight champion, train for a fight. Patterson was a gentle man for a fighter—when he knocked someone down, he'd actually help them up. Dad worked Friday and Saturday nights, so my brothers and I usually watched television with our mom, who, oddly enough, loved boxing. The Friday night fights were a television staple for us, and we got to see all the great boxers, like Gene Fullmer, Carmen Basilio, and Sugar Ray Robinson.

But the fighter we really loved was Cassius Clay. We loved his crazy antics, his predictions, his poetry, and, most of all, his skills. His rise to fame echoed that of the Beatles, who hit America at the same time he was hitting anyone who stepped into the ring with him. In 1964, he beat the "big ugly bear" Sonny Liston and became the new champion. Things quickly took another twist after that upset victory. He became a Muslim; then he changed his name, first to Cassius X, then to Muhammad Ali. He became a polarizing figure, confusing many of his fans, including me. My family didn't know much about Black Muslims; we just knew we were scared of them. Later, Ali refused to join the armed services when drafted, saying, "I ain't got no quarrel with them Vietcong." He claimed he was a conscientious objector—the fighter who wouldn't fight. He was convicted of draft evasion and immediately stripped of his boxing title and his passport. It was an enforced exile. Howard Cosell became his great defender during the three years when Ali wasn't allowed to fight. And this is when I looked at him in a totally different light. He was more than the greatest fighter of all time; he was a cultural phenomenon. While his appeal case moved through the court system, Ali spoke out on college campuses and wherever he could to protest the war. My mom admired him for that.

One day while I was still in high school, a white envelope from the Selective Service arrived at our house for my brother Joel. It sat on the table while he stared at it. Finally, he opened it, and sure enough, he was going to be drafted. Mom was beside herself. She had recently lost her husband, and now the army wanted her son. She wrote an impassioned speech to the draft board, and in a switch from our usual roles, she performed it for us in the living room. Finally she appeared before the board and told them, "You can't have my son. He is my sole support. I have another boy in college and another on the way. I don't believe in this war, and I just can't let you have him." Talk about a heavyweight fight. Mom versus the draft board. She won by decision. Ali was her inspiration.

Whenever she saw him on TV, my mom would say, "This is a great man. He gave up everything for what he believed in. It's a lesson in life. Whatever you do, make sure it's what you believe in."

Cosell was in my vocal and nasal range, and once I was doing stand-up, I studied his cadence, his attitude, and, yes, his pomposity. He was an easy send-up. Finding Ali's voice was pure accident. I had just seen *The Godfather* and was so mesmerized by Marlon Brando's performance that I tried to imitate him. To my surprise, one day Vito Corleone's "I'll make him an offer he can't refuse" became Ali's "I am the greatest of all time!" The voices, it turns out, are close, and one leaked into the other. Once I had that, the rest—the eyes, the mouth, the attitude—just followed.

The Ali impression was a big thing for me in the beginning. If I was having a rough set, I would make a sharp right turn into Ali. It always worked, because I was a little white guy doing a really good impression of "the greatest" black guy.

One afternoon, I was feeding eighteen-month-old Jenny in

her high chair when I got a call from my agent. She'd just received a call from Dick Schaap, who was not only a great sportswriter and broadcaster but also the editor of *Sport* magazine. The publication was doing a TV special honoring Muhammad Ali as the Man of the Year, and Schaap had called to see if Robert Klein was available to do some sports-themed comedy. Klein was one of the best stand-ups around, but he was unavailable, so she'd told him about this substitute teacher in Long Beach who did a killer Ali imitation. "He wants you," she told me. "Friday night at the Plaza Hotel." I was so thrilled I didn't realize I was putting mashed peas into Jenny's nose. If Janice had walked in, I would have said, "I think she has a cold."

Dick called me a few minutes later to introduce himself and give me the particulars. "Do you want to hear my Ali?" I asked.

"No, not now—I'll see you Friday."

"Will Ali be there?"

"Of course—you'll be sitting right near him on the dais. This is going to be great."

I was more scared than excited. Dick had explained that *Sport* did these yearly dinners honoring the best athlete in each sport, and all those stars would be there as well. Muhammad was the overall Man of the Year for beating George Foreman and reclaiming the heavyweight title. You must understand that, other than Mickey Mantle, to me Ali was the greatest athlete of any time, of any era, and, for reasons beyond sports, the most important. With Bobby Kennedy and Martin Luther King Jr. both gone, Ali had become the hero for my generation. Or at least the portion of my generation who hated the Vietnam War and what it was doing to our country. Now I would have a chance to perform for him.

"Jenny, we're going into show business," I said in my Ali voice, as I kissed her green pea–covered face.

I always performed in casual clothes, and the only suit I owned was a black velvet "mod" cut I had bought on Carnaby Street in London. Very hip and appropriate if I was singing with Herman's Hermits. I ran to the local men's store and purchased a formal velvet bow tie and dress shirt, so the suit would look like a sort of cool tuxedo. When I arrived at the Plaza three days later, everyone else was in business attire.

I met Dick, who I instantly realized was one of the nicest, most charming, and unassuming people I would ever know. He told me I'd be performing for three to five minutes, and then he asked how he should introduce me. Considering that up to this point *I* wasn't sure who I was, I told him to just introduce me as one of Ali's closest and dearest friends. I figured I'd be too nervous to set up the routine, so I'd get off to a fast start by going right into my Cosell imitation.

The crowd filed in, all excited about the evening. To be in Ali's presence at this time in his career was a thrill. He was at the top of the world once again. Many people had thought he'd be killed in the ring against the mighty Foreman, but he had "rope-a-doped" George into exhaustion and knocked him out. The Terrace Room at the Plaza Hotel was packed with New York's elite.

It wasn't just Ali—I was surrounded by sports stars: Gino Marchetti of the Baltimore Colts, Franco Harris of the Steelers, the Heisman trophy winner Archie Griffin, and, to top it off, two other legendary heavyweight champions, Neil Simon and George Plimpton. All in business suits and ties except yours truly, Mr. Velvet. We were asked to take our seats on the dais, and then there he was: Ali awash in his magical glow, greeting fan after fan. Sometimes when you see someone you idolize in person, they can seem smaller. Ali seemed bigger. He seemed to know everyone, and everyone wanted to know him. Then everything went into slow motion: that smile, those eyes. I kept thinking of how important he was to me. As I settled into my seat, the great Ali stared at me with a "Who the fuck is this?" look on his amazing face. Maybe he was thinking, "Who invited Joel Grey, and why is he wearing velvet?"

I was only a few seats away from Ali as the special officially started to film. Two-hundred-and-seventy-five-pound Gino Marchetti was seated on my left, and Melba Moore, who would sing the national anthem, was on my right. I liked sitting next to Melba; she was the only one at the dinner close to my size. I watched as members of the audience surveyed this dais of sports stars; when their eyes came to me, they all got that same confused look Ali had.

Dick Schaap was a genial host. Plimpton followed splendidly, and then Neil Simon came on and was really funny. It was my turn. Dick, at the microphone, looked at me and said, "And now, one of Muhammad Ali's closest and dearest friends." I walked to the podium to a hesitant but polite smattering of applause. I passed right behind Ali, feeling his confusion, and got to the microphone, where I launched right into being Howard Cosell in the ring in Zaire.

"Hello, everyone, Howard Cosell talking to you live from Zaire. Some would pronounce it 'Zare'—they're wrong." The audience laughed hard.

At this point, someone started yelling at me from the audience: "YOU GOT 'EM!" Two lines into it, and I'm being heckled? He wouldn't stop yelling. I realized it was Bundini Brown, Ali's flamboyant cornerman. So as Howard, I told him I'd handle it. He got quiet and I got good laughs, but it was awkward, to say the least. I'd always had the ability to think on my feet, even as a little kid, except this was my first time on television and Bundini was getting in the way. I continued as Cosell:

"Muhammad—may I call you Mo?"

More laughs; then I switched and became Ali.

"Everybody's talking 'bout Joe Frazier!"

Screams, applause.

"Howard," I said as Ali, "I'm announcing I'm changing my name again. I have new religious beliefs. From now on I want to be known as Izzy Yiskowitz. Chaim the greatest of all time! It's Jewish boxing. You don't hit the guy, you just make him feel guilty." BIG LAUGHS. If this was a fight, I was way ahead on points.

Ali was fantastic. He started joking around with me during my act, hiding his face with his napkin. When I was done, the crowd gave me a huge round of applause, Dick told them my name, and then Ali hugged me. "You are my little brother," he whispered. That is what he calls me to this day.

••••

One night Jack Rollins came to see me at Catch a Rising Star. This was the first time since that fraternity house that Jack would see what I was doing. A quirky, interesting man, he came off more like an eccentric English professor than the dean of comedy managers. I was nervous that he was there, but I had a great set. We met afterward, and I thought for sure he was going to tell me he was giving up Woody for me. We had settled into a booth in a quiet restaurant when Jack said, "I didn't care for what you did tonight." I wanted to stab him with a fork. "Why?" I spit out. "Listen," he said, "the audience loved it, and you can do very well with what I saw, but I have no idea what *you* think about anything. You didn't leave a tip."

"A tip?" I managed to ask.

"Yes, a little extra something you leave with the audience: *you*. I know what Ali thinks—what do *you* think? Don't work so safe, don't be afraid to bomb. Come back tomorrow and don't use any of this material; we know it works. Just talk. Let me know how *you* feel about things. What it's like to be a father, what it's like to be married, how you feel about politics—put *you* in your material. Leave a tip."

At first I was angry, but somewhere inside I understood what he meant, and I did just that the next night. I bombed, but I knew why. I started to talk about what was going on in my life. A few nights later, it started to click. It's the best advice I have ever been given.

Once I had a solid half hour of material, Buddy got me playing tasty small clubs like the Exit/In in Nashville, the Boarding House in San Francisco, the Great Southeast Music Hall in Atlanta, and Larry Magid's Bijou in Philadelphia. In Manhattan he booked me into the famous Other End (formerly the Bitter End) for weeks at a time. Under the guidance of club owner Paul Colby I went from an opening act to a headliner. It was on Bleecker Street in the West Village and was the home of Cosby and Woody and other great comedians. I got some good reviews, and people started to come down to see me. There's an excitement that you can get only from performing in a storied venue in New York City. Being a part of the heritage was a thrill.

One night, as I was doing my set in front of the club's famous brick wall, I saw a familiar face in the back watching me. It was Bill Cosby. He was the best stand-up comedian of any generation. I aspired to his skill at storytelling and his ease with a joke. Yes, he did great pieces like "Noah," but it was his anecdotes about his family and the kids he grew up with that stayed with me. He always left a tip. After my show, he came backstage to introduce himself, and we went out and talked. He did this a few times, and it meant the world to me that someone of his stature would take the time to mentor me. He would call me occasionally after a television appearance to tell me that he liked what I had done or to give me advice. "Just talk," he said. "Don't let them see that you're working."

Buddy also had me play different kinds of places, to give me some muscle. I played a lot of Playboy Clubs, which were not cool but paid well. All the Playboy Clubs around the country looked the same, sort of like McDonalds with cleavage. Businessmen in ties and jackets "enjoyed those Jewish skits." They certainly weren't my core audience, but if I could reach them and not give up my integrity (too much), I was way ahead of the game. Buddy then got me my first big job, opening for the hot band Blood, Sweat & Tears. David Clayton Thomas, their mercurial lead singer, had made "Spinning Wheel" a huge hit. The gig was at a theater in Scranton, Pennsylvania. I was to be paid $125 dollars for my twenty minutes. I didn't care that the tolls to Scranton were almost that much.

I kissed Janice and little Jenny good-bye and, after taking care of the garage door, drove to Scranton. Backstage prior to the concert, I met the band and loved the feeling of being part of a big show. But when I was introduced to the eager crowd—eager for BS&T, not *moi*—I got a very skeptical response. I had yet to do any network television or anything beyond Catch a Rising Star—no one knew who I was.

In those days it was difficult to open a show for a rock group because the audience had timed their drugs for the headliner. I started fast and the audience warmed up quickly—a really hot crowd. Twenty minutes later, I earned a big ovation from them and I was ecstatic. *I can do this!* I thought to myself over and over again. This wasn't just working a small club, this was for a paying crowd of a thousand people or so, and I handled it easily. I stood in the wings feeling a tad cocky and totally thrilled. The excitement in the house built when the lights went down and Blood, Sweat & Tears gathered onstage behind the curtain. Bobby Columby, their dynamic drummer, counted them down and the horns started to kick in, the curtains opened, and the crowd went berserk. If this is a rock and roll movie, the close-up is now on me, the young ingénue watching with anticipation as David Clayton Thomas takes the stage. He eyes the panting crowd and starts to sing "What goes up . . ." The audience goes crazy but then he abruptly stops, curses the sound, throws the mike down, causing a terrifying noise that blasts from the speakers, and then he storms off. The band keeps playing as Columby motions for the curtains to be closed. "Shit," moans the promoter who's standing next to me. Columby runs up to me and asks me to go back out there and do a few minutes while they talk Thomas down. "I don't have anything else," I tell him. "Make something up, just talk to them, we're losing the house."

I go back out to the confused and murmuring crowd and start to say there's a sound problem and the band will be back soon, but in the meantime, I spot someone in the crowd. "Where are you from and what do you do?" I ask. I keep doing the same thing with different people; I don't remember what anyone said, but it got really funny with me just improvising with the crowd, which now likes me. After a few minutes, Columby catches my attention in the wings with a thumbs-up and I introduce the band again. Curtains part, music starts, David Clayton Thomas comes back onstage, starts singing "What goes up, must come . . . Sorry, fuck this shit"—and *leaves again*. Columby looks at me and I mime *no*. The promoter begs me to go out there, and with the promise of other jobs that would give me a chance to net another $8 out of the $125 after tolls, I go out again.

"We have to stop meeting like this," I say as I saunter out onto the stage. I get some more laughs from the crowd and just before I'm about to ask, "Who'd like to see my act again?" Columby whispers to me, "We're ready." I say good-bye to a big ovation now, and . . . yes, it happens for a third time. When the curtains close this time, the crowd starts chanting my name. "BILLY, BILLY, BILLY." I turn to the promoter and say, "I can't do this again. I know where everyone is from." He gives me a check for $150, a $25 dollar tip for the extra time on stage.

Finally the band got through the first eight bars of "Spinning Wheel" and I ran to my VW and drove the four hours or so to Janice and Jenny. I grew to love driving home alone late at night in my VW after a good show. It was the beginning and I knew I was on the right road. Then I started opening for big-time music acts like Billy Joel, Sha Na Na, Melissa Manchester, Harry Chapin, and Barry Manilow, and I got some television spots as well. Mike Douglas did a wonderful talk show in Philadelphia. He had me on many times, and it was so exciting to be picked up in a limo and driven down to Philly to perform on his show. Like Merv Griffin and unlike Johnny Carson, he always had you sit and talk with him after your spot, no matter who else was on the show. This was so important to young performers.

The day after my first appearance on Mike's show, I went to visit my grandma Susie. "How come you didn't mention me? I gave so much money to charity," she complained. She was also a tad confused that I wasn't on the next day as well. "Did you get fired?" she asked. One time on Mike's show, I sat between Jimmy

Stewart and Lucille Ball. Mike said, "Nice pair of bookends, huh?"
I turned to Jimmy Stewart and said, "I love Lucy of course, but I
have seen *Gone with the Wind* fifty times." Lucy fell out of her
seat, and Jimmy just held a stare during the huge laugh and
winked at me, letting me know he had a line. "Yes," he said, "I
did some of my best work in that one." The great Norman Lear
saw me perform at the Comedy Store in Los Angeles and created
a part for me on *All in the Family;* I played Rob Reiner's best
friend, "Al, the Nut Boy." It was the week after Rob and Sally's
baby was born, and this show would be one of the highest-rated
All in the Family episodes ever. People tuned in hoping to meet
Joey, but instead they got to see me get married on the show. It
was the start of a great friendship between me and Rob. We
instantly felt like we had known each other forever. It would also
begin a creative relationship that would change both our lives.

....

In 1975, two important things happened that had polar opposite
effects on my career. First, on October 11, I was booked to do a
guest spot on a new NBC show called *Saturday Night,* produced
by Lorne Michaels. We had met a few times at Catch a Rising Star,
and I'd realized that Lorne wasn't your typical television producer. He was a young, cool funny man, not the middle-aged-
comb-over types I had been meeting. When he started talking to
me about this new show he was developing, he said, "It's a show
for us." The idea was that after regular programming ended, at
eleven-thirty, these young funny people would take over. He was
putting together an ensemble of sketch players for the cast, and a
guest would host the show each week. It would also feature the
best musical acts in the world. He didn't want me for the regular
cast but asked me to do stand-up spots on the show and suggested that I would make several appearances and perhaps, in
time, get to host the show myself. This was the break I'd been
hoping for. It was an opportunity to be with the kind of talent I
really admired on a show I knew would be important. I met some

of the cast. John Belushi had started to come down to the Other End to watch me work. I became friendly with Gilda Radner and some of the writers, like Alan Zweibel, who to this day is one of my closest friends and wrote *700 Sundays* with me. One night, Lorne brought the head of NBC, Marvin Antonowsky; the head of talent, Dave Tebbet; Gilda; and Chevy Chase to the Other End. I couldn't have been more excited.

Lorne asked me to be on the premiere. The Friday night before the first show, there was a full dress rehearsal with a live audience. George Carlin was the host; there were two musical guests, Billy Preston and Janis Ian, and three new comedians. me, Andy Kaufman, and Valri Bromfield. The run-through was a little spotty—George was funny, of course, yet the sketches didn't play very well. My piece was very strong, and Andy as "Foreign Man" did "Mighty Mouse," which brought the house down. I felt great. Afterward, during the notes session, Lorne not only asked me to cut my six-minute spot down to two minutes, since the show was running long, but also told me that my spot would be on at twelve fifty-five. After having it play so strongly, I was confused; more importantly, I couldn't figure out how to take that much out of my piece and keep it funny. I had nothing else that was only two minutes long that would be effective. I was suddenly in a terrible position.

On the day of the show, Buddy and Jack and Charlie Joffe came to the set and talked and argued with Lorne about my piece behind closed doors. They asked for five minutes and a more reasonable time slot. They were trying to protect me, and Lorne needed to protect his show. I had no idea what was happening until just before the run-through, which started around seven P.M., when Buddy came out and said that I had been bumped from the show. In a state of shock, I left 30 Rock. I watched the show that night and knew that a major chance had been lost.

The next month, I was booked to do three shots on Howard Cosell's *Saturday Night Live*. It was an Ed Sullivan–like variety show, actually coming from the Ed Sullivan Theater (now the

Letterman theater), not the ground-breaking show that *Saturday Night* was. The shots went very well, but the show was a bust, and once Cosell was canceled, NBC renamed its show *Saturday Night Live*. Little-known fact: Howard's show featured three funny semiregulars who did sketches. Called the Prime Time Players, they were Bill Murray, his brother Brian Doyle-Murray, and Christopher Guest. Their name inspired Lorne to call his troupe the Not Ready for Prime Time Players.

I was still reeling from the lost opportunity when the second important event of 1975 occurred. I was booked to do my first *Tonight Show*. At that time, doing a good *Tonight Show* shot could make your career. Johnny Carson was and is still the greatest comedy star of all time. He was a god to young comedians, and if you could get on the show and make him laugh, it meant everything. I was to do *Tonight* on a Tuesday, and on the Sunday before, I was in Las Vegas to appear on a Dean Martin roast for Ali. Dean had taken the Friars Club roast concept and made it a weekly event. My Ali imitation was my big-ticket item, and there I was with Ali, all of these legendary personalities, and, of course, Dean, who was a thrill to meet. It went great, and as I walked backstage after the taping, I saw Orson Welles, who at this point in his career was a regular on these roasts. He was sitting on a stool going over his jokes for the next show, which would tape shortly. At NYU, Scorsese had taught us about Welles and his amazing body of work, which included *Citizen Kane,* and I was in awe of him. Sky-high from my performance, I couldn't help myself, and I walked over to the massive man on the stool. He was smoking a smelly cigar as he rehearsed his new jokes: "Jimmie Walker was born a clarinet."

"Excuse me, Mr. Welles," I broke in. "I'm Billy Crystal. I was on the roast with you, and I want you to know that I studied your—" He cut me off and bluntly said, "Films, and you're an innovator and a great director and blah blah blah. I'm busy, go fuck yourself." I didn't know what to say, so I just walked away. I flew to Los Angeles and met my now good friend Christopher Guest and told him what Welles had said. Chris said, "You just walked away, you didn't say anything?"

"I was too stunned."

Chris said, as only he could, "Why didn't you say, after he finished, 'No, that's not what I was going to say. I was going to say, You're a fat piece of shit who peaked when he was twenty-five"?

It took us about an hour to stop laughing, and the next day I arrived at NBC's studio in Burbank with as much pressure on me as I could ever imagine. I got to my dressing room and was too tense to even sit down. Then from the next dressing room I got a whiff of a smelly cigar, and through the door I heard that unmistakable voice. It was Orson Welles! He was also a guest that night. My anxiety increased to a full panic. The show started, Johnny did his monologue, and then he brought Welles on. They did a funny segment, and I was led to my mark backstage, behind a curtain, to make my entrance. My routine was called "The Mood Comic." I played a comedian who did his act like a late-night lounge singer. There weren't many jokes in it; it was attitude and timing, not the kind of one-liner monologues other comics were successful with. It was what I closed my sets with, and now I would be opening with it.

Before the show the stage manager had told me that when I was done, to stay on my mark and watch him. If his hands were up, it meant stand there and take a bow; if he pointed to the desk, I was to go over to meet Johnny. The odds of that were almost nil. You really had to earn your way to the couch. As far as I could recall, only Freddie Prinze had ever done a first *Tonight Show* spot and been called over. Every other new comic had this painful look on his face as he took in his applause while his anxious eyes fixed on the stage manager, who had his hands up.

I heard Johnny introduce me, the curtains parted, and then, as if I were a bull rider in a rodeo, I was let out of the stall and into the ring, trying to hold on for dear life. The band played me on, and I walked to my mark on rubbery legs, feeling like I had to cough up a hair ball. *Wow, there's Doc and the band, I see Johnny to my right*—it was very surreal. I had been watching this show for so long, and now I was on it. The piece played very well, and when it was done the audience gave me a big hand, and I looked over and son of a bitch if he wasn't waving me over. I tried not to run, to act like I did this all the time, but inside I was a parade. I thought of my first home run in high school when I yelled, "Oh baby!" and my coach said, "Don't say that again." In essence, act like this has happened before. I shook Carson's hand and then Orson Welles's. We looked at each other and I stopped myself from saying, Go fuck *your*self.

Johnny said a few nice things about my performance, and we went to a commercial. They had told me not to talk to Johnny during the break if I did sit next to him; he doesn't do that. Doc and that fantastic band were playing, and there was the great man drumming away on his cigarette case with his pencils. I found myself staring at him. Johnny had very sharp features, blue eyes, gray hair, and other than Ali and Cosby, he was the first superstar I had been this close to. He must have sensed that I was staring, because he looked over and gave me a quick smile and I blurted, "How's it going?" He laughed and said, "It's going pretty good."

Craig Tennis, the segment producer, joined us and asked what I wanted to do in my short segment. "Let's go right to the Ali question," I answered; that would lead me into the imitation and I'd be okay. "We're back," said Johnny. "This Thursday you're on the Dean Martin roast with Ali—what's the connection?" At which point Welles said something like "He's terrific on the show" and patted me on the back. I'd like to think it was his way of saying I'm sorry. Johnny fed me the Ali line, I did the impression, Johnny laughed a lot and said, "Come back anytime," and I was in heaven. They don't all turn out like this.

····

In 1976 Michael Eisner and ABC signed me to a development deal and I put the plug back into the garage door of my building and we moved to Los Angeles. It was hard to leave our families and the town where I'd grown up, but it was time.

We arrived in Los Angeles on the evening of August 2, and that night I went into a supermarket to get some food. In the frozen food section I saw one of the actors from the film *West Side Story*. He wasn't the cool member of the Jets anymore. He had a belly and a bald spot and was reading the label on a bag of frozen peas with a cigarette dripping from his mouth. "Rough town," I murmured to myself. The next morning we were awakened by a lot of commotion outside. I opened my door, and Buddy Ebsen was sitting in the yard. They were shooting an episode of *Barnaby Jones,* and the front of our small apartment complex was the location. Welcome to Hollywood.

I was very excited and nervous when, a few months later, *Saturday Night Live* asked me to do a spot on the show, which was to be hosted by Ron Nessen, press secretary to Gerald Ford. That night, Dan Aykroyd did the Bass-o-Matic sketch, where he put fish in a blender and drank it. I did "Face," which was a funny and poignant monologue where I played an old jazz musician friend of my dad's who had seen me on television. When I was little, he was the first one to call me "Face," which became my nickname. Now he's older and down on his luck, and we have a bittersweet reunion. The hook he kept saying was "Can you dig it, I knew that you could." It played beautifully; it was great to be back there. And I didn't do the show again for eight years.

I was soon sent a pilot script for an ABC series called *Soap.* The producers wanted me to play a character named Jodie Dallas. Jodie was funny, he was charming, and he was . . . gay. There hadn't been a homosexual lead character on a series, so taking the part was a real gamble. I had been out in public with Rob Reiner many times when people called him "Meathead"; I didn't want to be the gay guy from *Soap*. But this was a great script. I decided to meet with its creator, Susan Harris; producers Tony Thomas and Paul Witt; and the director, Jay Sandrich, who, following his great run with Mary Tyler Moore, was thought of as the best director in television. They laid out the "bible" for the show. We talked about where Jodie would go as a character—emotional places that had never before been reached with a gay character on television. We went over the pilot, which was two half-hour shows. In the first I had only one line, but in the second, I had a very funny scene with my mom, played by Cathryn Damon. Jodie was caught wearing one of his mother's dresses, high heels, and a blond wig. When she saw me she said, "Stop wearing my dress— Oh, you wear it belted."

It was a risky scene, having Jodie dress up like this, but the plans for Jodie were to make him more of a subtle character, a compelling guy who just happened to be gay. I agreed to do the show because of that meeting. Susan Harris was a genius writer, and Paul Witt and Tony Thomas were really smart producers. It felt like we had the chance to do something special and important. Also, now that my stand-up career was taking off, I would be able to go out and be myself on talk shows and personal appearances, so I wouldn't be trapped in the character.

We shot the pilot and were put on the fall schedule for 1977. The show became the talk of the industry. Religious groups condemned it without even seeing it. It was on the cover of *Time* magazine before it was broadcast. Society's mores were a lot different then. The lead character, Jessica Tate, who was played by the brilliant Katherine Helmond, was having an affair with a younger man, Robert Urich; women didn't do that on television. Diana Canova's character tried to seduce a priest in church (women didn't do that, either), and then, of course, there was this young gay commercial director who liked to wear his mother's clothes and was secretly dating an NFL quarterback. Sponsors were picketed, gay groups were initially unhappy, fearing that Jodie was a stereotype, and with all that working against us, we still were a ratings success, finishing in the top ten shows. Suddenly I was in the national spotlight.

That first season, ABC executives were putting me on any show they could, sort of the Billy's Married (but His Character Can't Until 2013) Tour. Dinah Shore had a wonderful program

Jodie and his stepfather, Burt (Richard Mulligan).
(© American Broadcast Companies, Inc.)

that I had been on several times already; I loved doing it because she was so natural and easy to be with. Her producer called me to say that Mickey Mantle was going to be a guest and wouldn't I like to be on with him? I was so nervous I didn't know what to do. Then I came up with an idea.

My dad had shot some great home movies of Mickey, and I still had them. I would intercut those with footage of my brother Rip's Bar Mitzvah and not tell Mickey anything before we watched it together. I also brought the program he had signed in 1956. My heart was pounding when Dinah introduced me. There was Mickey, looking great and smiling at me as I shook his hand. I took out the program and told the story of how he had signed it but said I had never seen him do it, so could he verify that it was his signature? He laughed and said yes indeed he did sign like that back then, but he agreed to re-sign it. So, twenty-one years later, Mickey Mantle re-signed my program. I then showed him and the audience the home movies. I set it up that these were treasured memories of my hero. Mickey was totally sucked in. We rolled the film; it started with him throwing on the sidelines of the great old park, and suddenly it cut to my relatives doing the bunny hop and eating chopped liver. Mickey and the audience went wild, and after I described all the strange faces of my relatives in the flickering film, it cut back to Mickey, who promptly struck out. He loved it. That was it. We became friends right then and there. And that friendship would lead us to many unlikely encounters.

Playing a gay man in front of a live audience was difficult. My boyfriend on the show was played by Bob Seagren, a former Olympic pole vaulter. We had scenes where we said we loved each other, and the audience would laugh nervously. That was new information for people in 1977, and it made them and me uncomfortable. The lines were difficult to deliver, and hearing that nervous laughter made me angry. I felt they were laughing at Jodie, not with him. Sometimes I wanted to stop the scene and yell at the audience, "What are you laughing at?" But as time went on, and the character developed, viewers at home cared about Jodie, even wanting him to get sole custody of a child he had fathered. In a great cast of insane characters, Jodie, along with Benson, became one of the more sane ones. We continued to build the character, and I will always be proud of the role, but it sure was hard in the beginning. To compound the confusion, I had done a movie called *Rabbit Test*, directed by Joan Rivers. I played the first pregnant man. It wasn't just that the movie didn't work; it came out at the same time *Soap* did, so now the gay guy was also the pregnant guy? I try not to look back and think about mistakes, but that was a big one. We should have been more patient and waited for the right movie to come along.

A month after *Soap* went on the air, Lindsay was born. Despite the success of *Soap*, I kept watching *Saturday Night Live* and couldn't help but dwell on what could have been. As I sit here playing connect the dots with the liver spots on my hands, I think that my twenties were the most tumultuous times of my life. In March, I turned thirty. Oy.

The Elbow

We're at the movies and I felt it: a sharp jab from Janice, who in her prime could have taken out Metta World Peace on a fast break. I just got the elbow.

"Ow! What was that for?"

"You're nodding off."

"No I'm not, I'm fine, I'm fine."

"Well, everyone's looking at you—your head was back and you were drooling."

I glance down at my shirt and there's a spreading circle of Red Vines juice. I nodded off for thirty seconds and it turned into a mob hit. Nodding off: a new thing to add to the Whitman's Sampler of fun items I'm developing, like the forgetting of names. That's always a great one. I try to handle it with the old "Hey, great to see you, long time no see, you know you have such an interesting and rare name, how do you spell it?"

"B-O-B."

Then you have to fake it. "Bob, I don't mean that—I mean your last name."

"S-M-I-T-H."

It's better when I'm with Janice as I'm blanking out on whoever it is who can't be more excited to see me. I can finesse the introduction. "You remember Janice," I'll say to the person who is hugging me, and then, of course, he introduces himself.

"Hi, I'm Magic Johnson." It works every time.

....

The forgetting of names started a few years ago. We were watching *Do the Right Thing* on television. It's a great Spike . . . uh, what's his last name . . . shit . . . *Lee,* whew, movie, and an actor I've known for years is on-screen, and I go blank. I mean totally blank. Janice also is dumbfounded at who this actor is, and it's driving us crazy. This is before Google and all the other aids I now can use when there's a cave-in in the main shaft. Who the fuck is that? We describe moments we've had with him, places we've been together, things he's said to me . . . nothing. Finally, I call my daughter Lindsay and start to describe the movie, and in two seconds she says, "Danny Aiello."

"Danny Aiello, of course—man, that was so weird," I say. Lindsay laughs, and before we get off, I say, "Thanks, Jenny."

It's such a stunning moment when it happens, like hitting a brick wall. So now when I can't remember an actor in a movie or who it is that's hugging me hello, or what's that thing I eat soup with, we call it a Danny Aiello. It's not just me. I find comfort in the fact that most of my friends—whose names I can't come up with right now—are having the same problem. My doctor says it's par for the course and not a symptom of anything sinister. He suggests that I have a physical, and I tell him we did one two days ago, and he says, "Did we?"

....

This nodding off thing is just the latest annoying development in my life.

If I'm at a play and the curtain goes up and I see a secretary alone in the boss's office, silently looking for something on his desk, I'm gone.

A stately manor with a maid dusting: I'm gone.

If there's a castle and an accent, see ya.

I can't help it; it's just the way my body is now. It's like I'm an addict and five minutes of public snoozing is my heroin.

Movies and plays are an important part of my life, and now every time I go I'm fraught with terror that I'm going to nod off. On the drive over I start to worry: Will I stay up, or will Janice break another one of my ribs? She doesn't mean to hit me so hard, but at my age, it qualifies as elder abuse.

....

Janice and I discuss what to do. "What do you want me to do if you start to nod?" she'll ask. My answer will depend on how badly I wanted to see this particular movie or play, if my ribs are healed, and do we know anyone in the show? Usually it's "You won't have to, I feel good," even though inside I'm actually looking forward to a quick nap: it was a tough day and I need a chance to catch up because, as usual, I've been up all night.

We get to the movie theater, and as we're buying the tickets, another thing happens that annoys the hell out of me. I ask the person in the box office for the senior discount and they go, "Really, you're over sixty?" Vanity causes me to say, "Just kidding," and now I'm mad that I'm out an extra couple of bucks. But on the plus side, maybe the adrenaline will keep me awake.

Once we get inside, I decide to take preventative measures. I order a double espresso. The problem with that is (1) I'm going to miss the second half of the movie running to the men's room every three minutes and (2) chemicals tend to have the opposite of their intended effect on me. Caffeine makes me sleepy. Aspirin gives me headaches. Pot used to make me energetic, and you don't want to know what Viagra does.

Broadway plays are worse than movies because they're not that loud and there are actual human beings onstage, some of whom I know, who can see me going night-night. In the last few years, I've never made it through an entire show.

I saw *The Music Ma* . . . I know there was trouble, I just don't know where.

Then there was *The Book of Mor* . . . *Death of a Sale* . . . and *Mary Pop* . . .

If I had seen my own show, I would have only made it to 100 Sundays.

What makes it worse when I nod off is that I'm recognizable. People will look to see if I'm laughing and instead they'll see me fighting to stay awake, with head bobs, lionlike yawns, and then sometimes my head will swing violently backward, into the top of the seat. I must look like one of those crash-test dummies when they hit a wall in slow motion. At least I am not alone in this. Sometimes I glance across the row I'm sitting in and most of the men look like they're heroin addicts on a field trip.

The only solution is to get Broadway to adjust to us. All shows should be half an hour long, with two intermissions.

Once the lights go down and the curtain rises—the moment when we're supposed to relax and give ourselves over to the magic of the theater—it's on. I dig my fingernails into my arm or give myself an Indian burn, hoping the pain will keep me awake. I cross my legs, I keep my legs apart, and I try tapping my foot. I even bury my head in the program like I'm going to read in the dark. Then, depending on how good or bad the play is, sometimes I make a decision to just embrace it and go down for the count for a while.

Finally I came up with what I thought was the perfect solution. I decided that the next play I went to, I would make sure to sit right up front, so that the intensity of the performance and the closeness of the stage movements would keep me alert.

The play was *Fences,* starring the great James Earl Jones. Mr. Jones is a legend, a towering presence on the live stage. He's so much more than Darth Vader and the voice of CNN. We walk into the theater, the usher shows us to our prime seats, and we're the only two people up front. There is no one else. I can't understand this at all.

This is crazy—our tickets are in the third row, and there's no one in the first two rows. The lights go down, and the play begins. Jones makes his entrance. He's mesmerizing. He's playing a loud, dynamic former baseball player and, as always, his diction is flawless; he pronounces every inch of every letter, his booming voice resonating throughout the theater. I am watching a master at work. Then it happens. My eyes get heavy—NO! They start to close—DAMN IT!! I force them open; they want none of that—they flutter to half-mast. Just as they close, it happens: THE ELBOW! If Janice were a boxer, she'd be the greatest body puncher since Joe Frazier.

"I'm okay," I lie.

"It's embarrassing—we're supposed to have dinner with him afterward," whispers Janice. I hold on for a few minutes, but then my head flops back, and suddenly I'm Jack Nicholson with the lobotomy at the end of *Cuckoo's Nest.* I'm out. Then *blam!* Something wet hits my neck. Then it hits me again. It's a saliva storm. I look at Janice, and she's holding her program in a defensive-shield position. I'm now awake, and I realize why no one is in the first two rows. Perfect diction and booming voice and pronouncing every syllable means a spit bath from James Earl Jones. Seriously, if this were Guantánamo, it would be considered waterboarding.

On the plus side, I stayed awake for the rest of the play.

....

I've also been on the other side. I've been onstage when I *wanted* to spit on people because they weren't watching. When I was doing *700 Sundays,* I'd be pouring my heart out and then I would see someone out cold. I wanted to jump off the stage and shake them: "Hey, fuckface, is my life that boring?"

The problem is, as a performer I'm annoyed and upset; as an AARP member, I get it. We just can't help it. When the darkness of the theater combines with the coolness of the air-conditioning, it's toxic. But it doesn't help if they raise the temperature: warm theater plus big meal before the show and it's the narcolepsy express.

My worst time being on the other side of the "nodders" was when I did *700 Sundays* in West Palm Beach. It was the Kravis Center, a beautiful place, and we sold out our five-show run in a very short time. On opening night, I was really excited because I knew that a lot of New Yorkers, including family and friends, were down in Florida and would be in the crowd. So as I made my entrance onstage at eight o'clock, I was really looking forward to a great reception.

Nothing. Crickets. A modest round of applause. It threw me. Audiences had been wonderful to me during my season on Broadway and on our tours, so I was used to a loud and cheering crowd when I walked out to begin the play. I looked out, and there was an ocean of seniors. From the stage, their hair colors looked like Vermont in the fall. There was every shade of brown and orange and yellow, plus a bluish color that can best be described as "old."

Meanwhile, in the second row, maybe ten feet from me, a guy with binoculars was staring at me like he was bird-watching. I had to keep telling myself, *Don't look at him or you'll laugh.* The first act was a struggle. I worked much harder for my laughs than I'd ever had to. At intermission, I asked the stage manager what was going on: Why had there been so little applause when I'd walked out? He said, "Billy, you woke them up—they were stunned. The show starts at eight; they got here at six so they could get first crack at the hearing devices. We open the house at six because they can't stand around for too long, and they come into the theater and fall asleep. You got the best reception any show has gotten here!"

Another night I was onstage, and in the opening minutes of the first act, I saw a red light blinking in the back of the orchestra seats. *Damn it!* I thought. *Someone's videotaping my show!* So at intermission I told the stage manager where I'd seen the camera light so we could stop this jerk from pirating the performance.

The stage manager went into the audience with a security guard and returned shortly.

"Did you get him?" I asked.

"Billy, that blinking red light is part of his life-support system in his wheelchair. That's how his nurse knows he's breathing."

"Can they put some black tape over the light?" I asked. "It's distracting."

"No, if the nurse doesn't see the blinking light, she'll think he's dead."

The nurse had also said that the blinking light keeps her from nodding off in the theater; apparently, staying awake is also a problem for her.

So maybe that's it. Maybe nodding off is just a precursor to what lies ahead. We nod off a little more each day, and soon the nodding offs blend together, until eventually it's one long permanent sleep. Which is why I've made some changes in my living will. If the end is near, I don't want to be hooked up to a machine; I don't want extraordinary measures or the elbow. Just wheel my hospital bed to a theater showing a movie with Danny Aiello, give me a kiss good-bye, a small popcorn, and a medium Diet Coke for fourteen dollars, and tiptoe away until the blinking light goes off.

Take Care of Your Teeth

shouldn't complain so much. Life at sixty-five is good. I have had one house, one wife, my real nose, my real name, and most of my teeth. And the last part is a major reason why life is pretty good. Because when you hit your mid-sixties, you have to take care of your teeth. It's a generational thing—I learned it from my eighty-six-year-old grandmother.

Susie Gabler had perfect teeth. White beauties with no cavities. She took great care of them—always kept them by her bedside in a glass of water. The first time I saw them come out of her mouth she was in bed, and I was sitting next to her. In the middle of saying how proud she was of me, she suddenly reached into her mouth and pulled out her entire set of uppers and lowers. Splash, into the glass of water they went, and suddenly my beloved grandma looked like an eighty-six-year-old hockey player, or a woman with a horizontal vagina for a mouth.

"Take care of your teeth, Billy. Take care of your teeth." I think that is what she said, because with her lips flapping in the breeze, she could have said, "Pass me the marble cake." I was shocked, and slightly nauseous. It was a terrible thing for a grandson to see, even though I was thirty-two years old.

She lost her teeth because she never went to the dentist. Mainly because the Cossacks had killed him. None of my grandparents had good teeth. Sometimes when he was eating the Thanksgiving brisket, my grandfather's dentures would be hurting so much he'd remove them at the table, keep them in his hand, and manually chew the rubbery meat until it was ground down enough to swallow. While we all watched in horror, he'd take the "chewed" meat, dip it in horseradish, put it in his mouth, and swallow it with a great sigh of satisfaction. He'd then say something inaudible, and Grandma would reply, "Don't talk with your hand full, I don't know what the hell you're saying."

Take care of your teeth! It's why we baby boomers should floss, it's why we should brush, and it's why we should go to the dentist, because we know dentists are important people, even though they weren't smart enough to get into medical school. It's sad . . . dentists don't get the respect they deserve. You never hear, "Is there a dentist in the house?" That lack of respect started back in elementary school, when we were frightened of the dentist. Not wanting to scare us even more, they made dental hygiene cute. It was always "Watch out for Mr. Tooth Decay" and then a cartoon of some unhappy-looking animated guy. We don't treat any other malady like that, except maybe for those cartoon yellow devils that live under my toenails. Which really exist, by the way. Come to think of it, if other serious maladies were treated in a fun way, they wouldn't seem so scary. Don't worry about erectile dysfunction, it's Mr. Softie. Instead of incontinence, you get a visit from Mr. Pudding Pants. And good-bye, schizophrenia, say hello to Mr. and Mr. Bipolar.

But let's get back to teeth. Think about what they mean to us! Women say the first thing they look at on a man is his smile. Men are slightly different; we figure we'll get to the smile after we check out her tits. But in the end, we all do love a good smile. Face it, the *Mona Lisa* wouldn't be the classic it is if she had a little gap between her front teeth. Then she'd say, "Ith's a niceth thpainting, ithn't it, I think it thaptureth my thmile."

You would think that taking care of our teeth in 2013 would be easier than it was in 1963, but it's not, and that's because the whole dental experience has changed. Back then a dentist was a one-man show. He would clean your teeth, show you how to brush, do bridges, take X-rays, pull teeth, fill cavities, drill root canals, make appointments, validate parking, and rub your leg when he thought you were under anesthesia. The only specialist in 1963 was the orthodontist, who thought his job was to ruin your puberty. Now the whole dental experience is painless drilling, but everything else is a pain in the ass . . . and it's all because of the specialists.

When I turned sixty-five, I decided to celebrate by making an appointment for my cleaning. I showed up on time and read the *Sports Illustrated* from 2010 until the maître d' (it's L.A., don't ask) escorted me to my examining room. The dentist came in, asked if I've been flossing, and, like we all do, I lied. Then he pulled a chunk of lobster meat from between my molars. I'm not sure, but I think he muttered, "Schmuck" as the jazz trio played him off and he left the room.

Then the parade of specialists began.

First it was the cleaning expert—the hygienist. She came in looking like one of the riot police in South Korea. On some people, a large Plexiglas face mask isn't flattering. You can't imagine the noise the tool made as she chiseled that stuff off my bottom teeth. I don't have tartar; I have a coral reef. That's why dentists' offices always have fish tanks. You could sculpt Michelangelo's *David* out of my plaque. Some hygienists use a laser; mine uses jackhammers. I feel like I'm being tortured. If Dick Cheney knew about this, we never would have waterboarded Khalid Sheikh Mohammed, we would have sent him to my dentist.

Next came the X-ray technician, because God forbid the

hygienist should have to do two things. The technician, Paolo (once again, it's L.A., don't ask), put a heavy lead blanket over my goodie basket and sprinted out of the room. That's comforting. I figure with sixty-plus years of X-rays, my balls have been covered with more lead than a kid's toy from China.

Then the dentist came back in, after looking at the X-rays, meaning that he would be charging me for a second visit. He said, "Billy, you need a root canal."

"Now?"

"Oh, I don't do them—you've got to see Dr. Jack Wu for that. He can fit you in, in about three weeks." As soon as he'd said that I needed the root canal, my tooth started to hurt. Freud would have had a field day.

"Three weeks of this kind of pain?" I asked.

"No, not this kind of pain—tomorrow you'll have a worse kind of pain," he assured me. "I'll give you these pills I got in Mexico. They may constipate you, and if they do, call Dr. Ari Weitzman."

Great, another referral.

"How about my wisdom teeth?"

"Right now, they're fine, but if you want them extracted, Dr. Abrams does uppers and Dr. Hunter does the lowers."

"So what exactly do you do?" I asked.

"Oh, I do fillings and crowns and sit by the pool you paid for."

I currently have six dental specialists. I've had more people in my mouth than a Colombian hooker during a presidential visit. My dentist farms out everything. I'm looking at the pictures on his desk and I say, "Are those your kids?"

He says, "Technically no, I didn't handle that. I sent my wife to Dr. Feldman."

But I'm lucky. I go to a very prominent dentist. My dentist is the fifth guy. You know when they say, "Four out of five dentists prefer" whatever it is they prefer? Mine's the one who doesn't. When people find out he's the fifth guy, they go crazy. "He's the fifth guy? What's he like? You gotta get me an appointment!"

Once you find a great dentist, never leave them. I know guys who have been divorced three times but have the same dentist. And the main reason I go to my dentist: he gives a great shot. You don't feel anything.

The guy I went to before always hurt me, even though he'd warn me. "You're going to feel a little prick in your mouth."

"If I do, I'm going to bite it the fuck off."

What was a twice-a-year visit when we were younger has turned into six months of appointments with specialists. Then by the time you're done, the six months are up and you have to start all over again.

But I go because my teeth mean so much to me. If I have all my teeth at sixty-five, it means I won't need a nurse to cut up my meat like Hugh Hefner's girlfriends do.

If I have all my teeth, it means I won't be mistaken for a twenty-two year-old meth addict. And most of all, if I have all my teeth, it means I won't be the only man in the world with a horizontal vagina for a mouth.

My Thirties

The girls were both fast asleep as I rearranged their blankets and softly kissed them on their foreheads. A great feeling of contentment filled me up. I was now a daddy with two beautiful daughters and a career that was picking up steam. After one last look at my sleeping angels, I joined Janice at our dining room table, across from the portly, red-cheeked man who had come to our home with the sole purpose of making me contemplate my demise. That was one of the perks of having more money: I could spend it on things like life insurance. As I listened to him drone on, I nodded and attempted to look interested, though in my mind I was stabbing him repeatedly with one of the new steak knives I had just received for my thirtieth birthday. That great feeling of contentment, gone in a flash. Nothing makes you feel older than sitting across from a life insurance salesman who keeps talking about your imminent death, making it seem like you're going to keel over during the meeting and your kids and wife will have to live in an internment camp in northern California. The insurance man's message was clear, however: you're thirty, so now you are slightly "at risk." Meaning you have the same chance of dying that the president of Iran has of showing up at a Seder.

This was also the time that the "estate planners" entered our lives. "Who would get the kids if you both were, say, MURDERED BY A MADMAN?" Awful things are possible, and we realized that, but just discussing who we'd want to raise the girls in the case of catastrophe caused a lot of anxiety. After running through all the familial options, we either got annoyed with each other or started to cry. So we thought of friends. "What about my fraternity brother Dan?"

"WHAT? Jenny asked him for a piece of gum once and he said, Sorry, it's my last one. He's selfish."

Janice's turn: "I could see the girls with Gwen."

"GWEN?" I snorted. "I can't see anybody living with Gwen . . . except for her twenty cats." Finally I made a peace offering: "Let's go neutral. What about Regis Philbin? Always up, great sense of humor. Might be fun for the girls . . ."

After seriously considering an orphanage in Russia, we ended up making plans we felt good about, but the process had forced us to realize that time was moving on and, worse, would eventually end.

Soap was a big hit, but problems were starting to emerge. With so many characters, each story arc came around so slowly that it was hard for me to get a lot of screen time. I'd come home from a frustrating day at the studio feeling edgy and walk right into "Daddy!" The girls were tons of fun, but a five-year-old and a one-year-old are a lot of work, which feels like even more when you're not happy. I was making the big mistake of bringing my work home with me. Meanwhile, Buddy kept nudging me to perform. "It's been over a year," he said. "It'll get your mind going."

Finally, one night I went over to the Improv on Melrose, a terrific comedy room whose owner, Budd Friedman, was a great friend to comics. Budd had created the original Improv in New York City, which was the mecca of all comedy clubs. That night, I went with the intention of just watching, but I couldn't help myself. When Budd introduced me, the audience gave me a huge ovation. Walking onstage as a television star sure was easier than as a nobody, but then you better be really funny. I wasn't at first, but I kept talking about the show and playing Jodie and the odd things people would say to me—"Oh my God, it's you, the fagelah"—and it got funny. I left a "tip" and was hooked all over again.

After putting the kids down for the night, I'd perform at the Improv as often as I could. I started writing new pieces, and after an uneventful day at *Soap,* going to the clubs was like getting in a great workout at a gym. When Muhammad Ali retired, I was invited to perform at a televised All-Star party for him at the Fabulous Forum, in Los Angeles. We'd done a few other television shows together in recent years as his boxing skills had started to wane. He no longer was the floating butterfly, and the sting of the bee didn't hurt as much. He'd lost an embarrassing title fight to Leon Spinks and then won the rematch, becoming the first man to win the heavyweight title three times. By this point I had developed my original impression of him so that it wasn't just an imitation of his voice, it was a total portrait of the man. The piece was called "Fifteen Rounds," and it covered fifteen big moments of Ali's life, including his relationship with Cosell, all punctuated by ring bells. I played Ali from the age of eighteen until the thirty-six-year-old Ali loses to Spinks and plots his comeback. The last speech was a monologue that rose to a fever pitch, underscored by a full orchestra playing the stirring *Rocky* music. I was the last to perform at his retirement party, and once again the least known. Richard Pryor, Chevy Chase, and Diana Ross were just a few of the superstars who preceded me. But when I got onstage in front of twenty thousand people, all I could see was Ali.

To this day, I think it was one of my best performances. The great Ali laughed and cried as he watched me play him—it was

"Little Brother, you made my life better than it was."
—1979, the Forum, Los Angeles.

surreal. I wasn't even finished when Ali himself led the standing ovation. Afterward, he came backstage. I was standing with Richard Pryor and Chevy Chase, and Ali just walked through them. He lifted me off the ground. "Little brother, you made my life better than it was," whispered the champ. He turned and left; there was nothing more to say.

The next night, I taped my very first HBO special. Michael Fuchs, the network's creator, was the executive producer for my show. A visionary, Michael would become a big part of my career. HBO wasn't yet the incredible network it is now, but it was already something unique. You had to pay to watch, and doing a special for HBO was just that: special. You could say whatever you wanted, uncensored, without commercials. At the time, mine was only the third or fourth stand-up show HBO had done. I didn't want to just walk out onto a bare stage, so we built a set to look like the backstage of a nightclub, and I gave the show a story. It opened in the Stand-up Comedians wing of the Motion Picture Home, where a young reporter, Jimmy Brogan, was interviewing the now eighty-year-old me. (Clearly, even then I was looking toward my golden years, and wondering just how golden they would actually be.) Robin Williams and the very witty Martin Mull played themselves as old-timers (great makeup jobs!), and a young actor named Michael Richards made his television debut; he played an old and confused Chevy Chase tripping over bedpans and muttering, "Did I leave the show too soon?" We also had a Steve Martin look-alike with a limp arrow on his head and deflated balloon animals littering his room.

The "interview" then became a flashback to the performance. Not thinking he'd say yes, I'd asked Ali if he would do a few minutes with me onstage as a surprise to the audience. "We will shock and amaze them, little brother," he told me. The special was being taped at a small theater in Santa Monica, only two hundred seats. The Forum event we had taped the night before was being aired that night, but Ali wouldn't let me down. He sat on an apple box in the alley of the theater, alongside our production trucks, and watched his tribute on a small black-and-white monitor until it was time to go onstage. The audience, of course, went nuts. I got him to imitate Cosell while I played him. It was hilarious. He even recited a poem to me before he left the stage: "I love your show and I admire your style, but the pay is so cheap I won't be back for a while." That night, onstage, I realized, *Holy shit, Muhammad Ali is my friend.* This was confirmed a few weeks later, when he called me to see if I wanted to run with him on a local country club golf course. "I would love to," I said. "But that club is restricted."

"What does that mean?" he asked.

"It means they don't allow Jews."

"I'm a Muslim, and they let me in. I will never run there again," he said, and he didn't.

····

The special got great reviews and came at the perfect time, sur-prising fans of *Soap* who'd never seen me do stand-up. It also reconfirmed that as good as *Soap* was for me, it was also holding me back. I felt like I was a racehorse trying to run with one leg tied to another. Some weeks on *Soap* I would have only one line, and staying focused and content became a problem. Increasingly drawn to performing my act, I was now playing college arenas, Las Vegas, and other big venues. Finally I decided that I would convince *Soap's* producers to write me out of the episodes in which my role was minuscule, so that I'd have more time to work on my stand-up. Never very good at confrontation, I rehearsed my speech over and over until I had it down. Then I arranged a meeting with Paul Witt and walked into the office with the usual lump in my throat. Behind his desk I saw a large terrarium. Walking slowly across the white sand was a tarantula the size of a poodle. The spider was the star of an ABC movie of the week called *Tarantulas: The Deadly Cargo,* and Linda Otto, the casting director who had also cast *Soap,* had given it to the producers as a present.

I sat down and nervously began talking. "Um, it's been hard to be happy here, um, especially when my story line is light and I have to be here all week for, um, one line, and it's been months of that now, so, on, um, those weeks, could you, um, write me out, so I can go off and play some dates—"

Paul stopped me: "I know we've hit a little dry period with Jodie," he said. "But we love you here, and you're a big part of this show."

At this point he reached for a small jar on his desk. "We have some new ideas that we're talking about . . ." He unscrewed the top of the jar, reached in, and pulled out a live cricket. Then he opened the lid of the terrarium and dropped the cricket onto the sand. "Just be patient," he said as the spider moved like a hairy hand toward the cricket, which now seemed more nervous than I was. "You're so popular on the show." In a moment, the spider RIPPED a leg off the cricket. "We need you here." OFF with his wings, the spider having a fine feast. Oblivious, Paul continued: "Let me think about it. I'm sorry you're so unhappy here, and we'll figure something out." The cricket seemed to be looking at me and crying as—BYE-BYE, HEAD—the spider ripped the cricket apart.

The metaphor was too much for me. "Paul, you know what? I'm fine, I'll get through this." I never asked for anything again.

••••

Janice and I bought our first house, and in December 1979 we moved in. We were supervising the moving men as they unloaded our furniture when two women in their late fifties approached us. "The house is happy it's back in show business," one of them said, as the other handed us a circular coffee cake. They told us they were sisters who had grown up in our house and now lived next door. Their parents were well-known vaudeville performers who'd had a mind-reading act. Their father, Harry Usher, was a magician as well and had helped create the famous Magic Castle in Hollywood. Their home—now ours—had been known as "the House of Usher." Cue the spooky music.

They showed us vintage photographs of the many stars who used to stop by the house. In our new backyard we saw Harold Lloyd, Walter Lantz (who had created Woody Woodpecker), Houdini's widow, George Burns, Red Skelton, Walter Brennan, and many others. "Will Rogers used to ride his horse here all the time," they told us, pointing to a spot in the front yard and giggling like cartoon mice. "Our folks would be so happy it's you."

Many years later, we did a quick renovation on a small section of the house, and when we knocked down a wall, we discovered a hidden room. The small space was filled with little clay pots for seedlings, and on the wall above a small desk was a corkboard with a newspaper clipping pinned to it. It was from the *Los Angeles Herald Examiner,* and it reported on the Oscars of 1948, the

year I was born. Not just the year, but the very week! That was
the only clipping on the board. In the single desk drawer, we
found two pieces of paper. They were the horoscopes for a
female and male Pisces. Yes, Janice and I are both Pisces. "We
told you the house is happy it's back in show business," said one
of the sisters when we showed her what we had found, again
laughing the high-pitched laugh of a cartoon mouse. A short time
later, we dug up the front yard to replant and found one of Will
Rogers's horseshoes. We didn't bring it over to the sisters; I
couldn't bear to hear that laugh again. Thirty-four years later, we
still live there because we're afraid that if we moved, the house
wouldn't be happy and it would come after us.

I started performing in Las Vegas frequently, and one night at
the MGM Grand I had a special guest in the audience: Mickey
Mantle. We'd stayed in touch since meeting on the Dinah Shore
show. He would call me when he came to Los Angeles, and we
would have drinks or dinner, and I would see him in Atlantic City
at the Claridge Hotel, where I performed and he was a spokes-
man. Once, I walked into my hotel suite and the message light
was blinking. I called, and the operator gave me my favorite
phone message ever: "Mickey Mantle called—he's in Room 777."

But this was a different Mantle now. No longer the iconic
player, he'd become a vulnerable, insecure man who drank too
much. I watched him be the special guest at a fifties-themed party
for high rollers at the hotel. It was sad. He narrated a highlight
film of his career and made inappropriate jokes. Then he posed
for pictures as all of these tipsy strangers dressed in high school
letter jackets, poodle skirts, and sweaters put their arms around
him. From the look on his face, I figured this was more painful
than his leg injuries. I think he drank just to get himself through
the agony.

That night in Vegas, we had dinner, and one of Mickey's
younger brothers soon joined us. Mick's twin brothers were just
average players; they'd never made it to the majors. Mickey seemed
uncomfortable as his brother, who was a dealer at one of the

casinos, sat down. I immediately saw why: the younger brother stuttered. Mickey looked embarrassed. As we ate, Mickey, three drinks in already, was quiet. At one point the brother said, "D-D-Did M-Mickey t-tell you wh-what was the long . . . est homer h-he ev . . . er h-hit?"

Mickey abruptly got up and excused himself. "Where's the john?" he asked the waiter.

Once Mickey was gone, his brother said, as clearly and as smoothly as anyone, "Mickey hit a homer in Joplin that went over the fence and into a car of a passing train that was on its way to Kansas City. So his longest home run was two hundred miles!" I was stunned. Mickey returned, as did his brother's stutter. Then the serious drinking started. After midnight, I got him to his room. My hero, the strongest, fastest man in the history of base-ball, needed help to get into bed. I was no longer the awestruck eight-year-old fan; instead I was the confident one, helping a friend who seemed so lost.

Another night, at the bar of the Regency Hotel in New York, my now good friend Bob Costas and I stayed up with Mickey for many hours as he again put one drink away after another. Bob was as devoted to the man as I was; in fact, he still carries a Mickey Mantle baseball card in his wallet. We spent the long night reminding Mickey of great things he had done on the ball field. These feats were as vivid to Bob and me as if we were watching them at that moment, but to Mickey they were faded memories. Some he didn't remember at all. Mickey's sadness was what upset me most. That he could be the biggest and brightest comet in the baseball universe and then crash like this on reentry was difficult to comprehend. At times, it wasn't even fun to be with him. This was my hero, and I wanted to help him; I just didn't know how.

One night we started talking about our fathers. Mick's dad had taught him how to play. He'd made him a switch-hitter; he'd even named him after a Hall of Fame player, Mickey Cochrane. Mantle idolized his dad, and when his father died when Mickey was just nineteen, he was crushed. His father was only thirty-nine, and an uncle of Mickey's also died young, both from Hodgkin's. Mantle had thought he'd never make it to forty. He used to joke, "If I knew I was gonna live this long, I would have taken better care of myself."

That night I told Mickey that I'd lost my father when I was fifteen. "He taught me how to play, too," I said, "and took me to see you, but he also taught me about comedy." I told Mickey that making my dad laugh had given me the same feeling Mickey must have had when he hit a homer or made a great catch and looked into the stands and saw a smile on his father's face or got a nod. He was very moved when I said, "We both spent most of our careers looking at an empty seat." The difference between us was that Mickey felt he had failed his father—that he'd never been as good as his father had thought he should be. We understood each other in a different way now. Even though he was the great Mantle, and my own career was now going strong, somehow we were both still teenagers missing our dads.

....

Soap continued to do well, but pressure on our sponsors caused us to be canceled after the 1980–81 season. We had done ninety-four episodes, and I was very proud of how far we had brought Jodie. I was glad it was over, but my sense of relief was tempered with *Okay, now what?* As much as I felt ready to do something else, something else hadn't materialized. Then NBC's president, Brandon Tartikoff, a young and brilliantly creative man, approached me with the idea of starring in a comedy variety show. Having loved my HBO special, he gave me a six-show commitment slated for the summer; if it worked, it would be added to the fall schedule. My own fucking show!

The producers, the network, and I started putting the show together. It was a struggle from the get-go. The network wanted a middle-of-the-road show, and I wanted something edgier. We compromised and assembled a good writing staff, a mix of veterans and younger writers. The pressure was enormous. On *Soap*

I'd been one of a great ensemble; now the entire show's success depended on me. It was called *The Billy Crystal Comedy Hour,* so who do you blame if it flops?

My brother Rip, who knew me better than anyone, was a writer on the show, and he made a great suggestion. Every time Latin actor Fernando Lamas appeared on *The Tonight Show* with Johnny, he made me laugh. His charming attitude was infectious, and I had started to imitate him. I would call friends on the phone impersonating Fernando. David Steinberg—not the comic, but a very funny man himself—was now working with Buddy as my manager, and when I'd call his office as Fernando, he'd improvise with me. "Fernando, how is Esther?" he'd ask, referring to Esther Williams, Fernando's wife. "Dahling, she looks mahvelous," I'd say, and for some reason we'd just crack up. No matter who David brought up, when he asked how they were, Fernando would reply that they looked mahvelous. Then David asked Fernando how he felt, and Nando replied, "It doesn't matter, because it's more important to look good than to feel good." Like a prehistoric kind of tweeting, it caught on virally, and soon people were calling the house asking to talk to Fernando.

In the office as we were creating the show, I was doing Fernando all the time, so Rip's idea was to run a skit called "Fernando's Hideaway," where I would play a Latin-lover talk-show host and interview our guests. The piece would be improvised, so the guests would have no idea what questions I would ask them. I wasn't sure myself, and I loved the spontaneity and danger of it. My Fernando wasn't as smart as Mr. Lamas. In fact he was a tad dim-witted and incredibly unprepared. Morgan Fairchild and Robert Urich were the first ever guests in the Hideaway, and Morgan was the first person I told, "You look mahvelous." I could feel the audience reaction to Fernando. They laughed every time I said, "You look mahvelous." The first two shows were a little rough, but they were helped by guests like Robin Williams, John Candy, Rick Moranis, and Dave Thomas and musical guests like Manhattan Transfer and Smokey Robinson.

After we taped the first two shows, Rock Hudson had a heart attack and, sadly, couldn't continue on his new series. Since we already had two shows in the can, NBC threw us on the air, with only two weeks of promotion. People mostly knew me as Jodie, not as an all-around performer, and there wasn't enough time to market the show properly. The time slot could not have been worse—we were up against *Fantasy Island,* which followed *Love Boat,* two huge hits at ABC. France had a better chance against Germany. Reviews were good, but our ratings for the first two airings, as predicted, were weak. It was a terrible situation, because although the show was slowly finding itself, the audience wasn't finding the show.

I arrived at my NBC production office to tape our fifth show feeling like we were starting to get better. Our material for that night was very funny, which boosted my confidence. But everyone looked down when I walked in. Earlier that day, I'd received phone messages from friends calling to see if I was all right. I didn't think anything of it, other than that my pals knew how tired and stressed I was. Then Buddy came in and told me that we'd been canceled after only two shows had aired. He handed me the trade papers and the *New York Times* and this was the toughest blow of all. Everyone had known but me. Just two shows? A show like this needed time to gain momentum. I wasn't even told directly that we were canceled? I felt as low as I ever had.

My mom had taught me never to give up, and Janice wouldn't let me feel bad about myself. It was very hard, but slowly I regrouped. I went back on the road and started writing new material. I would go to the Improv and work tirelessly until I had new pieces. Little by little, performing took some of the sting away. The imaginary whispers—"His show was canceled, he's finished"— when I walked into a restaurant started to fade away.

I then got a dream job, opening for Sammy Davis Jr. at Harrah's in Lake Tahoe for one month. We had met briefly once a few years before, but this was to be twenty-eight nights with the greatest entertainer I had ever seen. He was also a fascinating man and an incredible storyteller. "One night I'm smoking weed with Gary Cooper," he'd say, and you knew you were in for a good one. I would get to my dressing room two hours early just so I could hang out with him. Along with Ali and Mantle, I idolized Sammy because he could seemingly do anything. I also started to realize something: I could be him.

When you spend as much time as I did with Sammy, you can't help but talk like him. I got to study his cadence, his vocabulary, his intonations, his different laughs, how he walked, and how he sang, and privately I started to do him.

Opening night, I did a strong set and Sammy followed me out on stage and told the audience a great story of how I had visited him in the hospital and helped get him well. The audience gave me a huge round of applause.

Wonderful story, except it had never happened. Next show, a different story with the same theme: Billy is a great guy and we're the best of friends. I went to the soundman, who had tears in his eyes. "Nice thing you did for Sam," he said, and after humbly thanking him, I asked him to tape Sammy's openings for me. I have twenty-five stories that Sammy told; none are the same, and all are about all the wonderful things we did together, which we never actually did. It was fantastic. I didn't mind at all; in fact, I looked forward to it every night because he just kept making me look better and better. It was show business to Sammy—that's it, and that's all.

I watched Sammy perform every night. He was electric onstage. Everything you've read or heard was true, except that being up close to the genius of it was like getting to look at a precious stone in perfect light. His energy, his love for performing, and his respect for the audience were simply astonishing. On our closing night, I had just started my act when I heard Sammy laughing in the wings. He never watched my show until the last moment, and then he followed me out onstage. I looked over and there he was, laughing so hard he was stomping his foot, and pointing at something on the stage. Sammy used a teleprompter so he could follow the lyrics of new songs. It was hidden in a speaker so the audience couldn't see it. It was also a video monitor, and that night, courtesy of Sammy, there on the screen was a porno film. For a full half hour that graphic film played while I did my act and Sammy laughed. I had to think of my grandmother to keep God from stiffening me again. Working with Sammy was like getting to be friends with Mickey, a dream come true.

••••

Soon after that, Rob Reiner asked me to play a small part in a "rockumentary" he was making called *This Is Spinal Tap,* the hilarious fictional documentary about England's "loudest band." Christopher Guest, Michael McKean, and Harry Shearer brilliantly improvised the entire film and wrote and performed all the songs. My scene involved a promotional party thrown by Spinal Tap's record company. I was the boss of the catering company, called Shut Up and Eat. We were all in whiteface mime makeup, and I engaged in a heated discussion with one of my inexperienced waiters (Dana Carvey); "Mime is money" was my big line. The movie, now a classic, launched Rob as a major director. After that, I did my second HBO stand-up special, called *A Comic's Line,* which attracted the attention of Dick Ebersol, who was now the producer of *Saturday Night Live.* In March 1984, Dick booked me to host *SNL.* It was nine years after I had been bumped.

I loved every second of that week. Walking into 30 Rock again and working with the cast in that studio was exhilarating. The show went well, and Dick asked me to host again later that season. That summer Dick called with a proposition: if he could get Martin Short and Christopher Guest to be regulars on the show, would I consider joining the cast, which also featured Julia Louis-Dreyfus and Jim Belushi? I knew instantly that I should do it. I was now thirty-six years old, I wasn't getting any movie offers, and being on the road and playing Vegas wasn't the career—or the life—I had wanted. Janice and I talked about it with the girls, and we all moved to New York for the adventure that would be my year at *SNL*.

The girls were eleven and seven, and the time in New York gave them the little "edge" that was missing from their California lifestyle. They experienced what it's like to live in the greatest city in the world. They were able to be around our family, and they got to watch winter turn into spring. We took them to museums and shows, the Bronx Zoo, Yankee Stadium, Radio City Music Hall. We showed them the places we'd gone to as kids, and we pointed out the statue of George M. Cohan.

Being home and doing the show reenergized me. Often I would walk from our apartment on Thirteenth Street to Forty-ninth Street, where 30 Rock is. The people, the noise, the smells, the chaos in the city gave me new ideas almost every day. The 30 Rock building itself is unique. An aura hits you when you walk into the lobby and carries you right up to Studio 8H, *SNL*'s home. The Yankee Stadium of comedy.

The plan was for me to do the show for just one year, so, to me, every week felt like a special. Plus, working alongside Chris, Marty, and the other talented cast members, I pushed myself to be as funny as I could. We created great new characters. There was Marty's Ed Grimley and the hilarious send-up of synchronized swimming starring Chris and Marty and Harry Shearer. There was "Lifestyles of the Relatives of the Rich and Famous," featuring Marty's phenomenal imitation of Katharine Hepburn. Marty is one of the funniest people I have ever met, and also one of the kindest. His energy is relentless, and his fearless talent always inspiring. To this day we are the closest of friends. Chris and I worked together beautifully. He has a lightning-fast, funny mind, perfect timing, and a great ear that enables him to imitate odd people, like Red Skelton and Alan Arkin. He also has the rare ability to underplay—not unlike Peter Sellers—and physically can do just about anything. When I made him laugh I felt like I had accomplished something important. The only problem was we

Christopher Guest and me as the Minkman Brothers,
Saturday Night Live.

would laugh on the air in most of our sketches. Chris and I had
big problems keeping a straight face.

Together we created the "I hate when that happens" masochists,
the seventy-five-year-old Negro League baseball players Leonard
"the Rooster" Willoughby and "King Carl" Johnson, and the Minkman brothers, who appeared in a hilarious spoof of *60 Minutes,*
with Harry doing a perfect Mike Wallace imitation and Marty
playing the Nathan Thurm lawyer character, who said, "It's so silly
that you would say that, why would you say that?" Makeup artist
Peter Montagna transformed me into all of my characters as well
as Sammy Davis Jr., who sang duets with Ringo Starr and Jesse
Jackson. Some people didn't realize it was me playing Sammy. My
mother thought Eddie Murphy was still on the show; I had to do
Sammy on the phone for her to convince her.

Sammy was so much fun to do. I even recorded my home phone machine message as Sammy. With some big band music in the background, I said, "Hey, it's Sammy, grooving with the band. Leave your name and number, and I mean that." Well, one night I come home and the message light was on. I pressed Play and heard the real Sammy say, "What the fuck is that?" Sammy called and Sammy answered. He said he wasn't pissed, but I erased it anyway.

Fernando really took off, and I always looked forward to playing him, because "Fernando's Hideaway" was the only sketch on the show that didn't use cue cards. The set would be brought out right in front of the audience at center stage, and the crowd could see that we were just winging it. My favorite episode was when Barry Manilow was scheduled as the guest and didn't show up at the last minute. Desperate, I convinced one of our crew, Bobby Ferracio, who weighed almost three hundred pounds, to play Barry, because as Fernando explained, he wouldn't want to disappoint his audience. I asked Bobby questions like "What's it like being a sex symbol?" He sang, "I Write the Songs," and the audience just loved him. That's what live television is all about. It was better than having Barry there. For a while we thought that for the rest of the season, Bobby would always be the only guest because everyone had canceled, but Bobby said no. "My neighbors made a big fuss," he told me. "I can't do it."

"You look mahvelous!" No matter where I went (and still to this day), somebody would tell me I looked mahvelous, as if I had never heard it before, from Bill Clinton and Ted Kennedy to Barbara Walters and my gardener. The encounter I'll never forget was with Henry Kissinger, who not only told me I looked mahvelous but then introduced me to his wife: "Honey, this is my favorite, Billy Joel." Other characters I did were Buddy Young Jr., an insult comic, who would become the basis for *Mr. Saturday Night;* Joe Franklin, a well-known talk-show host; and a character named Lew Goldman, an old Jewish weatherman who only gave the forecast for where his family lived. A writer on the staff named

"Three Amigos" with Martin Short and Jesse Jackson,
when Jesse hosted *SNL*.
(Photograph © Fred Watkins)

Larry David created him with me. I'm not sure what became of him.

We were older than the usual cast, the only drugs we did were antacids, and our comedy sensibilities were different, but it worked. People were talking about *SNL* again. All these years later, fans think that we were all there for a few years, when in fact it was just eighteen shows. Midway through the season, I started to feel that one year wouldn't be enough. I was having too much fun. Nine years after getting bumped and slinking out of that great studio, I was thriving in it, and I finally had the career I wanted, doing the work I had always hoped I would get a chance to do. For four years I had only played Jodie; now every week I got the chance to play four or five characters.

It was exhausting as hell. The cast and writers would meet the host on Monday and get their ideas and thoughts, and then the cast members would have only two days to write the bits we wanted to do on the show, while hopefully the writers were writing parts for us as well. All proposed sketches had to be ready by Wednesday afternoon, which was read-through day. The entire cast, the writers, and the crew would meet and we would read every piece, and then Dick, who was the best producer I have ever worked with, would pick the sketches for the show. Before we knew it, we were rehearsing on-camera or shooting promos or a film piece or writing a feature for "Weekend Update."

It seemed that I lived at 30 Rock. One Tuesday night around three A.M., Marty and I were in our offices on the seventeenth floor, staring at the driving snow that was falling on the sleeping city. I poked my head out of the door: "Marty, you have anything?"

"Nope, I'm dry."

"Want to grab a cab? It's late and it's snowing—let's get out of here," I said. Totally wiped out, we got into a cab and headed down Seventh Avenue. We were talking about how tired we were as the cab stopped for a light at Thirty-third Street. Marty was saying something when I heard it: the roar of a giant animal. Marty's eyes lit up, and I turned and saw a huge tiger outside the window. I knew I was tired, but this was ridiculous. It roared again, and we wiped the condensation off the window and saw not only tigers but lions in cages and elephants walking in the snow. The circus was loading into Madison Square Garden. Led by his handler, the tiger joined the animal parade into the great arena. It was one of the most beautiful and surreal moments I've ever experienced. Marty and I had just left the office, and these animals were on their way to work.

After all the time I had put into comedy, I was finally where I had set out to be, and it was the time of my life. If nothing came out of this year, so be it. I had given it my best shot. As the season was winding down to its finish, I got a call from Peter Hyams, who was directing a movie called *Running Scared*. He wanted me to star in the film with Gregory Hines. I was overjoyed. It was a solid action-comedy script, and I flew to California to screen-test for the part. Then, the night before the test, Brandon Tartikoff called and asked me if I would be interested in hosting *SNL* on a permanent basis. He was toying with the idea of a wheel: four different rotating shows to run on Saturday nights, one of which would be *SNL*. I was thrilled but confused—everything was happening at once.

"Brandon, if this is real," I said, "I have to know, because I'm screen-testing for this movie tomorrow, and it's going to shoot when the show would be on, and I can't do both. I won't do the test. We'd have to start working on the show right away!"

"I'll call you back," Brandon said.

He never did. What happened was that Dick Ebersol suddenly stepped aside as producer, and Lorne Michaels came back to rebuild *SNL*. He wanted to start from scratch, so not only was I not going to host the show, I couldn't go back to *SNL* even if I wanted to. I did the screen test and got the part.

My experience at *SNL* had been like getting lost in a snowstorm, retracing your steps, and then starting off again, this time in the right direction. Getting my first Emmy nomination was the icing on the cake. That was the most important year in my career, and I was very proud of the work we all did there and grateful for the chance, but it was time to move on.

....

In *Running Scared,* Gregory and I had a natural chemistry that Peter Hyams was able to orchestrate and capture on film. It was Peter's idea to team us together, and he brought out the best in us. I got into great physical condition to play Danny, a tough, street-smart, wisecracking cop from Chicago. Gregory and I did most of our own stunts, and both of us, not being the biggest guys in the world, had to train intensely. This would also be the first time I would have to shoot a gun; before that I'd never even had one in my hand, unless you count using my index finger as a kid to shoot the bad guys: "Bam bam bam."

We trained at a shooting range, and I was surprised and a

Running Scared with Gregory Hines.

little frightened by the power of a pistol and an Uzi submachine gun. The first day of filming was a shoot-out scene in a dingy drug dealer's apartment. With movie bullets flying around me, I would have to run into a room, dive onto the floor, and shoot my pistol three times. I did the first take, hit the ground, and fired the pistol. Peter yelled, "Cut," the crew applauded, and he called me over to the monitor, where he was cueing up the video playback. I was jazzed—this was a real movie! We watched the playback, and there I was, Mr. Tough Guy. I flew into the room, looking like a real cop, hit the floor, and when I fired the pistol, I shouted, "Bam bam bam!"

"You don't have to make the sound—the gun will," joked Peter. I had no idea I'd said a word.

....

Earlier that spring, I was asked to host an NBC special to be shot at the Baseball Hall of Fame, in Cooperstown, New York. *A Comedy Salute to Baseball* would air the night before the All-Star Game. Mickey Mantle was going to be a guest, along with Willie Mays. They had both been banned from baseball because they worked for casinos in Atlantic City as greeters and had just been reinstated by new commissioner Peter Ueberroth.

The show was to be a funny look at baseball and would feature Mickey and Willie doing sketches with me. When I arrived in Cooperstown, I was told that Mays had canceled at the last moment and it would just be Mickey.

The night before shooting, there was a production meeting at a restaurant directly across from the Hall of Fame. The director looked like a Hollywood stereotype: purple sweater tied around his neck and matching sunglasses . . . indoors! We were waiting for Mickey, who had been flown up privately. The man picking him up was a kindly older gentleman. He and his sweet wife were the owners of the bed-and-breakfast where we were all staying. A former neurosurgeon, he had undergone a major cancer surgery that had left him with a gap between his shoulder and his neck. He handled this huge deformity with dignity. It didn't bother him, so why should it bother you? was his mantra. Well into the meeting, Mickey arrived. Still wearing the golf shoes he'd had on in Atlantic City before he got on the plane to Cooperstown, he kept pawing the young waitress as she led him to our table in the back; I knew right away that he was smashed. She pushed his groping hands away again, saying, "Mr. Mantle, please . . ."

Mickey slurred back, "No, not Mr. Mantle—I'm your uncle Bob."

He saw me. "Hey, you little son of a bitch!" he said, which is how he usually greeted me. He nodded to our staff, and then he saw the director. "Fuck you!" he laughed.

"What did I do?" asked the Hollywood stereotype, now clearly uncomfortable.

"Look at ya," Mickey snorted and sat down, and the meeting went on as best it could.

As we were leaving, Mickey asked if we were staying at the same place. "Yes," I said, "it's a great old inn."

"Good," Mickey replied. "I guess Shark Bite took my bags there."

"Who?"

"Shark Bite," Mickey said. "Ain't that what happened to him?"

I explained what I knew about our host, and Mantle felt bad for a moment and then started laughing hysterically. It was locker room banter. Players always make up a name for someone with a distinctive feature. Guys with big noses were usually "Hook," big-eared players were "Rabbit," and so on. So I'm guessing in his boozy state of mind, when Mickey saw the huge indention in the outline of the fellow's shoulder, he was thinking there was only one reason: shark bite.

At the inn, Mickey and I had adjoining rooms with a common bathroom. It was a rough night for Mickey—I could hear him thrashing about. In the middle of the night, he knocked softly on my door. "Hey, you still up?"

"Yeah, but, Mick, it's two A.M. and we have to be at the hall at seven."

"I can't do this. I'm too nervous."

I let him in. There we were, me in my pajamas and Mantle in his boxer shorts. We spoke in hushed whispers. He was visibly upset.

"You'll be fine, Mick, it's all on cue cards."

"No, that's not what I mean. I've never been in the damn place. When I got inducted in '74, I left after my speech. Had a hundred friends and family, Merlyn, the boys, and I just left. I don't belong in there. I wasn't good enough."

"Are you kidding me?" I couldn't believe the legend was having an anxiety attack.

"No, I should have been so much better. I can't do this."

I talked Mickey down and finally coaxed him back to bed.

At the breakfast table the next morning, our host was pouring Mickey some juice and Mickey couldn't look at him. He kept staring down at his eggs like a kid in church who'd done something wrong. I knew he felt bad for calling him Shark Bite.

We headed over to the Hall of Fame. Mickey stopped me again.

"Please, I can't do this. I've never even seen where my plaque is."

"Well, let's go find it," I said, " 'cause that's where the first shot is."

"Shit," Mickey muttered. We met David Israel, one of the producers for the show, and we walked Mantle to his plaque. "There it is, Mickey," I said.

He stared at the plaque and looked at the others on the wall, and then suddenly he said, "Why the fuck am I with that guy? I should be with Willie and Whitey. What the fuck is going on?"

So now the man who didn't think he should be in the Hall of Fame was mad about the positioning of his plaque. It was a curious juxtaposition, and we all felt a little uncomfortable.

We shot some funny skits together, including a version of "I Hate When That Happens." He was a natural. On a break, the director of the hall, Bill Guilfoyle, took us upstairs. A preacher type with wire-rimmed glasses and a kind shyness about him, he was obviously thrilled that the great Mantle was there. We went to a floor dedicated to Babe Ruth and his amazing career, and we stared at the accomplishments: 714 home runs, .342 lifetime batting average, over two thousand RBIs, 94 wins as a pitcher. Ruth was the greatest player in baseball history. His locker from the stadium was sitting there, poetically alone.

"Some career, don't you think, Mickey?" said the president.

"Yeah, but I got more pussy than he did."

I thought the president would have a stroke. I wasn't far behind. Guilfoyle didn't know what to say. His glasses fogged up, his voice cracked. "Uh . . . yes, I guess you did, Mickey. . . . Would you like to see Gehrig's locker?"

It was a perfect Mantle joke. Totally wrong, but really funny. I put it into the script of *61**, the film about Mantle and Maris I later directed for HBO.

At the end of the day, we were taping my good nights on the field where Abner Doubleday was said to have invented the game. I said, "When you're a kid learning how to play this glorious game, you dream of a time when Mickey Mantle and you would be having a catch, and he'd say, 'Nice arm, kid.' " With that, Mantle stepped in behind me holding two gloves and a baseball. "Hey, quit talking—let's play catch."

I turned to the camera and said, "I love when this happens." The credits rolled as we were throwing the ball to each other. When it was over, we just kept throwing. I started to cry.

"What's the matter?" Mickey asked.

"I got something in my eye."

A lifelong dream. I had thought about playing catch with Mantle from the first time I saw him, in 1956. We moved farther apart, as he seemed to really enjoy throwing the ball again. Mickey couldn't move too well, and I didn't want to throw the ball where he couldn't get to it. Sure enough, the harder you try to make something perfect, the more likely you are to screw up. He limped after my next toss, the ball falling at his feet. "Sorry," I said, feeling awful. "No, I am," he said. "If I could get that, I'd still be playing."

We finished the taping, and "Shark Bite" drove us to the airport in Albany. The Mohawk Valley was in fine form; the spring rains

∧

With Mickey at the Hall of Fame,
a comedy salute to baseball.

had turned it into a green wonderland that would become a stunning red-and-gold watercolor in the fall. Mickey sat in the back-
seat with a six-pack of beer. I was up front with a tuna sandwich.
After a while, Mickey said, "Pretty . . ."

"You should see it in October," said Shark Bite.

"Yeah," Mickey muttered, "maybe I should come up here more.
When they put the new guys in, maybe I should come."

"Of course you should," I said. "Williams comes, Musial, Bob
Feller . . . they all come . . ." I continued, and as I turned I saw
Mickey staring out the open window, the breeze blowing his now
thinning blond hair. "Hey, driver," he said. "I never got your name."

"Ted," the sweet man answered softly, his eyes, still focused on the road, now misting up.

"I'm Mickey, nice to know you. If I get up here, maybe you'll drive me again."

"Anytime," said Ted. Mickey soon fell asleep. He looked like a kid who'd had a big day and conked out in the family car on the way home. We drove in silence now. Ted and I looked at each other and smiled as we headed through the lush hills of upstate New York.

••••

Soon after, I recorded a live stand-up album at the famous Bottom Line nightclub in New York, and wrote a single called "You Look Marvelous" with Paul Shaffer, which was nominated for a Grammy. We made a fun video of the song for MTV, in which I played Grace Jones, Tina Turner, Sammy, and, of course, Fernando. On the promotional tour I met a young Chicago talk-show host named Oprah Winfrey, who called me "the designated Negro" because I could play black people so realistically. I think what made it work was that they were characters I loved, and having been around all those great musicians growing up, playing African Americans just came naturally to me. I did a concert tour and made another HBO special, called *Don't Get Me Started,* which I also codirected. It was a parody of Sting's movie *Bring on the Night,* where he rented a mansion in France to write music and rehearse for his new tour and made a documentary of the experience. For my show we rented a house in Pasadena and Rob Reiner played Marty DiBergi, his director character from *Spinal Tap,* who this time was making a "yockumentary." The show also featured Chris Guest, Eugene Levy, and a strange older German comedian named Brother Theodore. I played Fernando, Whoopi, Sammy, and Buddy Young Jr. The show was mostly improvised, and working with these incredible talents was inspiring. Sammy (the real one) particularly loved the scene where I as Sammy show some footage of "himself" in the Jack Nicholson part in

One Flew over the Cuckoo's Nest, which he was fired from after one day for "creative differences."

Rob was in the midst of doing a string of terrific movies: *Spinal Tap, Stand by Me,* and now came *The Princess Bride,* from William Goldman's classic screenplay. Rob asked me to play Miracle Max, an ancient gnome of a medicine man. Carol Kane was my equally ancient wife, Valerie, and we made a magic pill that helps bring the hero back to life. No director had a more varied slate of films than Rob, and this trend would, of course, continue. His trust, sense of humor, and timing were sensational. He would always get the scene as written but would never stop finding new places for me to improvise. For instance, in a take when Rob told me, "Say whatever you want," I came up with "True love is the greatest thing in the world, except for a nice MLT, a mutton, lettuce, and tomato sandwich, where the mutton is nice and lean, and the tomato is ripe. Mmmm. They're so perky. I love that." We'd become the closest of friends and could talk about anything with each other, which in a few years would figure in a unique way.

For Max, I asked Peter Montagna, my makeup artist from *SNL,* to make me look like a cross between Casey Stengel and my grandmother. After five hours of makeup, I was that funny-looking little old man. I hope if I get that old, I'm as much fun as Max was. To this day people will say to me, "Have fun storming the castle." The movie wasn't a big hit, but it is now considered a classic. I'm so proud to be in it. (If only for three minutes!) The film means something to people. I've now watched it with both my kids and my grandkids. In 2012, we had a twenty-fifth reunion at the New York Film Festival. The screening at Lincoln Center was raucous. A thousand fans applauded everyone's entrance in the film and said their favorite lines with the actors on the screen. It was like going to a midnight showing of *The Rocky Horror Picture Show.* Tears came to my eyes as they chanted Mandy Patinkin's line "My name is Inigo Montoya. You killed my father. Prepare to die" and my "Have fun storming the castle." Generations of

"Have fun storming the castle." In London with Carol Kane.

families came to see the film and pay tribute to Rob and the cast. Sadly, André the Giant and Peter Falk had passed away, but the rest of us were there, united forever by this special film.

Next came *Throw Momma from the Train,* directed by Danny DeVito, who was also my costar. I learned a lot by watching Danny act and direct himself. A funny, dark movie, it opened at number one at the box office. After that, I cowrote a movie with my great friend Eric Roth. It was called *Memories of Me* and starred Alan King and JoBeth Williams. Alan and I played an estranged father and son. Working with Alan was like going to the Museum of Comedy every day. He had a big personality and an endless wealth of stories, and we became fantastic friends. The movie didn't do well, but I had learned how to take body shots and keep moving forward. Eric is now one of Hollywood's best writers; he won an Academy Award for *Forrest Gump* and has been nominated for Oscars numerous times.

In 1986 HBO's Chris Albrecht along with Bob Zmuda created

At *Comic Relief* with the cast of *Your Show of Shows*,
Sid Caesar, Howard Morris, Carl Reiner, and Imogene Coca.
These are the people who made me want to be funny!

Comic Relief, a telethon featuring every comedian they could get
to raise money to help the homeless. Robin Williams, Whoopi
Goldberg, and I hosted it, and by the time we had finished all nine
of our shows, we had raised over $50 million to supply medical aid
to homeless people on the streets of America. We also cemented
a friendship that will never fade away. They are powerful talents
who go about being funny in different ways. Whoopi is smart,
outspoken, and fearless. Robin is simply a comet. The challenge
of keeping up with him onstage is one I relish.

The first time I saw him was in 1977. I was asked to be part of
a benefit concert in San Francisco for the Boarding House nightclub. David Allen ran the club, and he was a most loved and
respected man, but it had fallen on hard times and many of its

regulars who were now big stars gathered to help David keep the club open. Steve Martin, Lily Tomlin, Neil Young, Melissa Manchester, and many others were splendid. I did a brief, strong set, and to close the show a young, local comedian named Robin Williams took the stage. He not only took it, he lifted it into space. Comedy, as I knew it, changed instantly. I had never seen anyone like him. He was Jonathan Winters but on warp speed. He was all over the stage, he was in the audience, and he didn't use a microphone, which made the two thousand or so in the audience listen even more intently.

In a short time the world would see what I saw that night, when *Mork and Mindy* aired and blew everyone away. We got to know each other, and now are the closest of friends. His mind still races at a speed few can keep up with. When we get a chance to riff together, it's as close to jazz as you can get without instruments. On our first *Comic Relief* broadcast, we left the stage after our opening and our producer Pat Tourk Lee said, "The phones are ringing." We all started to well up. People were watching; people were giving. I now had a career that, after my show had been canceled, I hadn't thought was possible. Right before I turned forty, I was asked to host the Grammy Awards. Oy.

The Five Stages of Forgetting Things

1.

2.

3.

4.

5.

Conservative

ately it's getting harder for me to feel optimistic about the world. Twenty-four hours a day, seven days a week, fifty-two weeks a year, this is why:

"Good evening, I'm Wolf Blitzer with bad news."

"I'm Chris Wallace, with even more bad news."

"I'm Rachel Maddow, don't even ask."

"I'm Brian Williams. They're wrong—it's worse."

It's become a race between what's falling apart faster, the world or my body. All the problems in the world have gotten me so angry that now I, Billy Crystal, a lifelong liberal, am becoming a tad . . . conservative.

Not on social issues; I'm still the pro–gay marriage, pro–civil rights, anti-war, feed-the-hungry-and-house-the-homeless, it's-okay-to-have-red-wine-with-fish, liberal-thinking guy I always have been. But in other areas, I'm drifting. It's like I'm my grandfather driving his car in the left lane of the freeway at twenty miles per hour (sitting as low as possible, so people behind him can't tell if anyone is actually behind the wheel), and s-l-o-w-l-y the car is drifting to the right.

And when did this drift to the right start? It started years ago when I was watching the news and saw that vile Richard Speck, who was in prison for life for killing eight student nurses, had been injecting himself with female hormones and was growing breasts and having wild sex with his inmate boyfriend. Some punishment. That's not prison, that's spring break. *Why is he still alive?* I found myself asking. I knew I was really driving in the right lane the day I saw Jared Lee Loughner pleading guilty with an idiot smile on his face to killing six people, including that beautiful little girl who'd had her whole life ahead of her, and critically wounding Gabby Giffords. Six people are dead, a great woman is permanently damaged, and he's going to spend the rest of his life in prison? We're paying to keep that sick smile on his face?

Up until then, I was against the electric chair. Now I'm for the electric stadium. Vendors and everything: "Last meal, get your last meal here." Everybody stands for the national anthem, and when they all sit down, we throw the switch and get rid of all the crazies at once. Think of the money we could save—think of the money we could make! We could sell rights to pay-per-view, and don't forget corporate sponsorships. Why not? People paid money to see *The Passion of the Christ,* and that was a snuff film. Okay, I'm kidding. I'm really not for the electric stadium. Let's make it solar-powered, because I'm an environmentalist.

There, I got the big conservative rage out of my system, but the little everyday things that annoy me are still there. These annoyances hang around and torment me like relatives who stay too long over the holidays, or that piece of food that gets stuck between your teeth and then you use dental floss and the floss rips, leaving that little bit of frayed floss that you can't seem to reach. The only thing you can use to work it out is a toothpick, and then you think, Why didn't I use this in the first place? I'm talking about the things you can live with but that annoy the crap out of you.

Honestly, I don't want to be the grouchy old man. You know: "Don't hit the ball in old man Crystal's yard, you'll never get it back!"—*that guy*. I just want to get rid of the frayed floss in the teeth of life.

Speaking of floss, fat people annoy me. I have compassion, believe me; I know obesity can be an addiction or a disease. But they drive me nuts with their excuses. They're not big-boned, they're fat. And they crowd me on airplanes and they eat excessive amounts of food that starving children need and they cause health-care costs to skyrocket. Worst of all, they let their kids get fat. Six-year-olds shouldn't be having bypass surgery. Obesity numbers are skyrocketing. Illegal immigrants can't get in anymore; there's no more room. Everybody eats too much. The only thing Jewish women won't swallow is their husbands. People are so immense, they can't even walk. They ride their Rascal scooters. Really fast. Have you been to Las Vegas recently? They roar through the casino buffet like a Harley gang tear-assing through a small town. One time at Caesars Palace, I got caught behind a whole flock of them and I thought I was in the Macy's Thanksgiving Day Parade!

Another thing that drives me crazy is when people use their cell phones in restaurants—and the restaurants that allow them to. About a year ago, Janice and I are out for our anniversary, we're having a nice quiet romantic dinner, and there's a guy at the table next to us. He gets on his phone just as my entrée arrives.

"That tumor weighed six pounds, it was benign, but I had to cut through his ribs and the abscess to get at it, all that pus. . . . Waiter can I have another chardonnay? The tumor was larger than I thought, it was like delivering a baby— Waiter, I'll have the liver and onions."

I wanted to kill him. And I could have, because I wouldn't get the death penalty, and I could live out my days with a sick smile on my face, far away from these annoying people.

I just want to tell them all, STOP.

Trolls: STOP. The crap you post on Internet forums and in comment sections is mean, it's vicious, and it's untrue. And if your parents knew you did that, they would ask you to move out of their basement. P.S.: If you're going to post, learn to spell.

NBA players who thump their chests and scream like mating dinosaurs after a dunk: STOP. I can honestly say I never do that after I dunk. If LeBron and I don't do it, neither should you.

Westboro Baptist Church: STOP. Stop protesting the funerals of our soldiers who died in action because you are anti-gay. When one of you dies, I'm going to show up with a couple of gay veterans and we're going to do a musical at your funeral.

Congress: STOP. I mean start. Do something. How can these politicians get to Washington, D.C., and actually brag that they're not going to pass anything? We pay their salaries! If you want to get paid for doing nothing and blocking progress, become a movie studio executive.

NRA: STOP. Or you'll shoot. Eighty-two percent of Americans want background checks, and the only reason you are against them is because you're afraid what craziness they'll find in *your* background.

People with so many tattoos that their bodies look like graffiti-covered abandoned buildings: STOP.

Iran: STOP. If you're going to threaten Israel, tell your president to wear a fucking tie.

People you love who die too young: STOP DYING. And people you hate who live too long: STOP LIVING. What do you know, Jared Lee Loughner made a return appearance in this chapter.

I'm annoyed at people who, every four years during the World Cup, tell us that Americans are dumb because they don't love soccer and that this is the year we all become soccer fans. So all of you announcers, here's your new life goaaal: STOP. Stop telling us how great soccer is. It will never catch on here. Americans like sports where the fighting is on the field, not in the stands.

I'm annoyed by Cats . . . the musical and the animal. People who like either, STOP telling me how great both are. One I ignored, and the other ignores me. If I wanted an aloof companion I would have married a Presbyterian.

I'm sorry Al Gore invented the Internet. They say the Internet is for everybody. Except the newspapers it put of business, the music industry it crippled, the bookstores that are now closed. And, oh yeah, I'm really annoyed at the Internet because it is responsible for the most annoying website of all time: WebMD.

WebMD: STOP. The truth is, we're all addicted to WebMD. It starts innocently. You wake up one morning and have a slight pain in your left side. You start to think, Is the appendix on the left or right side? So you go to Google, enter the word "appendix," and up pops WebMD. So you click through. You enter the words "appendix pain," and in a millisecond, there are twenty-two million articles to look at. After a four-hour search through the top five hundred, you realize two things: (1) the appendix is on the right side; (2) you had it out when you were ten years old. So you go to log off, but all that staring at the screen has made your vision blurry. So you look up blurry eyes. Blurry eyes are a symptom of twenty-six thousand diseases. It could be a stroke, a brain tumor, a detached retina, it could be you were bitten by a tsetse fly. With each cross-reference you find out that you have the symptom of . . . everything. And then your eyes drift to the side of the web page and there's a banner ad for the Jacoby & Meyers wills specialist. How did they know! Now you get ready to call him, because without even spending one second with a trained medical professional, without one day in med school, without even passing high school biology, you have successfully diagnosed that you have: sleeping sickness, a carcinoid tumor of the lymph glands, beriberi, scarlet fever, diverticulitis, and Lou Gehrig's disease.

Super PACs: STOP. The Supreme Court decision to allow this has disenfranchised all of us and ruined our country. It's now a game show: *The Country Can Be Yours, If the Price Is Right* or *Who Wants to Be Owned by a Millionaire.* We used to have Lincolns and FDRs and JFKs, now we have . . . who cares? Big money and corporations have made all voters feel like Jews do every election. That's right. Jews feel disenfranchised. Other than in New York and Florida. Everywhere else, elections involve nonstop talk about Jesus this and Christ that and how we are a Christian nation. I get it, but do you have to rub it in my face? Don't make me feel like, well, like a Jew at the Easter Parade. Look, I know there aren't many of us, but there aren't a lot of penguins either, and they get more attention and respect than we do. At least Morgan Freeman narrates their lives.

And I am really annoyed at teachers who have sex with students. STOP. It seems like once a week you hear of a thirty-five-year-old math teacher who had sex in her car with some sixteen-year-old. I am furious. Where was she when I was growing up?

Climate-change deniers: STOP. Look out the fucking window. How much evidence do you need? People who deny climate change are probably the same people who still think O.J. was innocent. And it's not just the climate deniers who annoy me. I'm annoyed at people who kill endangered species for profit, as well as those who eat them. There are less than one hundred Javan rhinos left. We can't take the planet for granted. The Earth is like that baseball you catch at the ballpark and it's so white and pristine and you take great care of it, but over time it gets brown and then you play with it on concrete, so it gets scuffed up, and finally it unravels and you can't play with it anymore, so basically it's worthless.

Pit bulls: STOP. Yes, I know they can be affectionate, and yes, I know that it's bad owners who make bad pit bulls, but guess what: there are a lot of bad owners out there. I never trust anything that even the North Koreans are afraid to eat.

Athletes who use steroids: STOP. Everybody knows that testing is mandatory, but somehow these guys are too stupid to realize that they're going to get caught. You would think that with a size 15 head, there would be a brain in there.

People not impressed by NASA: STOP. When we were growing up, space flight was a wonder. The Mercury astronauts were my heroes, and I followed every flight obsessively. Now we land a rover on Mars and people don't even care. Neil Armstrong's death got very little notice. He walked on the moon! Meanwhile, Anna Nicole Smith dies and she gets twenty-four/seven coverage on five cable networks. Wake up, everyone. One day after we've ruined the Earth, we're going to have to go live on another planet, and you know where we'll be forced to turn to for space travel because no one cared about NASA? Scientologists.

Ageism: STOP. What is it with American society? In Asia, they revere their elders and venerate anything old. Over there, one-hundred-year-old eggs are a delicacy; here, it means Madonna is trying to get pregnant again.

It's hard to believe that in 2013 there are still professions with mandatory retirement ages. If you're not physically or mentally capable of doing the job, sure, I get it—but decide on a case-by-case basis; don't lump us all together. Why do all FBI agents have to retire at fifty-seven, but J. Edgar was still wearing his heels and red evening gown to work until he was seventy-seven? I'd trust Sully Sullenberger to land a plane even if he were eighty. Maybe I wouldn't let him drive me home afterward, but land a plane on the Hudson, sure.

Now, I get that there are people who can't wait to retire; they've put in their time. For instance, I went over to a friend's house for a retirement party. He was seventy-one years old and in his pool just walking back and forth, back and forth. I said, "Al, what are you doing? Why not swim?"

He said, "I worked all my life so that I could walk in a pool."

But not everyone is like Al. Some people want to keep working, but even those in professions that don't force them to retire are often encouraged to leave their jobs. When it comes to fighting ageism, I'm pro-choice. Each of us should choose if we want to retire or keep going. Sure, some jobs we can't do physically. But there are plenty of jobs we can do. If we can't continue in the jobs we've pursued all our lives, let us stay active; put us to work doing something meaningful. Not bagging groceries, not being crossing guards, but something where we can make a real difference.

Fellow baby boomers, this is our new battle; this is our new war. We fought imperialism, we fought racism, we fought sexism, and now we need to enlist in the war against ageism. But if we are going to, we have to stay on top of our game. We have to meet the challenges. We have to show that we are better than those sprightly fifty-eight-year-olds. We have to challenge ourselves every day. And that starts with setting goals and having dreams of glory, and by that I don't mean getting our triglycerides under 150.

If you want to run a marathon, walk one.

If you want to bungee jump, don't.

If you want to learn Italian, forget it. Learn Chinese—they're the ones we owe money to.

And if we really want to stay current and relevant, we have to use social media. And by that I mean Facebook.

There are one billion people on Facebook. Maybe older people should have our own social media. We can call it What Did That Doctor Do to Your Face Book? In fact, we can have our own text and Facebook abbreviations. We can have our own WTF, LOL, and LMAO.

GNIB: Good news, it's benign.

OMG: Oh, my gout.

DMMLIMNWD: Don't make me laugh, I'm not wearing Depends.

WAI: Where am I?

ITIHSBCR: I think I had sex but can't remember.

ILI: I like Ike.

TKDC: The kids didn't call.

DTLSTY: Does this look swollen to you?

CTDMELOFM: Call the doctor—my erection lasted over four minutes.

PAMUHNASIHSB: Put a mirror under his nose and see if he's still breathing.

Bottom line: we can't be dial-up in a Wi-Fi world.

And to win this war against ageism, we're going to have to

implement economic sanctions and use our power of the purse and not just to buy those stupid products they scare us into thinking we need. They prey on our fears to sell us things we think we have to order right now because tomorrow could be too late. Snuggies, Rascal scooters, med-alerts, diapers, no-spill cups, elastic shoelaces, ring zipper pulls, anti-scalding devices, and reverse mortgages. Other than reverse mortgages, it's the exact same list you would buy for three-year-olds. Meanwhile, for anyone in the coveted eighteen-to-thirty-five demographic, they make cars, clothes, electronics—you name it. I've got news for these companies: the only reason our kids and grandkids can afford any of your shit is that we lend them the money to buy it.

You want to know what else upsets me?

Now you have to say, "What?" People who ask rhetorical questions: STOP! I'm annoyed when they make me a participant in their own monologue. Don't ask me, "You want to know what I think?," forcing me to say, "What?"

Just fucking tell me.

But of all the annoyances, of all the things that push me over the edge, of all the things that bug the shit out of me, there is one THAT IS GONNA CAUSE MY HEAD TO FUCKING EXPLODE.

TSA: STOP!

I'll give you a hint: if she's a ninety-year-old grandmother from Des Moines who smells like Febreze, she's safe. I came close to being restrained when an agent searched an eighty-eight-year-old wheelchair-bound relative of mine as if he were a known terrorist. On the whole, Homeland Security and the TSA are doing a great job, but it's the attitude. Before one flight not too long ago, I walk up to the security screener at LAX and she says, "Billy, you are the best. I love you. Can I see your picture ID?"

So I hand over my driver's license. After looking at it for thirty seconds, she stares back at me. "Five foot nine? I don't think so. Step over here, please.

"Now, *Running Scared,* I liked you with that cute Gregory Hines. *Mr. Saturday Night,* I didn't care for. Could you raise your arms while I run the wand over you? Miracle Max in *Princess Bride,* was that makeup or did you just make your face look like that? My kids love *Parental Guidance.* Could you take off your belt, please?"

"How about just an autograph?"

She cracks up. "You are so funny. Open them up. I need to make sure you're not carrying a concealed weapon."

Meanwhile, five feet away, a man with a Pakistani passport pushing a surface-to-air missile gets waved right past a security guard. The supervisor runs over to me. "Hey, Billy, my wife and I loved *When Harry Met Sally* . . . . We watch it all the time."

"Thanks. Do you know Verna?" I ask, pointing to the wand now traveling between my legs. "She's also a big fan."

"*That's* funny. Step behind that curtain; we're searching people who fit a certain profile."

"Well, that's not me—I don't have a good profile," I say.

Nothing, stone face. "You bought a one-way ticket to New York with no return flight booked," he says.

"I'm flying to New York and I'm not coming back for a month or two," I explain. "I'm not booking a round-trip flight at this point."

"I understand. No problem. We'll be finished right after a quick thorough search."

I think he's kidding.

He's not.

I keep trying to joke with him as he frisks me a little too eagerly. "I thought you'd buy me a drink first," I say. "I guess the only people drinking fifteen minutes before a flight are the pilots."

"You're a funny man. We searched Chris Rock last week—he's taller than you think," he says.

The last pat-down actually hurts me as he bangs into the jewels. I start to protest, but the large marshal behind him shakes his head quietly, as if to say, "I wouldn't." I tuck in my shirt, put my belt back on, slip on my shoes and my dignity, and walk to the gate, really pissed off.

On the plus side, he did find two benign polyps.

So that's where I am in life. I no longer live in the state of California, I live in the state of permanent annoyance. Remember Billy Joel's song "Angry Young Man"? It's a great song, but the lyric "he'll go to his grave as an angry old man" now has a troubling resonance.

So I guess that's what I'm really upset about. The world is moving faster and I am moving slower and technology is changing how everything is done and I still can't find my fucking keys.

Iron Balls—My Forties

Forty sounded old to me. It's a bad number for everything: pants size, IQ, blood alcohol . . . forty is just bad. As I approached it, I found myself feeling more anxious and scared than at any other time in my life. My career, despite the bumps and bruises up to this point, was going well, the kids were healthy and happy, and Janice and I were great, so what could be keeping me up at night, besides my reflux? In retrospect, it was simply that life *was turning into a 3-D movie* with every significant moment getting closer than I would like. I'd look at Jenny, who was fifteen, and she'd suddenly be thirty; Lindsay was eleven, but I'd see her with children of her own. Aches became MRIs, headaches became CAT scans, this hurt more than it used to, that didn't heal as fast. I was more than half done with my life, and that was not a pleasant thought. Midlife crisis or call it whatever you want, but I felt scared; *life was like a speeding train,* and I was standing on the platform watching it whiz by. Oddly, despite—or maybe because of—all of this anxiety, my forties would become one of the most fertile and successful times in my career.

In 1987, I agreed to host the Grammy Awards. I'd grown up around great musicians, and being a part of their celebration seemed like a perfect fit. Only one writer worked with me, and that was Robert Wuhl. Robert is also a fine actor (*Arli$$*) and a very smart comedian.

The show came from Radio City Music Hall, and at one point I was to introduce Miles Davis. Miles was a particular idol for me. His innovations and technique were to jazz what Richard Pryor's stand-up was to comedy. I wrote a heartfelt intro for him and looked forward to his reaction. In the middle of my short speech, the audience started to laugh, and I heard what sounded like wind chimes. I turned to my right and saw Miles walking onstage wearing a suit constructed from pieces of colored glass, with large sunglasses that made him look like a very cool fruit fly. He then played "Time After Time" with his back to the audience. I waited in the wings, and when Miles greeted me I said, "Sergeant Dinkus said to say hello." Without missing a beat he said, "That Ronald McDonald–head motherfucker. He'd impound my car and drive it to the Hamptons and bring it back with no gas."

Backstage, I watched the show near a personal "dressing room" that had been created especially for the legendary pianist Vladimir Horowitz. It was elegantly appointed with items the eighty-three-year-old maestro had requested, like precut meat and a doughnut pillow. But before Mr. H. (as I had quickly come to call him) arrived, Michael Jackson took up residence in the dressing room, not knowing it was reserved for Horowitz. No one backstage had the guts to tell Jackson it wasn't his, especially since he was sitting with Bubbles the chimp, who had eaten all the precut meat and left a gift Mr. Horowitz had not requested.

When Michael was seated in the audience, I have to admit it was kind of cool to see him but a little distracting. Most of the music stars were eclectically dressed but none like Michael, who seemed to be the general of some bizarre army sitting next to a large monkey. No matter where I looked, that iconic face was somehow in my vision. He was a good sport, which was a relief because Robert and I had created a parody of the *Young People's Concerts* television specials Leonard Bernstein hosted, one of which had illustrated how the different instrument sounds could tell a story. I was excited about doing something like this piece. I wanted to expand the role of the host and not simply introduce the presenters.

We'd asked Bobby McFerrin to use his genius vocal talents and "be" all the instruments in the orchestra. The sketch began with Bobby creating an ancient kind of rhythm, to which I said, "In the beginning, cavemen would make sounds by banging rocks together, and they could never imagine that someday Michael Jackson would own all their publishing." It got a big laugh from the audience, but the gloved one laughed more than anyone— except for Bubbles, who thought it was hilarious.

The next month my fortieth birthday arrived. The day was kind of quiet, and I was gripped by a very cloudy mood. *I'm forty, dammit. How the hell did this happen?* My young birthdays had always been filled with great excitement. My mom would wake me up at the time I was born and go through the whole story of my birth. We always did something a little special: we'd meet Dad in Manhattan and go to the Roxy movie palace or Radio City Music Hall, maybe meet Uncle Berns at a restaurant in Chinatown, where he would not only speak Chinese to the waiters but also teach me the art of using chopsticks. Now I just felt pissed off, and I didn't want my lousy mood to ruin the entire day.

I had, however, planned a big party, so that night we crammed as many friends as possible into the old Spago on Sunset Boulevard. Wolfgang Puck made his usual sensational food, the great jazz trumpet player Jack Sheldon jammed with a sextet, and a bunch of my pals and I got up to sing with him. Gregory Hines sang, Alan King sang, and then we all improvised a blues piece.

Rob Reiner started it off, and we passed the mike around and everyone made up a verse. It was sensational fun.

Then something happened that literally took my breath away. A few large television monitors were wheeled in, and there *live* on HBO was a filmed happy birthday greeting, hosted by Rob and featuring everyone I loved: Janice and the girls, my mom, my brothers and their families, Sammy Davis Jr., Mickey Mantle, Gregory Hines, and even a classroom of my brother Joel's students at Long Beach Junior High. Mantle said, "Happy fiftieth, Billy," and then Dick Schaap's off-camera voice corrected, "He's forty," and Mantle quipped, "I know." I just couldn't believe what I was seeing. Michael Fuchs had put this on the air! I started to laugh and cry at the same time—I must have looked like John Boehner giving a speech in Congress—but it was a joyous, disbelieving wail. When the film finished I felt an enormous sense of relief. I held on to Janice and the girls and then hugged my mom, Rip, and Joel. I realized that I was in a very positive and powerful place in my life, and suddenly everything felt okay.

....

A few months later, I heard that Rob was developing a romantic comedy with Nora Ephron. All I gleaned was that it featured a man and a woman my age. Rob never mentioned it to me, but I knew from agents and managers that he had met with almost every male actor my age, except me. I was not happy about that, but what could I do? We were the closest of friends, and I thought he was a great director, but if he didn't think I was right for it, then so be it. I didn't want to jeopardize our friendship by pushing the issue. One day, he called and said, "Listen, I want you for this movie. I had to go through a process with other actors, and you are this guy. I'm sending the script over—it's called *Boy Meets Girl*."

I read the script instantly, and honestly, it just didn't pop for me. The idea was great: a twelve-year relationship between a man and a woman who become friends, have sex, it ruins every-thing, and then they realize they're really in love. But it didn't seem fully formed yet. I thought about ways to make it better, and when I met with Rob and Nora, they admitted that they were in a sort of creative stall. I was a fresh voice for them. I told them my ideas for certain scenes and lines, and things started to click. Many of the moments Rob and I had experienced as friends, we felt could become moments for Harry and Sally. Rob's divorce from Penny Marshall had been a very difficult time for him, and we'd talked constantly, either in person or on the phone. We were inseparable. Often, Rob would have the sort of headache that became, in the film, the "twenty-four-hour tumor," where Sally said, "Go to a doctor" and Harry replied, "He'll just tell me it's nothing." About a year before, sitting with Rob at Dodger Stadium one night, I'd had an idea for a sketch called "Caught in a Wave." My idea involved two guys at a baseball game talking about a breakthrough one of them had in therapy and every time he's about to describe the big moment he had with his shrink, the stadium wave gets to them and they have to stand up, throw their hands in the air, and say "Whoa." That became the scene with Harry and his friend Jess at a football game talking about how Harry's marriage broke up. I also suggested the singing machine scene, where Harry sees his ex-wife and the music of the karaoke machine underscores the awkwardness, and Nora put that into the script as well. It was thrilling to collaborate with Rob and Nora, who were so smart and funny and open to new ideas. Then we had to find Sally.

Meg Ryan had auditioned to play my girlfriend in *Throw Momma*. I'd thought she was great and a perfect compliment to me, but Danny DeVito had seen her as a tad young and cast Kim Greist. This time, when Meg came in to read with me, we all knew instantly that we were Harry and Sally. She was beautiful, she was adorable, she was really funny, and she had that awkward kind of grace that is found in only the best screen comediennes.

I often wonder if Meg had gotten that part in *Throw Momma,* which I had done just before this, would Rob have cast her? Would he have thought, *I just saw this?*

Once Meg was on board, Rob, his producing partner Andy Scheinman, Nora, and Meg and I would have lengthy meetings where we just talked about men and women and relationships and tried to come up with fresh dialogue and create new scenes. I think this process is what made the movie so personal, because what Harry and Sally went through was so real. When Nora brought up the issue of women faking orgasms during sex, Rob couldn't believe it. "Well, they haven't faked one with me," he said. It was Meg's idea to have a scene where Sally tells Harry about this and, like Rob, Harry can't believe it, so she fakes one in a public place. I said, "Like a restaurant," and then Rob said it should be a loud orgasm, with everyone watching her, and then I said, "When it's done, an older woman says to a waiter, 'I'll have what she's having.'" And that's how it happened. In retrospect, it may be the longest orgasm in history.

Once the script was finished, we renamed it *When Harry Met Sally . . .* and the cast was completed with the excellent additions of Bruno Kirby and Carrie Fisher. We started filming in Los Angeles, then moved to Chicago and finally New York.

Rob was the perfect director for this movie, although sometimes he was too good of an audience. He would break out laughing and ruin takes, but in my heart I knew that if I had made him laugh, we were in the right zone. Early on, I had a very honest talk with him. This movie was so personal to him, I'd been starting to feel a little restricted. I didn't want to play Rob; I wanted to be Harry. I told him that he needed to move out of Harry so I could move in. He totally understood and gave me more freedom with the role, as well as the best gift an actor can get from his director: trust.

One day we were shooting at the Temple of Dendur, in the Metropolitan Museum of Art. I'd had this thought that when you start to get really comfortable with someone, you show them your

It doesn't get any better.
(Photograph © Andrew Schwartz)

funny "voice." Usually it's a silly-sounding character that you use
in your "special moments." You let your guard down and trust the
person to listen without judgment, because you're probably falling in love with them, and they with you. It became the "pepper
pepper" scene, where Harry uses this crazy voice and gets Sally
to repeat, "I would be proud to partake of your pecan pie." It was
all improvised. At one point—you can see it if you Google the
scene—Meg actually looks off to where Rob is standing. Harry
then asks her out, in his silly voice, and she tells him she has a
date, and then Harry, his feelings kind of hurt, flirts with her by
telling her to wear a skirt, that she looks really good in skirts. It's
one of my favorite moments in the movie, and it only happened
because Rob was so open to trying ideas and Meg was so damned
talented.

The night before shooting the orgasm scene in Katz's Deli,
Meg was nervous about it when we talked on the phone. After

most of our shooting days, we spoke on the phone as Harry and Sally would, discussing what the day had been like and how we felt about the new one coming.

The orgasm scene was worrisome because she would have to have one thirty or forty times that day. Which would have tied my all-time junior high record. I was as reassuring as I could be, and frankly, being the one sitting across from her, I was looking forward to it.

The next morning, we met on the set and did a rough quiet rehearsal. She seemed nervous and wasn't happy with her wardrobe, and she ended up wearing a sweater of mine. Once Barry Sonnenfeld, our outstanding director of photography, was done lighting, we walked onto the set, which now was filled with the "atmosphere." (I don't like the term "extras"—that means we ordered too many. "Background artists" is better yet.) Rob's wonderful mother, Estelle, was sitting at a nearby table. She would be the "I'll have what she's having" lady. We started to rehearse, and Meg seemed tentative. First orgasm, so-so; next one like we'd been married for ten years. Perhaps she was nervous about sharing her orgasm with so many strangers. Rob, getting a bit impatient, then asked her to step aside for a moment so he could show her what he wanted. Now I'm sitting across from this large, sweaty, bearded man. It looked like I was on a date with Sebastian Cabot. He then had an orgasm that King Kong would have envied. He was screaming, "YES! YES! YES!" and banging the table so hard, pickles were flying and cole slaw was in the air. When he was done, the background artists applauded and Rob took me aside. "I made a mistake," he confided. "I shouldn't have done that."

"Meg will be okay. I don't think you embarrassed her," I said.

"That's not what I meant," he said. "I just had an orgasm in front of my mother."

Once we started shooting, Meg was spectacular. All day with the camera either on her or on me, she had sensational orgasms. My reactions to her became more fun to do as she came up with

new little moans and groans. Months later, when Rob had finished his first cut of the picture, we had a test screening in Pasadena, California. The movie was playing really well, and then
came the orgasm scene. The laughs were enormous, and when
Estelle said her line, the place exploded. I was sitting in the back
with Rob and we just grabbed each other's arms. We knew we
had something special.

....

After *When Harry Met Sally . . .* came out, Michael Fuchs asked
me if I'd be willing to go to Moscow and do a stand-up special
for HBO. Michael had created HBO and was always looking to
expand television's boundaries. If people were paying for TV, he
felt, they should be getting something they couldn't see on network television. It would be the first time an American comedian
would perform in the Soviet Union. Gorbachev was in power,
and the wall had not yet come down. I found the prospect daunting but intriguing, so I joined Michael and a small group of HBO
executives that included Chris Albrecht, who was Michael's right
hand at the time and would become the programming genius
behind *The Sopranos* and *Sex and the City,* and we made a trip to
Leningrad and Moscow to get a feel for the country and its people
and see if performing there was possible.

Leningrad—St. Petersburg now—is a beautiful city, with lovely
bridges spanning the Neva River. We met with "humor officials,"
who told us of their concerns about this proposed show. It was
very similar to what I was used to, actually: Russia's humor officials were the same dour comedy-development execs we have in
the States. What was I planning on talking about? they asked.
Could they see the script? We explained that we were just doing
research at this point. We had a KGB man with us at all times, and
probably a few others watching us.

While we were there, the Jewish holiday of Yom Kippur arrived,
and the Jews in the group who were feeling guilty that they
weren't home with their families, or just merely feeling guilty,

wanted to go to synagogue. We found the only temple in the city still standing, which was moving in itself. Leningrad had once had twenty-four synagogues, but all the others had been destroyed over time, a stark reminder of what had happened to the Jews in the Soviet Union. Our group of ten or so men tried to go in, but we were refused entry by an elder of the temple because we didn't have head coverings (yarmulkes). We explained that we were Americans whose roots were in Russia and asked, in the spirit of our ancestors, would the rabbi make an exception and let us in to say our Yom Kippur prayers? Again he refused us, pointing to our bare heads. We left angry and frustrated, but across the street we found an outdoor market, and somehow somebody was selling a black velvet painting of Elvis, which we bought for two dollars. With a Swiss Army knife we cut some circles out of it, and we put the new "Elvis yarmulkes" on our heads. We confronted the elder with our new yarmulkes, and reluctantly he let us in. Elvis had entered the building.

The aging interior of the temple was still beautiful, but it had that musty aroma of an old apartment. Though it was a large place where men traditionally sat downstairs and the women upstairs, only a handful of people were there. On this, the holiest of days, most synagogues in the United States are jammed, so we all felt the same sadness. If the pogroms and the anti-Semitic Stalinist regime hadn't happened, this place would be full. There weren't many Jews left in the city, and those who were still there were apparently reluctant to be seen going to synagogue. I imagined what it must have been like to be a Jew living here in my grandparents' time—it seemed dreary and scary enough in 1989. As we boarded the train to Moscow, I still wasn't convinced I could do the show. The train leaves at midnight, and when you wake up you are in Moscow. *Midnight Train to Moscow* sounded like a title to me; I thought, *Now if I only had a show to go with it.*

The people in Moscow were more open to us. The lines we'd heard about, of Russians waiting for goods, were everywhere.

Around three each afternoon, when work was done, the longest lines were for the liquor stores—or as I called it, "Unhappy Hour." Soon the streets were littered with tipsy Russians. One evening we had arranged a meeting with one of the Soviet Union's top comedians at a restaurant overlooking Red Square. We were going to videotape our conversation and perhaps use it in the show. Sitting at our table, we watched the entrance to the restaurant, not knowing who we were looking for. Man after man entered and glanced around for a table, and I somehow knew that each one wasn't "him." Then a thirty-five-ish beleaguered-looking man walked in and paused. He slouched a little and had a tinge of anxiety in his eyes. "That's him," I said, and it was.

We greeted each other warmly and, through his translator, started talking shop. He and I had many things in common. He also didn't sit down before a show and instead he paced in his dressing room, he ate at the same time I did before a performance. He said he made love to his wife the night before every big performance and asked if I did. I said I didn't know his wife, but if he insisted, I would. I asked if he liked it when his family was in the audience, and he responded through his translator, "No, I am Jewish, too." But a few nights later, when we went to see him perform in a large theater, he simply sat down and read a text of his comedy that had been approved by a committee! He wasn't a stand-up; he was a sit-down comic. It was hard to fathom that his material had been censored.

One thing I did keep thinking about was my own Russian ancestry. My grandmothers were both from Russia, as was my dad's father. What if I made the show about finding my roots? The idea started to percolate. It could be funny but also have a soul. With another family member's help we found thirty or so distant cousins still living in Moscow. It was by chance—and choice—that some of my family remained in Russia while others flourished in America. Some saw that the revolution was coming and decided to flee, while others thought, "We will stay, it won't be so bad, and we'll come later." They never did. Who would I have been if my grandmother didn't get out at the age of fourteen? Probably a really funny tractor driver in Minsk.

When we returned to Los Angeles, I started to write the show with Paul Flaherty and Dick Blasucci. Our idea was to begin with a parody of *Field of Dreams,* with the voice that said, "If you build it, they will come" instead being the voice of my grandmother, urging me to go to Russia and find my roots. "If you go there, take a jacket," the voice—Christopher Guest—whispered. For the stand-up portion of the special, I studied Soviet television to see what people were watching. Charlie Chaplin movies were being shown almost every day, and he was referred to as "the Little Jew." Which, by coincidence, is the same thing they called him when he tried to join a country club in Hollywood.

I created a Chaplin "silent movie," wherein I would imitate Charlie live onstage, underscored with Tchaikovsky played by the brilliant and funny piano player Marc Shaiman. We wrote a scene where Gorbachev, looking to westernize his country, has a meeting with an American producer. With a makeup job complete with bad hair plugs, I played the slimy producer who brings the concept of creating a theme park called Lenin Land. We built a scale model of the Disneyland-like park, and a disbelieving Gorbachev watched a tiny roller coaster go right through dead Lenin's head.

And speaking of Lenin, in a fantasy of who I might have been if history were different, I played a guard at Lenin's Tomb who is a practical joker. One is not allowed to make a sound inside the tomb, but I use a hidden fart device to crack up the stoic soldier next to me, while I blame it on an American tourist. My favorite piece was a monologue where I played a man waiting on line, inspired by the thousands of stone-faced Russians I had seen standing on lines for goods. Many times, they didn't know what the line was for; they'd merely joined it. My character is hoping for food, vodka, or raspberries that don't have worms in them, all the while talking about what it's like living there. It was a ballsy piece to do for the Russians, because it confronted them with the reality of their own lives. Finally I wrote a postconcert scene that has me leaving on the midnight train, and I bump into a young girl, who, in the magic of *Field of Dreams*, turns out to be my grandmother on her way to America. My sixteen-year-old daughter, Jenny, would play her own great-grandmother.

The story was strong, but I was worried about the actual performance. How do you do stand-up for the Russians? I decided I needed to speak Russian for the first few minutes, and remember, this was before Rosetta Stone. I wrote about ten minutes of welcoming jokes; then David Bromberg, a Russian American comedian who was our technical adviser, translated them into Russian, and I learned them phonetically. For the Pyshkina Theater, a lovely old building with a long history, we created a backdrop of a poster of a Russian worker, and then before I knew it, we were ready, rehearsed, and, weirdly enough, very confident. We made a visit to the American embassy, and upon meeting the ambassador we were advised to talk in a whisper and were moved to a corner of the room so the conversation wouldn't be bugged. The only request he made was for me to work clean and not embarrass anyone. Next we shot some handheld reality video on the streets of Moscow from my point of view. Standing at the entrance to Lenin's Tomb in Red Square, we witnessed the changing of the guards. High-stepping soldiers with guns on their shoulders marched by us, their kicks almost reaching the level of their chests. I softly started singing "One" from *A Chorus Line* in time with their steps: "One singular sensation, every little step he takes." I had to sing softly because our KGB man was standing near me; from the look on his face, I figured he had not seen the musical. I played other characters as well, including my NYU professor Martin Scorsese, who commented, "I told Billy to gain forty pounds and call the show *Raging Bolshevik*."

The Russians were always looking for a "taste"—in other words, a bribe. If we needed something that had been promised but not delivered, the KGB man would tell us that giving him

$500 and a dual-track ghetto blaster might help. We provided exactly that a few times, most notably when we'd been promised that the lights of the Kremlin would be on in the background of a late-night scene. Of course they weren't. We came up with the loot and even threw in a second ghetto blaster, and lo and behold, the lights were on for two weeks, even after we left.

Sometimes it seemed that the only thing the Soviets had in common with us was that over there, the conservatives also thought all actors were socialists. The country, for all its great literature and music and scientific accomplishments, was unsophisticated. The windows of the big department stores were crudely decorated. Stylish clothes were rare. News coverage was scarce. It was 1989, but it felt like 1956. Chernobyl had shaken the nation a few years prior to our visit. Good food was now hard to find; at the few nice restaurants, a meat dish was more than likely horse. Several times we had to admonish the crew members for stuffing cheese and other goods from our catering truck (it had come all the way from England, of all places) into their coats at the end of the day. As scary as we found the Soviet image, they were a vulnerable people who seemed to want what America had. I sensed that the citizens were starting to realize that they had been handed a bill of goods and unrest was growing.

One night Janice, Michael Fuchs, and I went to dinner at the home of one of my new cousins. It was very emotional. They looked like all the relatives I'd known as a child. Their facial structure, even their personalities felt so familiar. As they showed us their family albums, I again thought about the twist of fate that had allowed me to live and thrive in America while this part of our family remained behind the Iron Curtain. We laughed at familiar family stories, and I invited everyone to the performance at the Pyshkina Theater. I started as a comedian by performing in front of my relatives. Now, halfway around the world, I would not only be performing in the country they'd come from—but once again in front of my family.

We were to do two shows, which would be cut together into one for the HBO special, but the size of the audiences was a mystery to us. We hadn't done much advertising, just a simple poster with a black-and-white photograph Janice had taken of me. It read, "An Evening with American Comic Billy Crystal." Which was better than the original poster: "An Evening with Another Little Jew."

As the beautiful sounds of Shaiman rehearsing his Tchaikovsky filtered into my upstairs dressing room, I looked out the window and was surprised to see a long line of people, young and old, waiting to get into the theater. I'm not sure how much they knew of me, yet they seemed excited that someone from America had come to perform for them. I had no idea what to expect. Would they laugh? Were they allowed to laugh? Would they be angry that an American was making fun of them? Getting off to a good start was the key, so I kept rehearsing my jokes in Russian.

The moment before I go onstage is always one of intense, quiet energy. I gather my thoughts, then let them go. I think of everything and nothing. Most comedians will probably describe the moment before they go on in the same way: Your brain opens up to a new part of you. It hears everything, it remembers everything; you feel powerful and intuitive. I always remain in good physical condition so my body feels strong, my legs always underneath me. I enter into a sort of hyperreality. I need to listen to every sound the audience makes, to feel what they are giving back, and then in milliseconds decide what and how to say the next line. That's a comedian's toughest challenge: saying one thing while thinking a few beats ahead and making decisions about what to say next without looking like you're going through mental machinations. In Moscow, these tasks would be coupled with an audience that might not have any idea of what I was about to do. If they were used to a comedian sitting onstage reading his edited script, what would they think of me? I simply kept looking at my notes, trying to remember key words. This wasn't

First moment on stage with Gorbo.

my honed act. Where could I have tried it out? The Russian Tea Room? This was all new material I had never performed before. Oh, and most of the people in the crowd only spoke Russian. Still, for some reason—perhaps the danger of it all—I felt relaxed and confident as I got dressed.

David Bromberg warmed up the crowd. "How many of you have relatives in prison?" he joked. He explained who I was, and what a big moment this was for Soviet-American relations and American television. He then introduced me, and I walked onstage to a strong round of applause. I went over to the wings, where it looked like I was shaking someone's hand. I was—it was a life-size cutout of Gorbachev with a movable arm. When the audience saw this, I could feel their astonishment. The American had already done something a Soviet comic could not do: make fun of the boss. A few people looked around, probably thinking that soldiers were coming to take them away for laughing. In fact, there were some soldiers in the audience, and they were laughing as well. I then launched into my jokes in Russian, my accent strong: "I am the first American comedian to come to Moscow, with the exception of Ronald Reagan." I told them how similar we actually are: "You have the Russian circus, we have Congress, you have Baryshnikov . . . we have Baryshnikov. . . ." Again the audience was delighted. They loved the Chaplin piece; I got them to do "the Wave" with me, hundreds of Soviets standing and throwing their arms in the air as the wave moved around the theater, something never before seen in Russia; and both shows went as well as any performance I had done in America. I had hoped I would be able to do twenty-five minutes or so, and in both performances I did an hour, ending with the man-on-line monologue, which brought the Soviets to their feet, cheering and throwing flowers to me on stage.

As I bowed and waved good night I saw my new family applauding their cousin. It was just like being in the living room in Long Beach.

The next night we finished our shooting at a lonely train station outside Moscow. Jenny and I did our scene together, and it was truly magical. Acting with my daughter, already a fine actress, portraying her great-grandmother on her way to a new life was the perfect ending to this whole experience.

....

After hosting the Grammys for three years, I was asked to be a presenter at the Academy Awards. The show that year was a disaster. The now infamous moment of Rob Lowe singing "Proud Mary" with Snow White opened the show, and the rest was chaotic. Still, when I walked out there that night to introduce Gregory Hines and Sammy Davis Jr., I felt that I was in the right place. I was now part of the movie community. A few months later, Gil Cates asked me to host the Oscars the next year. He was producing the show for the first time. The Oscars had become a laughingstock, and together our goal was to make the show something special again.

By then *When Harry Met Sally . . .* was a big hit, and Nora had been nominated for Best Screenplay. The movie had also been nominated for the Golden Globe as Best Comedy, and Meg and I were nominated for Best Actor and Actress in a Comedy or Musical. At the Globes I was sitting near Steve Martin, who was nominated for *Parenthood.* When our category came up and we both lost to Morgan Freeman for *Driving Miss Daisy,* I ran over to Steve and said, "Let's go up there and ask who finished second." As Steve and I approached the stage and asked the question, the look on Cybil Shepherd's face was priceless. (Yes, we did it, and you can Google this one, too!) Steve is one of the truly great original funny people. I'm sorry that moment at the Globes is the only chance we've had to work together.

As the Oscars approached, I had this strong feeling of *Wow, I'm really going to do this. I am hosting the same show Bob Hope and Johnny Carson did.* When I was growing up in the fifties and early sixties, the Oscars was always a special event. We gathered around our black-and-white television set to watch the glamorous Hollywood stars sitting together having a wonderful time. The show had such class and dignity. Back then, the only awards shows were the Emmys and the Oscars, and watching them, I felt as if I'd been granted a special one-night pass to sit in the palace with the legends. Bob Hope was usually the master of ceremonies and appeared almost regal in his formal tails. He was funny and charming, and although I didn't get most of his jokes, it didn't matter because the camera cut to Gregory Peck laughing, or to Jimmy Stewart or Jack Lemmon or Anthony Quinn sitting with some gorgeous movie star on his arm. Even though our DuMont TV set was black-and-white, I could see every color. Now I felt that I had been handed the baton in a relay race and it was my turn to run. Following in the footsteps of Hope and Carson was a huge responsibility, and I wanted to be great.

Robert Wuhl was again writing with me, and we set out to give the show the same kind of unpredictable feel we'd given the Grammys. Jack Nicholson would be in the audience and had just made a fortune as the Joker in *Batman*. We decided to write jokes about that, like "Jack is so rich, Morgan Freeman drove him here tonight" and "Jack is so rich, Jon Peters"—the former hair stylist and now studio head—"still cuts his hair." I also had the idea to create a musical medley that would parody the usually lame musical numbers at the Oscars, especially the "Proud Mary" moment from the prior year. Marc Shaiman and Bruce Vilanch came on board, and we wrote the first of what would become a favorite feature of my hosting appearances: the medley. I would sing special lyrics for each of the five nominated films. It wasn't easy to write a funny lyric for a serious movie. Oliver Stone's *JFK* was the most daunting. How to pick a song and rewrite it with funny special lyrics about the murder of our president? We wanted to parody "Tradition" from *Fiddler on the Roof*—"A gunman on the knoll. Sounds crazy, no? Suspicion!"—but we couldn't get permission from the composers. Instead, to the tune of "Three Coins in the Fountain," I sang, "Three shots in the plaza, who done it, Mr. Stone?"

Walking out there that first time as the host of the Oscars was one of the best moments of my life. With each challenging experience in my career, I felt I had grown more muscle. I'd come a long way from the nervous, dry-mouthed kid at his first *Tonight Show*. I wasn't overwhelmed; I could feel that the audience wanted me there, and I wanted them to know I loved being there. I also walked out there not just as a comedian but as one of the stars in a movie that people loved. I felt proud and, more importantly, I felt ready; in fact, I wasn't even nervous. I was excited. The monologue was strong and loose, and the medley really scored.

I had a long break during the show and was in my dressing room freshening up my makeup and looking at my notes when somebody knocked on the door. I opened it, and there stood Jack Nicholson and Warren Beatty. "Thanks for talking about my money," Jack said.

"You're doing great, and we wanted to tell you," Warren said. This was the first time I had met these two icons, and this gesture of theirs blew me away. Since then I have spent a lot of time with Warren, who is one of the smartest and most charming people I have ever met, and Jack and I have gone on to be friends. It's like being pals with Babe Ruth.

····

After the success of *When Harry Met Sally . . .* , Rob and his partners Martin Shafer, Alan Horn, and Andy Scheinman formed Castle Rock, a new film production company, and came to me and said, "We want you to be part of our company. Create movie ideas, and if we like them, we'll make them. If you want to direct, you'll get a chance to do that as well." What could be more perfect?

For the first time I had a nice office, an assistant, and a discretionary fund with which to develop projects. Stand-up would have to be put on hold for now. Coming up with material for my act is difficult enough, but creating and developing movies is much harder, so I wanted to focus on only that. One day while sitting at home watching television, I saw a show about fantasy vacations. This one was about a scuba diving resort with a sunken ship that you could dive into and explore. Groups of friends were going, and when interviewed they talked about how much it meant to them to do the trip together. One diver said, "It helped the midlife crisis I was having. Going with my friends on an adventure was just what I needed." I picked up my pen and pad and started writing: "*City Slickers,* three friends go on a fantasy cattle drive. City guys who have to learn how to be cowboys. Crusty trail boss (Jack Palance) dies during the trip and they have to bring in the herd themselves. Metaphor for what's missing in their lives. My character, like me, in his 40s . . . midlife crisis. Secrets that friends have from each other."

The Castle Rock group loved the idea of a "coming of middle age" film and we met with Lowell Ganz and Babaloo Mandel, who had not only written *Parenthood,* but *Splash* as well. We were all the same age and had similar feelings about turning forty. We spent a few weeks knocking out the beats of the story, and they went off to write the screenplay. It was that fast. No studio interference, no midlevel executives, no notes on every page, instead, it was simply: Go do it.

One day, as I was driving to the office, someone on the radio was talking about the running of the bulls in Pamplona, which would occur in a few days. *Bingo!* I thought. *Let's open the movie at the running of the bulls.* These three pals always did stuff like this, and wouldn't it be a great opening if we could pull it off? We went up to Martin Shafer's office and told him the idea, and without missing a beat he was on the phone getting a crew, hotels, and stunt people, putting everything in motion so we could shoot in Spain in just a few days. To this day, I've never seen a studio executive move that quickly.

That also put into motion an aspect of the movie I am asked about all the time: Why did I wear a Mets hat? Okay, here's the story. HBO brought Comic Relief to Radio City Music Hall, in New York, that year. We asked the Yankees to do a Comic Relief Day at Yankee Stadium—let us sell our T-shirts and give away our "Groucho" glasses, and Robin, Whoopi, and I would sing the national anthem and do an inning or two on TV. The Yankees, for whatever reason, turned us down. The Mets not only gave us the day but made a big contribution to the charity. So when it was time to shoot the stuntpeople in Pamplona as they ran with the bulls, something we would re-create at Universal Studios (it's not easy to run with Hollywood bulls; they're always on their cell phones), we needed to dress the man who was stunting for me. In Spain, the stuntman had a Mets jersey and hat and a Yankee jersey and hat. The Mets would waive the licensing fee, which was $40,000, and the Yankees wouldn't, so we went with the Mets. That's how the decision was made. The Mets deserved it.

Look, I love the Yankees. I was a Yankee (more on that later). I will always love the Yankees, and there's a scene in the film where I'm asked to describe my best day. Riding on horseback and not wearing the hat, I talk about my first game at Yankee Stadium, *not* Shea, watching Mickey hit one, *not* Ed Kranepool.

Later, when I got friendly with George Steinbrenner, he asked me why the Met hat, and I told him the whole story. He understood. I hope no one was fired, because shortly thereafter, the Yankees did a terrific Comic Relief Day and made a large contribution to the charity.

Training to be a cowboy for *City Slickers* brought about a bizarre case of déjà vu. In 1975, Janice and I had made our first trip to California. We knew that at some point we might move there, so it was sort of a scouting trip. One day while driving through Joshua Tree National Monument, near Palm Springs, I pulled over because I was having a strange anxiety attack. The western landscape suddenly looked very familiar. I had the strongest feeling that I had been there before. Specifically, the feeling was that I'd once been a cowboy and had ridden this same territory, not in a rental car but on horseback. "It's *not* a pleasant feeling," I said to Janice. "I know this place."

Okay, stop muttering "Bullshit." This is exactly how it happened. It threw me for a few days because, let's be honest, there weren't many Jewish cowboys. Growing up, you never saw Hopalong Chassidy.

So fifteen years later, when we were writing the script and creating the river chase where Mitch ropes Norman the calf, who was swept away in the rapids, Lowell Ganz asked, "Can you do that?"

"Yeah, I can do that," I answered. I don't know why I said that—I hadn't been on a horse since I was nine years old. When we started training on horseback, I took to it very quickly. One day we were working on roping a steer from a galloping horse, the first step in learning how to do it for the river sequence, and sure enough I chased the sprinting steer holding the reins in one hand and twirling my lariat like the rodeo boys do with the other. When the steer was in range, I threw the rope, and damn if it didn't go right around the steer's neck. I pulled the horse up and jumped off and tied the steer up. Jerry Gatlin, a veteran cowboy and stuntman who was teaching us, came running over, patted me on the back, and said, "Wow, you must have been a cowboy in your first life!" I wasn't sure what to say. Was I? Had there been a first life? Are we all recycled as time goes on? And if so, why do we get buried—shouldn't we be put into the green bin? Big questions, no answers. So I just accepted that maybe I had had a previous life and enjoyed this life's experience of being a cowboy.

The three "slickers" had to be unlikely cowboys, everyday men who are thrust into a tough situation. Bruno Kirby would play Ed, a pudgy sporting goods salesman, and Rick Moranis was set to play Phil, the introverted henpecked supermarket manager. The role of Curly, the old cowpoke who would lead this motley crew, was the plum role in the picture. Jack Palance was our only choice. The first movie I had ever seen was *Shane,* where Jack played Wilson, the bad guy who gets it in the end. I never forgot how scary he was.

Ron Underwood, our terrific director, set up a meeting with the man himself at the bar at the Hotel Bel-Air. We arrived early, and when Jack walked in, we were both a little starstruck at first. His large head was the perfect finish to his long, athletic body. He had a certain natural spookiness to him, and as we talked I could see that he loved to play on it. He was very well read, smart, and, in a word, classy. He loved the script and wanted to do it, but he had a scheduling conflict with another film and wasn't sure it was going to work out. We were crushed, and since shooting was to begin shortly, we needed a backup. With a twenty-four-hour window facing us, we secretly reached out to another icon, Charles Bronson. His agent assured us that he would read the script right away. The thought of Bronson in this role was in its own way very appealing. He was an intense actor—scary, of course—and would make a tough and hilarious Curly. The next day I was told to be at my office at a certain time as Mr. Bronson would be calling me. I sat by the phone, nervous about talking to him. The phone rang.

"Hello," I said cheerfully.

"Fuck you," he replied. I waited for the punch line. There wasn't one.

"Fuck you. I'm dead on page sixty-four! How dare you send this to me."

I wasn't sure if he was joking or not.

"You have a lot of nerve," he went on. "I don't die in my films." I was about to remind him that he died in *The Magnificent Seven,* but before I could, he said it again: "Fuck you."

"Mr. Bronson, I'm sorry you feel this way. It's a great part."

"No, it's not—I'm dead on page sixty-fucking-four." And he hung up.

I sat there, stunned, and then the phone rang and it was Jack's agent saying he'd blown off the other film because he wanted to do this one, and we were home safe.

We went into full rehearsal, and then tragedy struck Rick Moranis. His wife had been diagnosed with a serious illness, and he had to leave the film. Danny Stern came on to play Phil, and the three of us made perfect sense together. Bruno was the unlikely pudgy tough guy, and Danny the tall and timid Phil. He arrived the day before shooting started and never had time to train on his horse. Bruno and I had become good enough on our horses to be able to look bad, but all Danny could do was look bad, which was perfect for the character of Phil.

My horse, Beechnut, would become my best friend on the shoot. A nine-year-old gelding cutting quarter horse, Beechnut had a beautiful black coat, with a white blaze on his nose and four white socks that made him pop on the screen. He had the instincts of an actor and the reflexes of a great athlete. Riding him at a full gallop was like driving a Porsche. If I had a seven A.M. call, I would come in an hour early just to warm him up and push our herd of cattle with our wranglers. One early morning, we were chasing some deer in tall grass, which at the time I didn't realize is not a good idea. You don't know what's under the grass—there could be holes, barbed wire, tree stumps, all sorts of things that could cause an accident. Suddenly Beechnut pulled *himself* up and whinnied. I almost flew out of the saddle. He grunted and stuck his nose down into the tall grass, then turned to show me that his white nose was covered with wet mud. He was warning me that he didn't want to run in this stuff, that it was dangerous and he was protecting me. Amazing animal, amazing friend.

I found a sense of peace on Beechnut. I could just walk him around or gallop him and not have to say a word. In between takes, I would sit with the cast and Beechnut would stand behind me, sometimes with his head on my shoulder. I didn't have to tie him up; he would just stand there. I loved being a cowboy . . . again. The only other times I'd felt this sense of peace had been while fielding ground balls or playing catch on a baseball field or doing stand-up when everything was working. When filming was over, my agent, Andrea Eastman, gave me Beechnut as a surprise gift. At first, I didn't want him. Owning a horse is an enormous responsibility, and I was concerned that my relationship with him was just a location romance. But I accepted, and I rode him until 2009, when he passed away at the age of twenty-eight.

Dean Semler was our director of photography. He'd won an Oscar for *Dances with Wolves,* but his first love was comedy. Many of the scenes we had to film were very challenging—most shots had a few hundred cows in them, and our real heroes were the cowboy wranglers, who kept the cows in frame. Our stunt coordinator, Mickey Gilbert, had been Robert Redford's stuntman in *Butch Cassidy and the Sundance Kid,* and he designed every shot with Ron Underwood to make the action look real and, at times, dangerous.

And it didn't just look dangerous: for the river crossing, Danny, Bruno, and I actually brought 450 head of cattle down a muddy hillside and into and across the swiftly moving river. Huge fire hoses and giant fans simulated a rainstorm and pelted us with water from above. Nets had been set up downriver from bank to bank, to catch any animals or actors that might get pulled away by the current. In the scene, Norman the calf would get swept away from the herd and I would ride along the riverbank and heroically rope him, only to take a fall into the surging river myself and then go after him when he got caught in the swirling rapids. My stuntman, Brian Burrows, did the majority of the white-water-rapids work, but I got in there as well. The water was fifty-two degrees, and I wore a wet suit under my clothes. Mickey kept telling me to pee in my wet suit when I got cold: "Remember, pee is ninety-two degrees." Holding the calf was very difficult; he weighed about seventy-five pounds, and you know how heavy suede gets when it's wet. The underwater rocks were the real danger—you couldn't see them, and breaking a leg was a real possibility. I was not only worried about me, but I had Norman to keep safe as well. At one point, I was in the middle of the river with the calf, and he went under. I grabbed him and, terrified, he started kicking me, which was really painful. The more he thrashed, the harder it was to keep him and me from going under. We got the shot, but I was covered with bruises. I don't think I've ever done anything that dangerous— oh wait, I did, just a few days later. In that scene, the herd hears the sound of my portable coffee grinder and stampedes. We wanted a moment when Mitch would be in a lone Joshua tree as the hard-running herd swirled around him. I thought the tree they found was too tall and didn't look dangerous enough, so we found a smallish dead one just above eye level for the steers. The herd was driven to its starting point, about a hundred yards away, and I mounted the barren tree, something I guess lonely shepherds have done for millennia. The steers had not yet been fed, and their food was in a large corral behind me. The wranglers fired some gunshots into the air, and the starving cattle started running, fast, toward me, the dope in the low dead tree between them and their breakfast. It was just like my relatives at a buffet—the difference being that cattle don't bring to-go bags. They went by me like a tsunami. A steer's horn actually grazed my foot, which is in the movie. We filmed the scene with no movie magic, no special effects, we didn't use three steers and digitally make them look like 450. That incident lasts for only a few seconds of footage in the film, but it felt like a lifetime to me.

After we'd shot for five weeks in Durango, Jack joined us for two weeks of shooting in New Mexico. We were a well-oiled machine by the time "the Big Cat," as we called him, arrived. The crew was as excited as I was about his arrival. When Jack, dressed all in black, arrived on the set, everyone applauded. Jack's first shot was to confront a ranch hand who was making lewd remarks to Helen Slater's character. He would rope the dude around the neck and then enter the corral and confront him and me, which would start our relationship. Ron, who is a gentle, sweet man, easily mistaken for a puppeteer, softly explained to Jack what he wanted: "Then you come through the gate and see Billy and give him a glare—"

Jack pounced: "What the fuck does that mean, give him a *glare*? I don't glare, I'm a fucking actor—tell me what I'm thinking, not what I'm doing!" He then took off his hat and threw it and a shit fit. The crew, just moments ago so excited, was now

I did this in my first life also.

confused and pissed off. Things had been going swimmingly, and now "the Big Cat" apparently had a thorn in his paw and was attacking Ron, whom they really liked. I quieted Jack down, and Ron apologized to Jack as best he could.

"Let's just fucking do this!" Jack yelled.

"ACTION!" Jack got off his horse, walked through the gate, and gave me a *glare* like a laser beam that went through my head and burned a hole in the fence behind me. "CUT, PRINT!" said Ron. It was a lesson to us all. Jack knew what he was doing, he knew who he was, and he needed to be talked to in a certain way. After that day, Jack and I were alone for ten days shooting all of our scenes together, including the one where we birth Norman, our little calf. That scene is one of the most talked about in the film. I'm asked all the time what it was like to birth a calf, because it looked so real. Our special effects crew created the rear section of a cow. (Apparently one of them was once a plastic surgeon in Los Angeles.) It was a perfect anatomical replica, complete with "lungs" that would breathe as a cow in distress would. They covered a few-days-old runt calf in realistic bloody jelly and folded the little guy up, and I pulled him out of the faux birth canal. He must have been thinking, *Didn't I just get out of here?* It was a lovely moment between Jack and me.

For a crusty, sometimes intimidating man, Jack was actually a very sensitive guy. He understood how to act on film better than anyone I had worked with up to that point. He knew how to hold the frame. More than anything, he knew that the size of his head was a powerful instrument. All great movie stars have big heads. Chaplin: big head; Spencer Tracy: big head; Gable: huge head; Meryl Streep: all head; Bogart: big head; Katharine Hepburn, Cagney—the list goes on and on. Jack found the right way to hold his big head, and Dean Semler understood exactly how to light him. He also was a poignant figure to me. Curly was meant to be the last of the cowboys, and Jack, at this stage of his life and career, embodied that idea of a dying breed. He had trouble remembering his lines at times. I would watch him

With Jack Palance in his last shot in the filming.

rehearsing his words with his wife, and I would walk over and say I was having trouble with the scene and would he mind going over it with me. He labored some days to get his seventy-year-old body onto his horse for all the hours we had to be in the saddle. He never complained. On the night we finished shooting Jack's work in the film, I had a quiet moment with him, and I told him what an honor it was to work with him. Then I asked, "Why did you go so crazy that day? Why did you yell at Ron like that and carry on?"

He looked at me and simply said in that gravelly voice, "It was my first day. I always get nervous on the first day."

"How many movies have you made?" I asked.

"Counting the shit I did in Europe? . . . About three hundred."

"And you still get nervous?" I asked incredulously.

"Only on the first day," he replied.

We said our good-byes, and a few weeks later we finished shooting the film. Once it was cut, we had our first test screening, and it went through the roof, as they say. Other screenings went even better, and when it was finally finished, we were invited to take it to the Cannes Film Festival. We weren't in competition; we were there to show it to foreign exhibitors for the European sale. Castle Rock threw a big party for the film and to honor Jack, who was an icon in Europe. We were booked at the Hôtel du Cap, one of the truly great hotels in Antibes, where everyone stays during the festival. Fresh from our party, Jack and I walked in together, and as the paparazzi's flashbulbs were blinding us both, through the blue dots in my eyes, I spied Charles Bronson sitting on a couch with Sean Penn. Bronson and I made eye contact, and I nodded slightly toward him (though I wanted to say "Fuck who?"), and he quietly got up and left.

City Slickers was Castle Rock's first movie and helped put the production company on the map, and to have gotten to make the film with my friends meant everything to me. Finally people stopped asking me if they looked mahvelous and started asking me what the "one thing" was, and how was Norman the calf? The Golden Globes honored us with several nominations, including Best Comedy, Best Supporting Actor for Jack, and Best Actor in a Comedy for me. We were sitting together when Jack won. I was elated—this meant he had a real shot at the Oscar. He made a short speech and came back to the table.

"Jack, you're supposed to go to the press room," I told him.

"No way—I'm gonna be here when you win."

I was very moved, but then shortly thereafter I lost. Instantly, Jack got up to leave. "Where are you going?" I asked him.

"The press room—you lost."

••••

Next came the Oscars—one of the best nights I ever had as an entertainer, even though I was suffering from pneumonia. A fever of 103 degrees, cough, stuffed-up ears and nose—you name it. I was exhausted. Gil Cates was so concerned about me that he had talked about having Tom Hanks stand by in case I couldn't do it. Janice's chicken soup helped some, but I had no energy, and the powerful meds I was on sapped my strength further. I made my

Oscars opening with Anthony Hopkins—love at first bite.

entrance being wheeled out by some medical personnel, strapped
to a gurney wearing the Hannibal Lecter mask that nominee
Anthony Hopkins wore in *The Silence of the Lambs*. I walked right
off the stage and greeted him in the audience, saying, "I'm having
some members of the academy for dinner—care to join me?"

During the show, from the stage I could see Jack's big head
above everyone else's. In my gut I knew he would win, and of
course he did. I was in the wings when he was named the winner, and I wanted to run across the stage to him, but I just watched
as he uttered, "Billy Crystal, I crap bigger than you," which was a
line from the movie that no one remembered at the time. Many
thought he had dissed me. He then, of course, hit the deck and
did a few one-armed push-ups, and the place went wild. Bruce
Vilanch and Robert Wuhl were in the wings with me. We hud-
dled during the commercial break and I said, "Let's run with this,"
and we did. "Jack Palance just bungee jumped off the Hollywood
sign," I said, and, later, "Jack won the New York State primary."
There was a musical number with thirty children in it: "Jack is the
father of all of these children." It was just perfect.

Later in the show, I introduced Hal Roach, one of the great pioneers of movie comedy. Hal was the creator of *The Little Rascals* and had teamed Laurel with Hardy and was that night one hundred years old. After my intro, he was simply to stand up in the audience and wave to the crowd. Well, he stood up and started talking, but he wasn't wearing a mike, and no one could hear his frail voice. He kept going on and on, and it became a little awkward. I was at center stage as they tried to get a mike to him, to no avail. My mind was racing with lines, and I knew the Cyclops was looking at me with its red light, letting me know that a billion people were watching me smile patiently at Mr. Roach and hope I could salvage the awkward moment. Suddenly, a line settled in my head, like the three cherries in a slot machine. "It's only fitting," I said. "He got his start in silent films."

The crowd roared, the moment was saved, and for me, it was a time that I can say I was a good comedian. Later in the show, my fever spiked and I got very woozy. As I tried to introduce Liza Minnelli, nothing came out of my mouth right, and I just stopped and said sarcastically, "Didn't inhale," a reference to Bill Clinton, who had recently claimed he had smoked pot but hadn't inhaled. The crowd laughed, but I felt seriously unwell. During a break they rushed me into Gil's production office to get some fluids into me. Paul Newman was there, preparing for his appearance. He took a look at me and said, "You look like shit, but you're having a great show." I lay down, and a paramedic gave me fluids as Paul put a pillow under my head.

"Great to meet you," I remember saying. I finished the show feeling better and went to the Governors Ball. People were very kind to me as Janice and I made our way into the celebration. Jack was standing at a bar with his lovely wife. He didn't embrace me, he didn't shake my hand; he simply put his hand, the one holding the Oscar, on my shoulder, stared at me for a moment, and said, "Billy Crystal . . . who thought it would be you?" I've thought about that line all these years. Of all the great parts he had, and all his fine performances, his career in Europe making countless B movies and then doing silly television shows like *Ripley's Believe It or Not!*, he finally, at age seventy-three, gets an Oscar for doing two weeks in a movie opposite a comedian and a calf. From seeing him in *Shane*, to being him when we were writing the script, to acting with him and finally having that craggy big-headed icon getting what he deserved, I felt like some sort of Rubik's Cube had been completed. We had a glass of champagne together, and I could only imagine what Charles Bronson was thinking as he went to sleep that night.

....

Mr. Saturday Night was the first picture I directed, and it was a backbreaker. Coming off *Throw Momma, Midnight Train, When Harry Met Sally . . . , City Slickers*, and the successful Oscar shows may not have been the right time to play a bitter seventy-three-year-old comedian, no matter how funny he was. I first did Buddy Young Jr. in the HBO special *A Comic's Line*, without any kind of special makeup to age me. Then at *SNL*, in a film piece, we made me look older, and the character became an insult comic doing a cheesy one-man show. I also did him on "Weekend Update," where he was a restaurant critic who would leave the desk and work the live crowd. One night Christopher Reeve, Waylon Jennings, and Johnny Cash were in the audience, and I went after them like Rickles would: "Waylon, nice hat—when did you go Hasid?" Still, I felt there was something more to Buddy, and when I did my *Don't Get Me Started* special for HBO, I knew how to go after that. The makeup design was great; it aged Buddy naturally. And I created a "life" for him. His family, his wife, his career. It gave him the sort of natural poignancy I often felt when I was around older comics. He was now a real guy rooted in the world of borscht belt comedians, like Alan King and Gene Baylos. I was very comfortable playing older characters. Maybe I was getting ready for this book.

I loved talking to comics like Milton Berle and Red Buttons as much as I did old baseball players. After all the years on the road, they were still sharp and almost smelled of the nightclubs they had labored in for so many years. Buddy was interviewed by Rob Reiner in *Don't Get Me Started,* and it plays as though he was being interviewed on *60 Minutes.* When I showed some footage to William Goldman, the ultimate screenwriter, he said, "He's a funny Willy Loman." I started writing the screenplay during the shooting of *City Slickers.* I wanted it to be a story of not only Buddy's up-and-down stand-up career but also of his relationship with his sensitive brother, Stan. David Paymer was one of the "ice cream" brothers in *City Slickers.* He's gentle and kind, and also very sharp and funny. He was the very soul of the character I wanted to create opposite the abrasive Buddy. We got along great while making *City Slickers,* and without him knowing it, I started crafting the part for him. When *City Slickers* was done shooting, I showed Ganz and Mandel what I had written, and they came on board to write the screenplay with me. Castle Rock was totally behind the picture. We had a sixty-three-day shooting schedule and on fifty-two of those days I would be in the old-age makeup. The other days I was Buddy in his thirties. This meant fifty-two days of five hours or so to put the makeup on, another hour or so during the day for touch-ups, and almost two hours to take it off properly without ravaging my skin. I don't know how Joan Rivers does it. That doesn't count the ten hours of shooting. The math was impossible. It was like a Republican budget plan: the numbers didn't add up.

We did tremendous research to capture the look and feel of each time period. One day we were shooting in the childhood home of the Yankelman family (Yankelman was Mr. Young's real name). The set was based on both my grandma's house and that of our production designer, Albert Brenner. When it was done, we walked the set and I said it was perfect except for one important detail: "It doesn't smell." Albert knew instantly what I meant. So we sent out for chicken livers and onions and garlic. We got a take-out order of chicken soup from a nearby deli, and we cooked up the liver and onions and kept walking the familiar concoction around the set. We left open bowls of soup out overnight and rubbed cooked onions into the doorways. We even smoked a few cigars. It was like a mini Jewish Woodstock. The next morning, when the background artists who would play the family came in, they couldn't believe how great it smelled. "It's my house!" one exclaimed. Another said, "It's my grandma's place." That's the level of detail I aspired to and demanded that we achieve.

We started shooting in New York in early November. The leaves in Central Park were perfect—faded metaphors, I thought, for Buddy's career. The first scenes to be shot were of old Buddy and Stan taking their daily walk and then having a heartfelt talk about the end of his career. The sunlight would be gone by four-fifteen, so we had to really hustle to make our day. We also had to get a night shot of Buddy walking alone on Seventy-second Street. I left the Regency Hotel at one forty-five in the morning to start makeup at two A.M. to be on set by seven. We had rehearsed

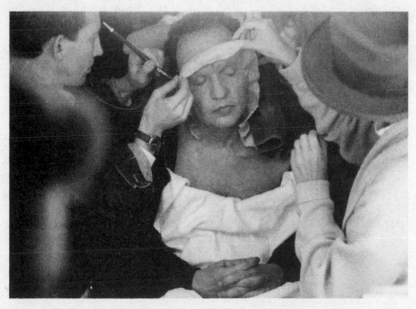

End of a long day. Iron Balls gets to go home.

the scene in the park days prior, and Don Peterman, our director of photography, knew the shots, so he would be ready when Paymer and I were done in makeup. Saying "Action" the first time was quite thrilling. The filming was on time, and when we finally finished shooting on Seventy-second Street, I went into makeup to get Buddy off my face. I had "old" hands, which were immediately placed in plastic bags filled with chemicals to melt the rubber and glue. Peter Montagna and Bill Farley, my terrific makeup artists, carefully removed the hairpiece, and when Bill cut a small hole in my bald cap, you could hear a whoosh of hot air escape. I got back to the Regency at eleven P.M., only to leave again a few hours later for a similar kind of day. This went on for nine days. The crew started calling me "Iron Balls," which is what my urologist calls me now.

After the first week, Martin Shafer and Andy Scheinman flew into New York for a meeting. After watching dailies with me, they said, "We love the footage. But with a schedule this punishing, you'll be dead in a week, so we're going to add ten days to the schedule and the corresponding amount of dollars." Believe me, this wouldn't happen today. The studio would let you die and then CGI you into your remaining scenes.

Making *Mr. Saturday Night* was one of the great experiences of my life. I was naturally drawn to directing and knew more than I thought I did about the camera. I guess some of the days with Scorsese breathing down my neck must have done some good. Actually, it was the relationship with Don Peterman and our sensational crew that made this such a wonderful time for me. Seventy-two days after shooting began, we wrapped in Los Angeles, and the moment I said, "Cut, print, that's a wrap," I got sick. My body wouldn't let me get sick during the shoot, so once it was done, all hell broke loose. That was the start of what would be the pneumonia I had when I walked onto the stage of that year's Oscars.

Kent Beyda, a gifted young editor who had worked on *Spinal Tap*, did the cut with me. We were able to play with time periods and flashbacks, and the first cut was over three hours long, but the story was playing, which was the most important thing. Once we got it down to a playable time, we had our first test screening, and it went very well. The movie was funny and poignant, but I knew it wasn't the commercial fare that *City Slickers* and *When Harry Met Sally* . . . were. As we went on through the testing process, we kept cutting and trimming; then Marc Shaiman wrote a beautiful score and we were done. The early reviews were great, and we had a fantastic evening at the Toronto Film Festival, where the movie got a standing ovation and the respected producer Scott Rudin introduced himself and said, "That's a big hit movie." Soon it was time for it to open. The early magazine reviews were positive, and then I spoke to Joe Farrell, the audience research guru of Hollywood; he said he thought the film would do $10 million the first weekend, which for this movie was a very big number. I'm always nervous before a movie opens, but things felt good.

Opening day came, and the reviews were very mixed, some good, some bad. Some critics thought it too sentimental; some said the makeup bothered them. I started to get really nervous. This birth wasn't going to be easy. We took in only $4.7 million that first weekend, which meant the movie was pretty much toast. All that work, all of that effort and care, and you're over with after one weekend. We hung around and eventually topped $27 million, but it was considered a box office failure, and I was dazed. I was sad, I was angry, but I was also really scared. I found myself rationalizing a lot, second-guessing our decisions: We shouldn't have opened in so many theaters. It should have been a slow release to get word of mouth, because once people saw it, they loved it; we just couldn't get enough people in to see it. *Mr. Saturday Night* has more laughs in it than *City Slickers,* but it isn't a happy comedy. Seventy-three-year-old bitter Jewish comedians are an acquired taste. I'd had a great run playing a certain kind of a guy. Audiences liked that guy; they didn't want to see that guy get old.

I didn't process any of this easily. It was similar to the cancellation of my show at NBC, but worse. Hollywood is a winners' town. When you're up, it's a great place to be. When you are a loser? Well, it's a self-imposed hell. Getting a Golden Globe nomination for Best Actor in a Comedy and David getting a Best Supporting Actor Globe nomination and then deservedly an Oscar nomination took a little bit of the hurt away, but not enough. I was thrilled for David, who totally deserved the recognition, and I took great pride in having directed someone to a nomination, but I was exhausted and disillusioned. After so many good things in a row, why didn't my audience trust me? I didn't want to host the Oscars that year. The previous broadcast had been so strong that I thought, *End it there, take a break—you can't top that one*. Gil Cates, whom I had great respect and affection for, talked me into it, and I did the show with mixed emotions, which is not the way to do anything. I knew halfway through the show that I didn't want to do it again for a while. Johnny Carson had told me that he did four years in a row, took a year off, and really didn't want to do it a fifth time, but he eventually did, and he regretted it. I loved hosting the show, but it ate up so much of my time. I needed to do something different. What I had to do, I thought, was get my movie audience back.

It wouldn't be easy. Even after *When Harry Met Sally . . .* and *City Slickers*, I always had to generate my own material, and thankfully I had great partners in Castle Rock. But the next string of films I did—*Forget Paris, City Slickers II, Father's Day*, and *My Giant*—didn't perform well. Most actors, even the most successful ones, feel that when they've finished a film, they'll never work again. After a few off years like this, I was convinced that I was done.

....

In the midst of this career angst came the loss of two great friends. In April 1995, Howard Cosell died. I had made my network television debut on Cosell's short-lived variety show on ABC. He'd always claimed he had discovered me, and I'd even played his wife in a sketch when he'd hosted *Saturday Night Live.* Also, my imitations of Howard and Ali had gotten me started in television. Howard was a very complicated and fascinating person, of course, but in his devotion to Muhammad Ali and Ali's struggle for vindication from the Supreme Court, he'd had his finest hours. He had become a close friend over the years.

At the funeral service, it was fitting that I sat next to Ali. In front of the closed casket, Ali nudged me and whispered, "Do you think he's wearing his hairpiece?"

I had to hold in my laugh. "I don't think so," I replied.

"Then how will God recognize him?"

"Once he starts complaining, he'll know," I said.

We both shared a muffled laugh. "He was a good man," said Ali—his last words to me that day.

....

Just a few months later, another sad good-bye. Mickey Mantle and I had seen less of each other over the last few years, and I knew he wasn't doing well. His drinking had continued to get worse, according to Bob Costas and other good friends who spent time with him. I'd encountered the problem firsthand when I'd invited Mickey to come to the New York premiere of *City Slickers.* I talked about him and my first game in the film, and I wanted him to be there to see it. Also, that night I was being honored by the Anti-Defamation League as the entertainer of the year. The award ceremony preceded the film, and I could see Mickey's empty seat as I was asked to come onstage and receive the award, which I assumed was a plaque. Instead, a large object covered with a cloth was brought out. The ADL representative explained that, knowing my love for baseball and the Yankees, they were giving me an original seat from Yankee Stadium. The ballpark had been renovated, so these seats were rare. It was the same kind of wooden seat I'd sat in back in 1956. Amazingly, it had the number 7 —Mickey's number—on it. I was onstage, overwhelmed by this gift, and I could see that Mantle's seat was still empty. After the premiere I went back to the hotel, and the doorman told me Mickey was in the bar and had requested that I stop by.

"Hey, you little son of a bitch. Sorry, got held up here. How'd it go?"

I told him about the seat. "A seat? I put asses in them seats, and I don't have one," he laughed. I asked him to sign it, which he agreed to do. "Where is it?" he asked.

I explained that he should call the man on the business card I handed him. As I pointed at the name, I could only imagine Mickey with his Oklahoma accent asking for Schlomo Abromowitz.

We said good-bye, and two weeks later the crate arrived at my home in Los Angeles. There it was, my Yankee Stadium No. 7 seat with this inscription: "Billy, wish you was still sittin here and I was still playing. —Mickey Mantle 6/7/'91."

It was perfect. Cowboy poetry, I thought. I'm looking at it now as I write this. I have a very nice art collection, but nothing comes close to this perfect piece of American folk art. Years later, I bought one of Mantle's gloves from the sixties at an auction, and I rest it on the chair. It's my own Hall of Fame.

Mickey's sons, Danny and David, were recovering alcoholics. Danny had gotten sober at Betty Ford, and in 1994 he convinced his father to go. Finally, Mick checked himself in. He came out of the program a changed man. Mickey and Bob Costas did a televised interview together that was just heartbreaking. Mickey sat there holding a handkerchief, using it to dab at his wet eyes. He seemed so much smaller in some ways, and so much bigger in others. He talked openly about his drinking, admitting that he was an alcoholic and that he now had a good feeling about himself and how he wanted to live the rest of his life. A few months later, I received a letter from him inviting me to play in his golf tournament. He closed his note with "Can't wait to see you now that I'm sober."

The tournament never happened. Mickey was gravely ill and

needed a liver transplant to survive. He got the liver, and with his life like a game that he couldn't possibly win, he rallied.

The last time I saw him was on television. He appeared at a press conference to announce the Mickey Mantle organ donor program, which would go on to become very successful. Mickey needed help getting to the podium. He wore a baseball cap and had the look of a very sick man. He said that he wasn't a role model. God had given him a body, and he'd blown it. Don't be like me, he said, and was then led away. I was shocked to see him this way. His demons had had their way with him for sure, but it was also clear that he had a new insight. He was honest and direct. He was even able to make a joke. Barry Halper, a friend of Mantle's and the biggest collector of baseball memorabilia, was in the audience. Mickey saw him and asked, "Barry, did you get the liver?" His joking gave me hope, but what I didn't know—what nobody knew—was that cancer had spread throughout his body and he was terminal.

I spoke to him once in the hospital and told him I wanted to come visit. "Not right now," he said "Give me a little time. I wanna be able to have some fun when I see you." A few weeks later, Costas called me to say that Mickey had taken a turn for the worse. He died the next day.

"Come to Dallas and help me write the eulogy," Bob said. I flew out with a heavy heart, jotting down some thoughts on the plane. Bob and I hugged each other hello like we were about to bury a favorite uncle, but in a way Mickey was much more than that to us. It's hard to explain to some people what it was like to grow up as a Yankee fan during those glory days. Mickey was ours. There was no one like him. The power, the speed—but there was something else. He was vulnerable, it seemed, even then. He had the perfect baseball name. He looked better in the uniform than anyone else. He was the symbol of a simple time in our youth. We jumped onto his broad shoulders and he carried us to middle age, and even though we got older, we didn't want him to. When I was with him later in his life, grown men would stand up and, with tears in their eyes, try to say how much they loved him. Mickey didn't understand that until the end, but I know he finally got it.

Bob and I stayed up most of the night working on the eulogy, which he delivered beautifully at the service. Giving Mickey Mantle's eulogy is like trying to hit a fastball on a cool October night with the World Series on the line. You don't want to foul it off, you have to get all of it, and only Bob could have done him justice. I sat there with George Steinbrenner and Reggie Jackson. The casket was covered with flowers forming the number 7. When the '61 Yankees approached the casket as pallbearers to lead their teammate away, I lost it. That was my team, now all in their sixties carrying the casket of their fallen prince.

Maybe it's the baseball magic. When Dad rolls a ball to you for the first time and you roll it back, it starts; but then there comes a time when you don't want Dad to throw it to you—you want Mickey to. I got that chance.

....

While I was shooting *Father's Day* in Reno, I got a call from George Steinbrenner on behalf of Mickey's family. They wanted me to speak at the unveiling of Mickey's monument in Yankee Stadium. Moved and honored, I agreed and flew to New York. It was a somber occasion as the Yankees and fifty-seven thousand fans gathered to remember the legend. Many former Yankee teammates were there, and after a few spoke, Bobby Murcer, a former Yankee and now an announcer, introduced me. He told the crowd that I was a great Yankee fan and a dear friend of Mickey's and that the family wanted me to speak. I almost tripped on my way out of the dugout, but I made my way to the microphone. At the home plate I always dreamed of stepping on after my World Series–winning home run, I spoke of my dad taking me to my first game in 1956 and asked the last row of the upper deck to stand up to show how far Mickey had hit the ball that day. I told them I was there representing all the fathers in the stands who were bringing their sons to their first game. I then introduced a film package of Mickey moments, which was shown on the big scoreboard screen. As it was playing, Murcer came over and said, "While you're there when it's over, introduce Joe DiMaggio."

Oh man, okay, I thought. In the dugout, Joe was pacing; I spotted his broad back, shock of white hair, and chiseled face. I had never met him, but he'd been my dad's favorite player. "Ladies and gentleman, please welcome Joe DiMaggio," I said.

Joe bounded out onto the field and got to me quickly as the crowd roared. "I'm not speaking—what do I do?" he asked gruffly.

"Wave and stand next to Whitey Ford," I replied.

When the ceremony was over and we were leaving the field, Mark McGwire of the Oakland A's called to me and tipped his cap as if to say, "Good job." Joe Torre, in his first year as manager of the Yankees, invited me to work out with the team. I spent some time with Yogi Berra and Whitey Ford. I greeted Mickey's widow, Merlyn, and their sons David and Danny. We were standing just outside the Yankee clubhouse when the door opened and Joe DiMaggio came out. He stepped toward me and, without warning, punched me in the stomach. Hard. I wasn't ready for it, and it knocked the wind out of me. He put his face inches from mine. "Greatest living player!" he hissed, and he stormed off. I didn't know what to do. Totally confused, I was escorted up to Mr. Steinbrenner's box, and when I arrived, George was laughing. "Well, you pissed Joe off—he insists on being introduced as the greatest living player."

"I didn't know. Can I apologize to him?"

George laughed some more. "Joe was so angry that he left the stadium, and not just because of that. He was jealous of Mickey and couldn't stand the fact that it was Mickey's day, even though Mickey's gone. I'll take care of it," he assured me. "Don't worry." But this would not be my last encounter with Mr. DiMaggio.

····

Meeting Joe DiMaggio at Yankee Stadium on
Mickey Mantle Day—a few minutes later he belted me.

In 1997, Gil Cates started pressuring me to do the Oscars again, after a gap of three years. I kept saying no. Then one day a large gift box was delivered to the house. I opened it, and inside was a prop horse's head with a note: "If you want to see the rest of the horse alive, do the fucking show." I was getting tons of mail from people saying they missed me, so I decided to go ahead with it.

We started planning the show, and I came up with the idea of filming myself in scenes from the nominated films, so it would look like I was in all of the movies. The story would be that after three years off, I'm coming back to the Oscars and I'm nervous about how to do it. We could shoot it to make it look like I was in the five movies, and that could surprise the crowd and give me a funny opening. We hired Troy Miller and his company Dakota

Pictures to shoot the piece. The movies that year were all small independent films, except for *Jerry Maguire*, which had been the lone big financial hit. The opening sequence began with a brief moment of Yoda telling someone, "You must go back," and when I appeared, asking, "To the Oscars?" it totally caught the crowd off guard. I was then edited into scenes from *Secrets and Lies*, *Jerry Maguire*, *Fargo*, *Shine*, and *The English Patient;* David Letterman, who'd had a tough time hosting the Oscars a couple of years earlier, graciously agreed to do a cameo at the end of the film, poking fun at himself. We shot him flying the biplane from *The English Patient;* David looked like he was after me and then insanely started screaming, "Here's what you have to do: introduce Uma to Oprah, and Oprah to Uma, and KEEP DOING IT!" The plane crashed into the desert, I ran toward the audience on film, and then at the precise moment, I burst right through the special screen the film was being projected on (which was a series of strips of fabric) and onto the stage. The audience stood up and gave me an ovation that was so emotional I had a tough time getting my first lines out.

After the Oscars, my agent, Andrea Eastman, sent me a script by the wonderful writer Kenneth Lonergan called *Analyze This*. It was the story of a Mafia boss who is having a midlife crisis and starts seeing a shrink; then at one point he realizes he's told the shrink too much and has to kill him. It was dark and funny, and I loved it. I brought in Peter Tolan to rewrite with me, and Paula Weinstein was to produce and I would be executive producer and play the shrink. I was convinced that Robert De Niro should play Paul Vitti, the midlife-crisis Mafia boss who can't kill anymore and cries at life insurance commercials. He hadn't done a mainstream comedy like this, but of course he was brilliant, and I kept telling everyone how many times he made me laugh in *Raging Bull*, *King of Comedy*, and even a dark movie like *Sleepers*. Over and over again studio executives told us that he would never do it. "De Niro? No way." I had met him socially a few times, just small talk, but I called him. I told him about the script and how funny I believed he could be in this part. He read it immediately and called me two days later and suggested that we do a reading. In a conference room at CAA, I sat across from the great De Niro and, with a good cast in the key parts, we read the movie. He got big laughs right away, and I could see him enjoying himself. We had a natural chemistry, and I couldn't get over the fact I was acting with him. "Let me think," Bob said. His concerns were legit: How far should he go with this character? Would it hurt his chances to play a mob character again? Would he be making fun of himself? I told him that audiences would love it if he winked at himself.

I was on pins and needles for a few months as he thought and thought. Finally he said yes. When it was announced that we were doing this together, there was a great buzz about the pairing—two actors so different in every way playing opposite each other. Harold Ramis came on to write and direct and he took what Peter and I had done and elevated it. We started shooting in New York, and Bob asked that we film all his anxiety-attack scenes first, so that when he came into my office for the first time, it would be in perfect sequence.

Eight days later, our first day of filming together arrived. We met on the set at seven A.M., and Bob looked sleepy and unshaved, his hair unkempt. After an easy rehearsal, Harold figured out the shots and then Bob and I went to our dressing rooms to get ready. Two hours later I'm called to the set, and Robert De Niro isn't there; Paul Vitti is. Wearing a silk suit, clean-shaven, with his hair slicked back and a menacing but needy look in his eye, Bob was ready to—pardon the pun—shoot. Just seeing him helped me get firmly into character. Ramis called, "ACTION," Vitti walked into my office and said his first few lines, I did mine, and "CUT." Bob motioned me over secretively. *Uh-oh,* I thought, *he's gonna say, "Is that the best you can do that? Where did you learn to act?"* Instead, he whispered into my ear, "Listen, if you see anything you think could be funnier, let me know, okay? Just take me aside with any ideas."

"You have a gift, my friend." The great Robert De Niro, *Analyze This.*

I was amazed. The world's greatest actor was saying it was okay to give him ideas, that he trusted me. We did the next take and after "CUT," I went over to him: "Is that the best you can do that? Jesus . . ." We laughed, and from that moment on, playing straight man to De Niro was as good as it gets. I felt like a trapeze catcher. One guy does the spins and somersaults, but he needs the other guy to catch him. De Niro's technique was fascinating. He loves to keep doing different versions of line readings, all of them coming at you at lightning speed. He would keep going back and starting over as he repeated lines four or five times, each time with a different spin to it. Bob made me better just by being great himself. I played a man who listened for a living. That's what I had to do playing opposite him: listen and respond in kind. When we'd finish a really tough scene together, Bob would hug me and say, "Good day today," which was better than any good review I could ever get.

After we wrapped the film, I started planning a big event: my fiftieth birthday party. This was a big one. Fifty is the last stop of middle age. I felt much more reflective. I wasn't as anxious as I'd been about turning forty; I found myself thinking that life is short. My dad had died at fifty-four, and I knew how hard he'd worked for us, but I wasn't sure he'd had enough fun in his life. I wanted that to be a goal for myself. I had been very fortunate in my career, doing all kinds of things I hadn't thought I would get a chance to do. Only one experience was missing: Broadway. I started making notes for a one-man show that I'd had in the back of my mind. I wrote a four-page blueprint of a show about me and my family and my relationship with my late father. I called it *700 Sundays*—for the number of Sundays (his only day off) we were able to share before his death when I was fifteen. When my mom came out for my birthday party, she brought tons of photos and audiotapes and home movies that she wanted me to have. Little did I know how much they would mean to me when, six years later, I would use them as I began the process of creating the show. But I didn't do anything with the four-page outline then, except file it in my desk drawer. I wasn't ready yet.

Doing *Analyze This* had put me in a good frame of mind, and I invited two hundred friends and family members to my fiftieth birthday party. Janice and I rented the ballroom at the Four Seasons in Beverly Hills and had a set designer turn it into an old-fashioned nightclub, complete with red leather banquettes, that we called "Club Fifty." March 14 fell on a Saturday that year. The day was normal. I worked out in the morning with my friend and trainer, Dan Isaacson. My mom joined us for a while. She had gotten heavy late in her life, and Dan said, "Helen, there are a lot of good diets for people your age." She replied, "I don't need a diet—I put on some weight after the last baby." Which was me. I went to get the mail, and my fucking AARP card had come. Did the card have to arrive on the very day I turned fifty? Did they think, *Hey let's ruin his day and send him this reminder that he's an old fart?* I said to Janice, "Hey, honey, I'm old now, which means you are officially a trophy wife."

That afternoon, I was reading the paper in the kitchen when the phone rang. Janice answered it and said, "Oh, he's right here. I'll put him on."

"Who is it?" I mouthed. Janice just shrugged. I took the phone and said hello.

"Kid, this is Ted Williams. How ya doing?" I had never spoken to him before, and that strong voice almost knocked me over. How had he known it was my birthday? Janice had this wonderful smile on her face as Ted continued: "Listen, your lovely wife tracked me down and invited me to your party tonight, but, kid, the good Lord is pitching me tight. So I can't make it, but I love what you do. When you do the Oscars, it's like watching a great hitter. You see the pitch and wherever it is, you hit it solid. You don't foul any off. I love to see that."

I was in shock to be on the phone with him, but I managed to say, "Ted, is everything hitting to you?"

"You bet," he said. "It's a great metaphor, isn't it?"

To this day I think he's the only Hall of Famer who has used the word "metaphor" in a sentence. He continued, "Hey, I read that you own a piece of that team in Arizona." Janice and I had bought a tiny interest in the Arizona Diamondbacks.

"Yes, I do, Ted."

"Well, that's where I'd like to play. With that dry air, you hit a ball with the right kind of spin, it's going to keep going. Man, I'd hit .285 there."

"Only .285?" I asked the last man to hit .400.

"Billy, I'm in a wheelchair," he replied. Before we said our good-byes, he told me he had sent me a gift and hoped I would like it. Like it? He'd sent a large photo of himself with Babe Ruth and had signed it to me. Wow.

The party was spectacular. Jack Sheldon and a fifteen-piece dance band were onstage, and Wolfgang Puck was in the kitchen. The party wasn't just for me; I also wanted to thank my friends and family for always supporting me. Marty Short sang a few songs, my hero Mel Brooks got up and sang with the band, my

brother Rip belted out a few, and then Rob Reiner went up
onstage and acted as a host as one after the other of my good
friends, including Richard Lewis and Christopher Guest, got up to
speak. Marc Shaiman performed a funny personalized song he'd
written. Janice also sang a song for me, Jenny and Lindsay made
a beautiful toast, and then Joel and Rip presented me with a large
gift-wrapped present, flat and roughly seven feet tall. It was the
door of my bedroom from our house in Long Beach, which I had
decorated with decals of ballplayers of the fifties. That fantastic
gift is now the door to my office closet. Sometimes when I'm having a bad day, I look at that door and wish I could open it and go
back in time.

Janice then announced a gift from George Steinbrenner. It was
a World Series ring from 1996! My name had been engraved
where the player's name goes. His card read, "To our 26th man,
Happy Birthday, your pal, George and the New York Yankees."
Wait, it gets better. Janice then told the crowd, "You know, I can
do impressions also. Here's Mrs. Muhammad Ali." She started to
do her own impression of Ali, which got big laughs, and then she
stopped and said, "Why am I doing him? Here he is." And Muhammad Ali walked out. Some people—like me—almost fainted. Janice
had arranged the whole thing. "Happy Birthday, little brother," he
whispered in my ear. "Gotcha."

My mom always said, "Do something special on your birthday."
The party was the perfect way to end my forties and start fresh in
my fifties. It was a time to take stock. Who was I? Was I the Oscar
host who did *When Harry Met Sally . . . , City Slickers,* and *Midnight Train to Moscow,* or was I the guy who got dissed by Orson
Welles, told to fuck off by Charles Bronson, and punched by Joe
DiMaggio? Oy.

Kiss Me Twice

I guess when you write a book covering your first sixty-five years, there has to be at least one scandal, so here's mine: for over three years I had an amazing affair with Sophia Loren. We made love everywhere. At her villa in Italy, in the back of a Maserati, on a hilltop overlooking the Mediterranean, and once behind the monuments at Yankee Stadium during a rain delay.

I was thirteen when our trysts started, and they went on and on, sometimes happening twice a day (once five times in an afternoon), until I was sixteen and saw Joey Heatherton on *Hullabaloo*. But that was a fleeting moment of lust compared to the enduring memories I share with Sophia. My Sophia. If only I could meet her someday, I said to myself. If only.

Funny how things work out sometimes. In 1992, I was now a grown man and had just hosted the Oscars for the third straight year. It was a great night for many reasons: the show was going well, I was in good form, and, most importantly, it was the only time my mother was in the audience. We had watched the Oscars together so many times, but rarely the whole thing. Proving that nothing changes, even back in the fifties the show would run long, and so this little New York schoolboy would be sent off to bed around—you guessed it—sound effects editing. Before getting into bed, I would brush my teeth and hold the toothbrush like it was an Oscar and thank people! "And to Clark Gable: man, we had fun." (Years later, whenever I hosted the show, I kept a toothbrush in my breast pocket, just to remind myself where I'd come from.) In the morning when I got to the breakfast table, I would find, in my cereal bowl, a paper napkin on which Mom had written out the names of the big winners.

You can imagine what it was like for me that night walking out onstage, the audience applauding my entrance and me getting to catch my mother's gleaming eye. I could see her smile and shake her head in proud wonder at me, her little Shredded Wheat eater, hosting the show it had once seemed I'd never be old enough to watch to completion.

I almost lost it; for at that moment as I walked out onstage, seeing my mom, thinking about my dad and my brothers, where this whole journey had started, my emotions ran wild like a rioting soccer crowd. But I held it together, and of all the times I've hosted (nine—which means that if I host every year from now until 2022, I'll catch Bob Hope), it was my favorite.

Once the show was over, my brain spun with a jumble of thoughts and questions. Was it okay? That worked, that didn't, should have, shouldn't have, glad I talked to Jack in the audience, good ad-lib there, I knew that joke would kill—man, that was fun! There was more adrenaline than blood in my veins as I made my way to the Governors Ball.

My family had yet to arrive, and sitting at my mom's place setting was an older man. From the back he looked familiar, and as he sensed I was standing there, he turned toward me. It was Burt Lancaster! Burt Elmer Gantry, *Sweet Smell of Success, Trapeze,*

Apache, Jim Thorpe, Doc Graham, and assorted pirates Lancaster! I'd never met him before.

He smiled that huge movie-star smile, which lit up his huge movie-star head, and out of nowhere asked, "Have you ever been an acrobat?"

"Uh, I did tumble a bit in school . . ." I weakly responded.

"You move like an acrobat," he said.

I had no idea where this was going, but before either of us could say another word, I heard a woman's voice with a beautiful accent call out, "Billeee, Billeee." It was the voice from my dreams. I turned, and there was Sophia Loren.

I flashed what in my mind was a debonair killer smile, which, as I think about it later, was probably the goofy grin of a thirteen-year-old. She motioned me over to her with her index finger, just the way all of our encounters had begun. I walked toward her like a zombie in a trance, and being the Jew I am, all I wanted to do was apologize.

She reached out her hands to me, and I grasped them as she pulled me closer to her. (Just writing that sentence almost gave me a chubby.)

"Billeee, kiss me twice . . ." She turned her head as I kissed first her right and then her left cheek. She told me how much she'd enjoyed my performance (as the host) and how she loved my acting in movies, that I reminded her of Cary Grant in a way, all the while holding my hands and looking at me with those seductive dark eyes. She was so beautiful, and yet something was different about her. Then I realized that this was the first time I was looking at her without a staple in the middle of her body.

I turned to see that my family was now sitting down and my mother was talking to Burt Lancaster, making motions probably showing him how I indeed could do back flips when I was seven. I didn't care. At that moment, it was just me and Sophia.

....

Kiss me *twice.*

The next year I was hosting again and was in the wings watching
the show and going over what to say during my next appearance
when I felt a mouth close to my left ear. "Billeee, Billeee . . ." The
gentle aroma of her perfume and her breathy whisper made me
break out into an instant sweat (another almost chubby). I turned,
and there she was, taking my breath away again. "Kiss me twice,"
she said. Then she looked me in the eye and said, "This is special, I want you to meet someone," and I'm thinking, *Threesome.*

   She left for a moment and returned with Federico Fellini!

   "He loves you, Billeee," Sophia said.

   "Mr. Fellini . . ." I began, but he put his hand up and shook his
head as if to say, "Don't talk."

"Billeee, you drive this show like it is a race car. You take the turns, you hit the straightaways, you are a maestro." Fed—we were now on a first-syllable basis—was then interrupted by the stage manager telling him, "One minute—I want to get you to your mark, sir."

"Billeee, before I go," he said, taking my hands in his, "please, kiss me twice."

That almost spoiled everything, but it was Fellini! They left together, and I stood in the wings and thought, *Oh my god, isn't this WILD!* I never want to lose that feeling of awe when I meet great artists. Later, at the ball, we had a drink together and I hobnobbed with the two of them. One more champagne and I would have asked Fellini, "Why 8 1/2, why not just 8?"

In 2011, Sophia called and asked me to host an evening honoring her at the academy. We showed clips of her magnificent career, and then I brought her up onstage and interviewed her for almost an hour. My first question to her set the tone: "You are Italy's greatest export to Hollywood. Why is there no good pizza in L.A.?" She laughed and relaxed and we had a great conversation. If this was a date, I was in. As I drove home that night, I couldn't help but think how rare it is that two former lovers— even if only one of us knew about the affair—can end up as friends. Funny how things work out sometimes.

Still Foolin' 'Em

I stared at myself in the three-way mirror. I was wearing an unbuttoned tuxedo shirt, underwear briefs, formal black silk socks to the knee—I call them talk-show socks because if you're on a show and cross your legs, you don't want skin to show—and my patent leather shoes. I carefully pulled my tuxedo pants on so as not to catch a heel on the newly sewn hem. One usually puts his shoes on after his pants, but Alan King taught me to put my shoes on first because you don't want to bend down to tie them as you'll break the crease in your pants. I silently went over my thoughts and jokes as I slipped the suspenders over the shoulders of my pleated shirt. On the mannequin form was a brand-new tuxedo jacket, its beautiful black satin lapels shimmering in the glow of my dressing room lights. I didn't put it on yet—not the right time. I stared at myself in the mirror. *Hmm,* I thought, *this is who I am now. A little older, a little wiser.* "Still foolin' 'em," I muttered, as I always do before facing the crowd.

That is always my ritual. I kept going over my lines in my head, *Start with this, go with that,* as I buttoned my shirt with my dad's silver tuxedo studs. I was nervous and had a little lump in my throat. Hosting an evening like this is not easy.

I've been accused of being sentimental, and this time I plead guilty—I think it's 50 percent because of my genetic makeup and 50 percent because there is something special about being the father of the bride. Jenny, my firstborn, was getting married today.

Jackie Kennedy once said, "If you bungle raising your children, I don't think whatever else you do matters very much." And it's true. The greatest compliments I've ever received are about how Janice and I raised our girls. Now, I know part of that is because I'm in show business. When your kids are in a show business family, people tend to give you credit for being a good parent simply if they're not on TMZ for being arrested for their third DUI in the past two weeks.

I sniffed the beautiful white rose before I slipped it into the buttonhole on my lapel, its familiar scent lingering for a few seconds. My feelings about the moments and milestones in my life with Jenny were starting to crystallize. Which is what happens if your name is Crystal. The first time I'd held all eight pounds, four ounces of her, I'd known this day would eventually arrive. But I hadn't known it would come so fast. Today I would walk my daughter down the aisle and then, with Janice alongside, stop as Michael, her husband-to-be-in-a-few-minutes, walked toward us. I would then lift her veil, kiss her on the cheek, shake the lucky man's hand, and give her away forever.

As I straightened my crisp white tuxedo shirt the way Alan King had taught me to do, by opening my fly, reaching in, grabbing the fabric, and pulling it down until it's smooth, I found myself jotting down notes on her "first sleepover"—the first time Janice and I were alone for a night in three years. All parents have that moment, when they realize they can have sex again and not worry about being noisy—if only they remembered how to have sex. Well, somehow we managed, and nine months later, guess what blessed little event occurred? That's right, exactly nine months to the day after we decided to send Jenny on another sleepover so we could have sex again, Lindsay arrived.

"Funny," I said to myself as I tied my bow tie. I thought back to one of the bigger decisions I'd made in my life. When the girls were nine and five, I was busy on the road doing my stand-up pretty much nonstop, and one night Janice said, "We have enough money—you don't want to be Uncle Daddy." I got it. Luckily, I stopped going on the road to be at home just at the point in my career when I was starting to get movie offers. Sure, with movies there were times when I was away, but in the end I rarely missed games or school plays or concerts or birthdays. However, despite the better schedule and less travel, one year I thought I was going to miss Lindsay's birthday. She was in Los Angeles turning eleven, and I was filming *When Harry Met Sally . . .* in New York. Her birthday was on a Friday, and I knew I couldn't make it home unless there was a drastic change in our shooting schedule. Then, miraculously, it rained and I found out I could make a three P.M. flight and get back home in time for her birthday. I called Janice and told her to go to the supermarket and get a giant cardboard box, gift-wrap it, keep the bottom open, and leave it by the front gate.

I called Lindsay from the airport to say I was sorry but that this year Daddy just couldn't make it home for her birthday. Right then an announcement blared over the airport loudspeaker.

"Dad, what's that?"

I did what all parents do with their kids when confronted with an awkward question: I lied. "We're shooting in Central Park."

I then told her not to worry, that Daddy was sending her a big birthday surprise.

I flew back to L.A., and the car dropped me off at the front gate. The gift-wrapped carton was right where it should be. Like a Navy SEAL, I crept up to the house. Unlike a Navy SEAL, I rang the doorbell, sat down, and pulled the box over my head. Janice answered the door and immediately began to do bad summer-stock acting.

"WELL, WHAT'S THIS? OH LOOK, LINDSAY, THIS MUST BE DADDY'S BIG PRESENT. WHAT COULD IT BE?"

I threw off the box and stood there.

Lindsay looked at me, jumped into my arms, and said, "Somebody pinch me."

"Save story for Lindsay's wedding," I scribbled now, underlining it three times. The satin vest was next, and I was relieved that it hid the little bit of paunch I just couldn't conquer. My notes said, "first kiss." Oh yeah, that's a big moment for a dad, when you find out. Of course, Jenny didn't tell me; I found out when she told Janice, who, after promising never to say a word, called me five seconds later.

"Billy, Jen was at a party and a boy kissed her."

I nervously asked the natural question that any man in my position would ask: "Tongue?"

As I put my cuff links on, it hit me: my little girl is about to get married, and her next kiss will be her first as a married woman.

"We need you," said Janice, poking her head through the doorway.

"Look at you," I was barely able to say, my glistening eyes meeting hers.

"Don't make me cry—I'll have to redo my makeup," Janice said.

"I didn't say anything," I replied.

"You didn't have to," my beautiful wife whispered.

"One second, I'll be right there," I promised. We held hands for a moment, stared at each other, and then she closed the door. I had to compose myself before I could leave for the wedding service. I took a deep breath and looked in the mirror one last time. Shirt, immaculate; bow tie, tied precisely; tux, awesome; pants, perfect crease; shoes, shiny. I started to leave, took a last sip of bubbly, and glanced at my notes once again. I folded them neatly and put them in my breast pocket.

Sometime after dinner, I would make a speech, and then Jenny and I would dance. Giving the opening monologue at the Oscars is hard; this was harder.

But I'd had plenty of practice. A lot of my milestones with my kids involved events where I gave speeches.

I spoke at Jenny's and Lindsay's high school graduations, Lindsay's NYU graduation, both their weddings, their engagement parties, their soccer team parties, and at their Bat Mitzvahs.

I gave a quick speech at Jenny's fifth birthday party at Chuck E. Cheese's. That was a Saturday afternoon to remember. I'm giving a happy birthday speech to fifteen five-year-olds bouncing up and down in a salmonella-infested plastic ball pit while a couple with his-and-her devil tattoos are staring at me.

"That looks like Billy Crystal."

"You're crazy—what the fuck would he be doing at a Chuck E. Cheese's?"

The first Bat Mitzvah speech was challenging. Not because of the emotion. When I was standing on the stage looking at the audience, all I could see was 300 people, 250 of whom I didn't know, all costing me $90 a head.

When I gave the speech at Jenny's high school graduation, I felt that things were really getting serious. Maybe it was "Pomp and Circumstance" or the caps and gowns or the look on my now seventeen-year-old daughter's face as she walked up to get her diploma, but that speech signaled the coming storm. The winds would blow and sweep Jenny across the country. The theme was all the changes the graduates would be experiencing. Most of them were now driving, and that is perhaps the most stressful event in any parent's life. Especially driving in L.A. You not only have to worry about them driving on the nation's busiest freeways; you have to make sure they know how to tell another driver to go fuck himself in five different languages.

Because we were all constantly worrying when they drove and asking them to "call us when you get there," that phrase became the closing thought in the speech. They were now on their way to becoming adults, with all the aspirations and pressures the world would bring. Work hard, don't take any moment for granted, and someday soon you'll be mature adults with a great education, a good job, and maybe even a family, and please "call us when you get there."

The summer after Jenny's graduation, we knew that our time together as the Crystals was dwindling. She was going off to college, and the family would never quite be the same.

There was a ticking clock that whole summer, an event countdown: this is the last time she'll sleep in her bed before she becomes a legal adult; this is the last time we'll have dinner together where Mom cooks; is this the last time she'll lie to you about what time she got in? As her boxes were packed and shipped, we got sadder and sadder. Sometimes she'd quietly walk into the room where I was and just hug me.

At Northwestern, we set up the room, met her roommate, walked around the campus, and then it was time to go. I was leaving my oldest daughter in a strange city to live with someone she had known for one hour. After we said good-bye, we watched her waving to us in the parking lot outside her dorm, and as we drove away our melancholy was tempered by the knowledge that we had raised her right and, more importantly, for the first time in eighteen years, we could walk around the house naked and play our own music. Then we realized, *Wait a second, we can't do that. Lindsay is still at home.*

....

Lindsay had been born when Jenny was almost five, so Jenny had had us to herself for a long time. Now Lindsay had *her* alone time with us. Everything we did revolved around her. Time flew by, and then it was time for her to go to college. That's a major milestone for parents: the empty nest.

It's the quiet that you first notice. The deafening quiet. From the baby cries when you first bring them home to the door slams when they're teenagers, the house is always noisy. They've been your life, and suddenly, they're gone. It was a huge adjustment for us. However, it then became a great thing. It was just us again; we had a chance to get reacquainted in a new way. We loved it. Then came the next important revelation: THEY NEVER STOP COMING HOME.

Here's some wisdom I can pass on to you from my vantage point of sixty-five years on this planet: From the time your kids are about three, they're always leaving . . . and then once they graduate college, they're always coming home.

They're home again, and sometimes you can't wait for them to leave, because when they come back from college, they don't come back the same.

You can't treat them like you used to.

You can't ask them, "What time are you coming home?"

You can't ask, "Who were you with?"

You can't ask, "Where were you, what did you do, and who opened my vodka?" The only thing you really have the right to ask is "Who didn't flush?" Basically, you have adult strangers living in your house. You can't talk to them like you used to. But don't worry; this is a transitional phase where you take a step from being only their parents to also being their friends. And that's kind of a good thing. You have to let go.

When the girls were little, I created a character named Mr. Phyllis, a flamboyant José Eber character without the cowboy hat, who would shampoo their hair during their baths. While I was blow-drying their hair I would style it into all these funny shapes, all the while chattering away. "This is a fabulous look for you. I call it the unicorn," I'd say as I twisted the wet hair into a horn. Mr. Phyllis would get nonstop giggles from the girls. It is one of the great times I had with them growing up . . . until the day Janice said, "Billy, you can't go in the bathroom."

"Why?" I asked.

"The girls are taking their bath," she said.

"I know, I'm going to shampoo their hair."

"Not anymore. They're . . . too big."

It was one of the saddest days of my life. But you have to let go.

As I finished my champagne, I thought of all of these things I missed already. I could hear the mingling guests, who were now being asked to take their seats for the ceremony. I left my dressing room and joined the wedding party. There were Michael's parents and grandparents, Janice's folks, my mom and my brothers, who would walk her down the aisle in the processional. There was stunning Lindsay, the maid of honor, the ushers, and all the beautiful bridesmaids, many of whom I had known since they were in kindergarten. Everyone was getting into position. Janice looked ravishing, a portrait of beauty and poise. And then there was Jenny, the late afternoon sun shining through the delicate lace of her wedding gown, giving her an angelic glow. What a lovely woman she had become right before my eyes. A glimpse of that face I first saw in the nursery was still there. The music started, and Jenny looked at me. "Ready, Dad?" I said, "Not sure." I then did something that from the time she was a little girl I had told her I would do on her wedding day. "What's on your dress?" I asked in a very concerned way, pointing to her waist.

She looked down quickly, and I raised my finger up to her nose. "Gotcha," I said.

We laughed. I told her I loved her, she put her arm inside mine, and then in a few moments she was Mrs. Michael Foley.

The speeches I gave at both girls' weddings had to be funny, heartfelt, and honest and, most importantly, personal, because you are really only talking to your daughter, with a big crowd watching. Standing there looking at my girls, I felt all the years, all the diapers, the fevers, the car pools, the spelling tests, the term papers, the Halloween costumes, the spaghetti twirled on forks, the first bicycle, the puppies, the volleyball games, the school plays, the boyfriends, the soccer games, the gymnastics practices, the giggles, the tears, the mean girls, the prom dresses, leaving for college, the "Dad, we're engaged." The life.

I managed to give the speech at each of the girls' weddings

without crying, and it wasn't the champagne. It had actually become simple. When Lindsay got married, as I looked at my now grown-up beauties sitting there with their wonderful husbands, I knew they were safe. Their men were perfect fits. I raised my glass and said what a good feeling it was to know that we'd brought them up to be intelligent, charming women who good men could fall in love with. They say the father of the bride gives his daughter away. But after searching my soul that day, I knew that this wasn't really accurate. For in truth, when you're a father, at each milestone along the path, you've been giving them away, piece by piece, little by little, their whole lives.

My Fifties

Leonardo DiCaprio spit on me. The large glob of phlegmy gook expelled from Leo's mouth in a scene from *Titanic* landed perfectly on my forehead and got a huge laugh in my opening film for the 1998 Academy Awards, which would turn out to be the highest-rated Oscar show of all time. I'd love to take sole credit for the show's success, but *Titanic* might've had a little something to do with it. Early the next morning, my assistant Carol Sidlow, an unflappable showbiz veteran, called me at home, sounding uncharacteristically excited and nervous: "Johnny Carson is on the phone . . . calling himself."

I broke out into a sweat, took a deep breath, and said, "Tell him to fuck off."

There was a pause. "Excuse me?"

"Carol, I'm kidding. Of course put him on."

"Here's Johnny . . . ," she said breathlessly.

"Johnny?" I said. Then I heard that unmistakable voice.

After the Oscars, my beautiful girls and their guys.
Howie, Lindsay, Janice and I, Jenny, Mike.

"Hey, I gotta tell you, that was a great show. I was watching with some friends, and I said to Alex"—his wife—"how great I thought you were, total command, and Alex said, 'Call him and tell him yourself,' so here I am."

"Johnny, thank you so much. I thought it went well."

"Stop being modest," he replied. "It was just great."

"Johnny, I can't tell you how much this means to me . . ."

"Billy, you just did . . ."

What a great way to begin my second of what I hope are three half centuries.

....

Spring came, and there was no other place I'd rather be than opening day at Yankee Stadium. I was sitting with Janice in the

Steinbrenner box. She left for a short period of time, and when she returned to her seat, I could see that she was upset.

"What's up?" I asked.

"Nothing," she said, but I know her too well. Finally, after much prodding, she told me that she had smuggled into the ballpark one of my prized possessions—a Joe DiMaggio uniform top—knowing that DiMaggio would be there that day. She'd just asked him to sign it, and he'd refused. He'd claimed he had an exclusive deal for his signature with a baseball bat company and that if they found out that he'd signed the jersey, they might cancel it. It was a foolish argument. I left Janice at our seats, swearing to her that I was going to the bathroom, but I went to talk to DiMaggio. I wasn't sure what I was going to say, but the sight of Janice so upset made me angry, and given that the first time I'd met him he'd punched me, things couldn't get much worse. Honestly, I thought I could take him. But when I found him, DiMaggio was disarmingly apologetic and told me about his concerns about the deal he'd made with the company.

"Joe," I said, "I'm not going to sell it. This jersey is very rare and important to my collection. Do you really think if they found out you did this for me, they'd drop you?"

"I'm sorry," he countered and handed me a ball with this inscription: "To a great Yankee fan, from your fan, Joe DiMaggio." It is a very nice inscription, but honestly, it didn't matter what he had written: twice he had shown me who he was. And by the way, I thought Willie Mays was the greatest living player.

....

Another opening day was about to happen with a lot more on the line than a baseball season. *Analyze This* was to be released, and I couldn't bear another movie not succeeding. Test audiences had loved the film, the trailer was playing well in theaters, the TV spots were funny, but as I had learned, you never know. Our reviews were positive; critics loved our pairing, and the big story was that Robert De Niro was funny. Our opening Friday box office numbers were good, but Saturday would tell the story. On Saturday night, Janice and I went to a birthday party for Bob's wife, Grace, at the restaurant Ago, where Bob is one of the owners. When I asked him what "Ago" meant, he joked, "It's Sicilian for 'Ago fuck yourself.'" This was thirteen years before the line was used in *Argo*, so please, no nasty tweets.

We started getting box office reports from the studio as the party progressed. It was like election night. The numbers kept going higher and higher, and when it was over, we had done over $18 million for the weekend and were the number one film at the box office. We were especially happy about that because we beat out *Cruel Intentions*, with Reese Witherspoon and Ryan Phillippe, which was expected to dominate the two old guys' flick. Bob and I had become good friends, and my respect and affection for him were tremendous. In some ways I was as happy for him as I was for me.

Two champs. Mom meets Ali.
Notice the lipstick on Ali's cheek.

In January 1999, the Hebrew University in Jerusalem had given me its highest honor, the National Scopus Award. The event was in Los Angeles, and Muhammad Ali was the dinner chairman. Not only did he lend his name and time to the evening, but he also came and sat with my family at our table. When he arrived, I introduced him to my mother. She told him how much he had inspired her. She told him about her speech to the draft board. She thanked him for being who he was and for being so kind to me. I've never seen Ali speechless, but for a moment he seemed overwhelmed. He gave her a big hug and called her "Mama" the entire night. I loved seeing them together.

....

Soon after, Ross Greenburg, a good friend and the head of HBO Sports, called and asked me if I'd like to executive produce a movie called *61** with him. It was the story of Roger Maris and Mickey Mantle and that dream season of 1961, when they both chased the ghost of Babe Ruth in their pursuit of the single-season home run record of 60. I went to many games that summer and could still feel the excitement as if it had just happened. Also, Mickey had told me about how he and Roger had lived together that year in an apartment in Queens, something not many people knew.

A movie about these two teammates and rivals, who ultimately became such good friends, was right up my alley. We worked on the script with an excellent young writer named Hank Steinberg. I imitated Mickey in our sessions. I knew Mickey's speech patterns, and I could use things he had actually said to me, so his presence in the script rang true. Ross kept pushing me to direct the film, but I wasn't sure I wanted to, until we made a scouting trip to Detroit to take a look at old Tiger Stadium.

To me, the biggest problem, of course, was who could play these two icons, and the next issue was finding a stadium that felt like Yankee Stadium of 1961. On a freezing cold day just before Thanksgiving, we toured the now vacant Tiger Stadium. Wind whistled through its empty seats, the November sun peeked through lonely archways. Like an old relative waiting for a visit from his family, the stadium seemed to be aching for a crowd to cheer one more time. It had been built in 1912 and felt very close to the Yankee Stadium I knew so well. We toured the abandoned clubhouses, and I stood where Mickey and Roger had stood so many years before. As we walked the dark passageway to the visiting team's dugout, tracing their footsteps, I started to put shots together in my mind, and before I knew it, I was directing the film. I had to. I didn't want anyone else to go near it. I had been thirteen that summer, and I wanted to return to that time, to re-create it for all the other thirteen-year-olds who were now my age.

Next we had to find Roger Maris and Mickey Mantle. When I saw Barry Pepper in *Saving Private Ryan,* I couldn't believe my eyes. *Roger Maris walks the earth,* I thought. Barry was very interested but was concerned about doing a film for HBO at that time. His movie career was just getting going. He'd recently finished an independent film and wanted to do more of them and thought making a movie for television might not be the best move. I tried to convince him that good work is good work, no matter where it is, and that this could be the part of a lifetime. Where else could he play such a misunderstood, moody man who becomes an unlikely hero? And with the way HBO promotes its films, more people would see this than any independent film.

While Barry was making up his mind, I met with Thomas Jane, a free-spirited up-and-coming actor whom I had loved in *Boogie Nights.* His natural boyish charm was perfect for the Mantle I wanted to portray, and his resemblance to Mickey, though not as strong as Barry's to Roger, was still stunning. He came to my office barefoot (he hates shoes, I later learned), smoking smelly French cigarettes, his hair to his shoulders. I had put together a presentation of Mantle photos and video clips—Mickey just being Mickey—and some home movies of the two of us, and I told him stories about how Mantle always greeted me with "Hey, you little son of a bitch, how ya doing?" and I watched Tom soak it all in.

Tom was too young to have seen Mickey play, but as I spoke, he became enthralled with the boozy, cowboyish baseball icon. I explained that this was not just a Hall of Fame player; this was a charismatic and complicated man whose fear of dying young had sent him on his way to becoming an alcoholic, and that's the portrait I was going after, warts and all.

Tom wanted the part badly, but this time HBO wasn't sure. The executives wanted stars in those parts. I told them that these parts would make someone a star, but at their request, I arranged a meeting with Matt Damon and Ben Affleck. I knew it was a long shot, and with all due respect, they were not as suited as Tom and Barry were for the parts. I wanted the audience to see Mickey and Roger, not Matt and Ben. At the meeting, Matt explained that as Red Sox guys, putting on the pinstripes would be too difficult. I got it and, frankly, was relieved because I so strongly believed that Tom and Barry would be sensational. Next, I secretly did a screen test with Thomas. I got him a vintage No. 7 Yankee uniform, pinned up his hair, put the Yankee cap on his head and a bat in his hand, and interviewed him as Mantle. I fed him the answers, lines Mickey had said to me, and Tom was perfect. I sent it to the HBO higher-ups, and their response was "Who is this guy? He's great!" I said it was Tom Jane, the guy they weren't sure about. Well, they were sure now. Tom was in, and not long after that, Barry agreed to play Roger.

Now they had to play ball. This was Mickey Mantle and Roger Maris, and they and every one of our players had to look real. There have been so many baseball movies where the actors are great but they throw like seven-year-old girls. I called on Reggie Smith, a former major league player and now a fine hitting coach, to be my technical adviser. Reggie, a switch-hitter himself, had played against Mickey, and he would have to teach Tom Mantle's swing from both sides of the plate. Tom had told me he had played baseball in high school; he lied. When I brought him out to Reggie's place, the first thing he asked was "How do you hold a ball?" I almost fainted. Reggie looked at me and shook his head.

He took the French cigarette out of Tom's mouth and said, "Let's go to work. Billy, come back in two weeks."

Two weeks later, I arrived at Reggie's workout field and said, "Where's Tom?"

"He's not here," Reggie answered. Then he put his fingers in his mouth and whistled toward the outfield. "MICKEY! SOMEONE WANTS TO MEET YOU," he yelled, and running in from center field, limp and all, was Mickey Mantle. "Hey, you little son of a bitch," he asked me, "how ya doin'?" He then got into the batting cage and hit the ball beautifully, right- and left-handed. The transformation was stunning.

I hired veteran casting director Mali Finn to work with me. The smartest, sweetest, and most talented casting director I had ever worked with, she had done such recent hits as *Titanic* and *L.A. Confidential.* She had a special relationship with all the actors she regularly saw for auditions; she cared about them and often coached them. Our research team made portfolios on all the ballplayers in the script, and Mali immersed herself in the details of that '61 season. Basically, this woman who knew nothing about baseball became fluent in Yankee.

Seventy-four-year-old eccentric genius Haskell Wexler joined the team as our director of photography. Even though he was a two-time Oscar winner and his son Jeff was my sound mixer, I hadn't thought about him doing the film, until Haskell called me himself and said, "If you want me, you got me."

"Let's talk," I said.

"Good, I'm standing outside your office." As he entered, Haskell announced, "This is not a baseball movie. It's the story of these two men. One shy, one not, teammates who become rivals who become friends. This has to look real. I'll make it beautiful, but real." How could I resist? As we cast the supporting parts with such pros as Bruce McGill and Richard Masur, the crucial role of Pat Maris, Roger's wife, went uncast.

When we were writing the piece, I'd been aware that my daughter Jenny was the right age, type, and personality. A talented young actress, she was currently on an ABC series called *Once and Again*. I told Jenny that I wanted her to read, as long as she was comfortable with the fact that she might not get the part. She said, "I want to earn it. I don't want you to feel bad if I'm not good enough. I'd like to read." Mali liked Jenny's work on the series and thought she even resembled Pat Maris. We agreed to bring her in to test with Barry, but we wouldn't tell him she was my kid. Jenny and Barry clicked immediately—their look was perfect; they felt like a couple. Their intimate scenes were splendid. When it was done and Jenny had left, Barry said, "Well, she's great! Who is that?"

"She's my daughter," I said.

"Oh shit, I kissed her!" Barry shrieked. I calmed him down. "It's fine, you were supposed to," I said. Mali loved her, too, as did HBO, and we cast her in the part.

Rusty Smith, our brilliant production designer, had the mammoth job of turning old Tiger Stadium into Yankee Stadium of 1961, painting fifty-five thousand seats the pale green used in Yankee Stadium that year and then, incredibly, turning it back into the blue Tiger Stadium of 1961 a day later! The fences were realigned and new ones built to perfection; the famous monuments to Babe Ruth, Lou Gehrig, and Miller Huggins, which stood in the outfield and had made this thirteen-year-old think it was a cemetery, were re-created and placed in center field. Every bit of advertising was removed from the park. We couldn't have Roger Maris at bat and an ad for the Keith Olbermann show visible in the shot. We had to strip it down so we could build it up. The upper decks of the original Yankee Stadium would be added digitally, so the ballpark I remembered would be whole once more.

To fill out the teams we would be featuring, we held baseball tryouts at a local university. Over eleven hundred men and one woman—"I wanna be Yogi," she said—came for a chance to be in the film.

We had photographs of the real players, but I didn't actually need anything to remind me—I remembered everything. In fact, the crew started to call me Rain Man. Each player we chose was as close as you could get to a match, not only physically but in ability. The day before we were to start shooting the baseball sequences, we held a team practice at three P.M. It was a hot August day, with beautiful mashed-potato clouds hovering over the ballpark. In their vintage uniforms, the 1961 New York Yankees ran onto that heavenly field with the sun bathing them in the most gentle way. Once again they were together: Ellie Howard and Yogi, Whitey Ford and Clete Boyer, Tony Kubek, Bobby Richardson, and Moose Skowron. As a surprise I had invited Yogi Berra and Mickey's widow, Merlyn, and their sons David and Danny to join us for practice and our preshoot party. Yogi walked in, took a long look at what we had done to transform Tiger Stadium, and with tears in his eyes whispered, "You put the old joint back together" as we embraced. Merlyn's entrance was equally moving. A lovely woman, she'd had a very complicated marriage

With Yogi Berra, Barry Pepper, and
Thomas Jane, shooting *61**.

to Mickey. They were separated for years but never divorced, even after Mantle left her for another woman. Despite everything Mickey had done to her and the family, she still loved him deeply. She walked in holding hands with her middle-aged boys, and when I pointed to center field, she turned and caught sight of Tom. He had his broad back to us, the summer sun hitting the 7 on it just right, so he looked like he was glowing. Merlyn let out an audible sigh and had to turn away. I called, "Mickey!" and Tom ran in from the outfield as the sound of the ball hitting the bat echoed around the empty ballpark. The boys greeted Tom, and soon Merlyn joined them, and she and Tom hugged and talked. I felt like a proud papa sitting next to Yogi Berra and watching this surreal reunion.

....

The experience making *61** was—apologies in advance—a total "home run." This was the third movie I had directed and as much as I had enjoyed the other two, this one proved that directing something so personal to you is the best job in the business. I don't think I ever had a part as an actor that touched me as much as directing *61** did.

Revisiting the summer of 1961, the time when I had started to find myself, while really finding myself as a director completed an important circle for me.

A few weeks before its debut on HBO, we were invited to the White House to screen the movie for President Bush. Barry and Tom came, as did Jenny and Janice and Pat Maris and Merlyn Mantle and the HBO brass. The president had invited several senators and other dignitaries. We ate a lovely meal on the South Lawn and soon were ushered into the White House screening room. I sat next to the president, who asked me to say a few words after he welcomed everyone. I started by thanking President Bush for hosting us and for the chance to be with so many people I hadn't voted for. W plopped his initialed cowboy boots on a hassock in front of us, and the movie started. Mickey has some risqué lines in the first few moments of the film, and I worried that the women in the room might find it offensive. "There's only a few more," I whispered to the president as Mantle said, "I like women with small hands—makes my dick look bigger."

"Bring them on," whispered W.

At a late point in the film, Roger, playing in Detroit, hits his fifty-third home run off a right-handed pitcher named Frank Lary. President Bush whispered to me, "I think he hit that one off Hank Aguirre, who was a lefty." I was in awe. He was right. On the day we'd shot the scene, our Hank Aguirre hadn't shown up, and we'd had to use our Frank Lary. "No one will ever know," I'd said at the time, but W saw it and knew it was wrong. Now, isn't it strange that he didn't know there were no WMDs?

When it was over and the lights came on, the president had tears in his eyes. "Well, that's the best baseball movie I've ever seen. Hell, it's just a great movie." Before the president had finished speaking, Tom, in his best Mickey, blurted, "Mr. President, I really want to hear what you have to say, but right now I have to pee like a racehorse."

"Me too," laughed the president, and we all ran down the hallway of the White House to the men's room, where Tom and I and the president relieved ourselves. I love this country.

A few weeks later, *61** premiered to huge ratings and went on to get twelve Emmy nominations, including best movie, best actor for Barry, and best director (which I lost to a young novice named Mike Nichols), as well as an extra-special honor for me: a nomination by the Directors Guild as best director for a movie made for television. Days after the premiere, Johnny Carson sent me a lovely note saying how much he'd enjoyed the movie; he'd also enclosed a DVD of some film from *The Tonight Show* of 1962 that he wanted me to have. There, in grainy black and white, was young Johnny in a Yankee uniform pitching to Mickey in Yankee Stadium. It is a most prized possession.

Also prized was a phone call from Matt Damon, who told me his mother was mad at him for turning down the part, because she loved the movie. "For a Harvard kid," she'd said, "sometimes you're just stupid."

In October 2011, the fiftieth anniversary of Roger's home run, *61** would be honored by the National Baseball Hall of Fame. The script and a print of the movie resides in the hall's archives.

....

Jenny got married in September 2000 (the joyous and emotional occasion I wrote about earlier), which was marred the next day when my uncle Berns collapsed at a family brunch. After my father's death, his brother Berns had become a giant force in my life. No words can really describe him. A Santa Claus look-alike (he actually played Santa in *When Harry Met Sally . . .*) with a hilarious personality, clownlike abilities, a booming baritone singing voice, and uncommon artistic talent, he was a rock for me. We were always intensely close. I needed his presence so much.

After his collapse, doctors healed his ailing heart with stents, and, fearing I would lose him, I made it my life's goal to make his life longer. Janice and I rescued him from his cellarlike dwelling, found him a new apartment, paid his bills, got him healthy, and took every worry we could away from him. We basically adopted an eighty-six-year-old son. For a while Berns had been creating stunning drawings of unusual animals. He'd mix up species—a cat with a lizard's tail, a dog with a fish body—and all were funny and, in a strange way, touching. I gave them to Tom Schumacher at Disney, and he hired Berns as a character creator. They would send Berns scripts from their animation department, and his job was to draw characters based on what he read. It was daunting at first, but soon he found his way, and his work at the age of eighty-six was as valuable as any of their young animators'.

I was very fortunate to be close to all my uncles. Sadly, my uncle Milt Gabler, who was a giant in the recording industry and in many ways a mentor to me, died the following July. I spoke at his funeral, as did my mother, and it was tough to see my aging

Uncle Berns in *When Harry Met Sally*—my own personal Santa.
(Photograph © Andrew Schwartz)

mom and her sister and brother weeping at the loss of their big
brother. Growing up, they were all like royalty to me: young
vibrant people who were electric to be around. Now my mind was
filled with dread as the running order seemed in place. Milt was
the oldest of the six kids. Who would be next? The fifties may be
a time of more wisdom about life, but along with it comes the
terrible knowledge that people you love will be leaving you.

After Milt's death, we found Berns an assisted-living apartment across the street from the World Trade Center and just a few
blocks from our New York apartment. "My night-light," he called
the towers. We moved him in on September 2 and wearily went
back to Los Angeles.

It was six A.M in Los Angeles on September 11 when my
daughter Lindsay called from her apartment on the Lower East-
Side of New York. "A plane hit the World Trade Center. I'm on
my roof watching the tower burn," she told us, disbelief in her
voice. We rushed to the television and watched the beginning
of the end of the world as we knew it. The horror unfolded as
the news of the other hijacked planes filled the airwaves. I
called Berns, who was watching the whole thing from his
apartment, a hundred yards away. Berns had been at D-day
and had seen mayhem like this before, but not on his doorstep.
"They want us to look at this; we mustn't look at this," he kept
saying. He assured me that he was okay. We tried calling Lindsay back, but the phones were out. Then a friend of hers called
us and told us to connect to her through instant messaging.
We had never used it before, and this was a hell of a way to
start.

As we got online, the first tower fell.

LINDSAY: Oh no! It's gone! I have to get to Uncle Berns.
Us: No. STAY WHERE YOU ARE. We don't know what this is
    yet. There are other planes in the air.
LINDSAY: What if it fell on his building?????
Us: I just spoke to him. He was in the apartment; an aide was
    with him.
LINDSAY: I'm going over there.
Us: No. There's nothing you can do. The area is sealed off.
    STAY WHERE YOU ARE.
LINDSAY: I can't believe what I'm seeing. I'm so scared. WHAT
    IS HAPPENING?????

The second tower fell shortly after that.

On television, the replays were staggering. As the second
plane got closer I could see the jet gain speed, as if the hatred of
the terrorist pilot were fueling the engines. Somehow the building absorbed the blow and remained standing, like a fighter on

the ropes. Horrifically tight helicopter shots of the inferno revealed people jumping to their deaths.

LINDSAY: OH MY GOD!
Us: The Pentagon was hit also and there is another plane, they think, heading for D.C. This is war.

I got Berns on the phone. He was with an aide from the building as the second tower came crashing down. I could hear it and Berns's labored breathing. "Bastards," he muttered, and then the phone went dead.

LINDSAY: I HAVE TO GET THERE.
Us: Stay where you are. Keep trying to call the desk of his building. That's what we're trying to do but it's always busy. Keep trying. STAY HOME.

The next hours were excruciating, and finally that night we were informed that the fire department had evacuated the elderly residents of Berns's building and taken them on a school bus to a sister facility in Yonkers. He was safe. Lindsay, moved by the thought that, if Berns had perished that day, she wouldn't have known who he really was, started to spend time with him and began to film their conversations. It became a beautiful relationship and ultimately a fascinating documentary called *My Uncle Berns,* which not only won a few film festivals but was also broadcast on HBO and led to her becoming a field producer on *The Daily Show with Jon Stewart* for four years. It was one of the few good things that came out of 9/11.

We had watched the murder of three thousand innocent people on television. We watched this vile act celebrated in some parts of the Middle East. We watched our world and our future change in moments of insanity. We were introduced to the madman

Osama bin Laden. Still reeling from my uncle Milt's passing, 9/11 was another huge blow. There would be others.

Dick Schaap, the noted sports journalist who'd been the first person to put me on television, had become one of our best friends. He was a special man with a great sense of humor and a gentle spirit. I had introduced him to Berns at a family function and they'd become fast friends and would often see each other while Janice and I were in California. He called to see how Berns was doing, and I put them in touch. Berns had left his building in his wheelchair, wearing slippers, and had no shoes and only the clothes on his eighty-six-year-old back. Dick not only bought Berns clothes, he found him some sneakers—which wasn't easy, considering Berns wore a size 17. Dick got them from a contact at the NBA and brought them to Berns in Yonkers. Dick called us when they were all together and then told me he was going in for hip replacement surgery the next day. He said he'd talk to me as soon as he could, and to let him know if Berns needed anything. Let him know? He was about to have major surgery, but he was more concerned about my uncle.

Dick had the usually routine surgery, but there were complications, including an embolism in one of his lungs. A botched diagnosis followed, and eventually he was put into a coma so his body could heal itself. We were devastated and worried. What more could go wrong?

····

Monsters, Inc. opened as a big hit, but the strain of the last few months made me feel like I was running in mud. I loved playing Mike Wazowski, the little one-eyed green monster, opposite John Goodman. To me, the movie was a classic, and I was thrilled to be in a modern-day *Pinocchio,* but I found it hard to enjoy anything. Pixar arranged a series of screenings for families of police officers and firemen and first responders, which John Goodman and I hosted. New York at that time was a nervous, grieving place.

Everyone had an ominous instinct that at any moment Al Qaeda could strike again. There were warnings of chemical attacks and suicide bombings, and the airports seemed like war zones. People thought twice about being in crowds, and those of Middle Eastern heritage were scrutinized. The smoking wreckage of the buildings was piled high, and bodies were still being removed. We all had a sick feeling, knowing that some three thousand souls were hovering over Ground Zero. At the *Monsters, Inc.* screenings, it was moving to see these young people have a laugh or two in the midst of their sadness. It was also a prelude for what would become one of the more difficult tasks of my career.

The Concert for New York City was being put together as a major benefit for the families who'd lost loved ones that day. The Who, Paul McCartney, Billy Joel, and the Stones were among the legendary musicians who would play, and I was asked to greet the huge crowd at Madison Square Garden. David Bowie opened the show, and then it was my turn. Gripped with fear about what had happened to our city and our world, and weighed down by the constant feeling of being on guard, I walked out onto the stage. All the moments of my career could not prepare me for what I saw. The members of the audience directly in front of me were all firefighters and police officers and men, women, and children holding up signs saying, HAVE YOU SEEN MY BROTHER? HAVE YOU SEEN MY FATHER? HAVE YOU SEEN MY MOTHER, MY WIFE, MY HUSBAND, MY SISTER, MY COUSIN, MY FRIEND, MY TEACHER? HAVE YOU SEEN . . . "

The pictures of the certain dead pasted onto the signs made for an eerie audience. Most of the photos were of a smiling face frozen in time staring straight ahead at me. Alongside them was the audience of loved ones, hurt and exhausted, each with the same expression: wounded, angry, confused, and scared. Usually audiences are happy to see me; this time I felt that they needed me. I like to make eye contact with the audience as I arrive onstage. I check them out and assess what kind of crowd they are. It's always interesting to gauge a reaction as they see me for the first time: sometimes smiling, sometimes giddy with anticipation, sometimes respectfully warm. There's usually one or two joyless souls, but this mass of humanity had just lived through a nightmare.

They had to know in their hearts that there was no chance that their special person had survived and was wandering the streets or lying nameless in a hospital, unable to communicate.

In the weeks following the attacks, lethal amounts of anthrax powder had been mailed to various notables, including Senator Tom Daschle, whom I was to introduce following my opening monologue. It was hard not to cry as I received the crowd's warm welcome. I tried to be funny—"I've never seen musicians run away from white powder before"—and I tried to be comforting and inspirational as I explained that this evening was for them and to show the world that we aren't afraid: we're New Yorkers, and we will move on. People were on their feet as I introduced Senator Daschle. I left the stage that night but really haven't in some ways. The looks on those faces still make their way into my dreams, and every time I visit Ground Zero, I don't look down into the cascading memorials; I look up, and for a brief moment, the towers stand again.

....

As Ground Zero continued to smolder and the rescue part of the mission ceased, the nation slowly moved on, and David Letterman proved to be an unlikely catalyst. David gave an impassioned speech when his show returned to the airwaves. I'd known him for a long time, our relationship at the time solely that between a guest and a host. There is no one I enjoy making laugh more than David. I think he is to many younger comedians what Johnny was to me. That off-the-cuff speech was very healing for millions. He wasn't just cranky, funny Dave. He was Dave, our friend who had a heart and a soul we hadn't realized existed. "There is only one requirement for any of us, and that is to be courageous, because courage, as you might know, defines all other human behavior," he said. At that point, every little bit of help, no matter in what form, was desperately needed, and David delivered beautifully the feelings and thoughts we were all experiencing, and in fact made it okay to move forward.

Baseball returned as well, reminding us of the powerful speech James Earl Jones gave in *Field of Dreams*. Through two world wars there was always baseball, he told us, and in 2001, once again the New York Yankees rose to the occasion and went to the World Series, this time versus the Arizona Diamondbacks. *Awkward*. A few years earlier, Janice and I had become minority owners (I don't mean Jewish) of the D-backs. I had always wanted to be involved with Major League Baseball, and owning a tiny share of the new Arizona franchise, only an hour by air from Los Angeles, seemed ideal. I had no idea that a few short years later the expansion team would be in the World Series, against my New York Yankees. But the heart is the heart, after all, so I was rooting for the Yankees. We went to the first two games in Phoenix. My dear friends Joe Torre and Commissioner Bud Selig got us great seats behind the Yankee dugout, from which we could see our business partners on the Arizona side. When a shot of me sitting in Yankee land appeared on the big video screen, the crowd booed me loudly. They were so hostile . . . but dry. Arizona destroyed the Yankees in the first two games, and Janice said to me, "Honey, we're beating us."

We flew to New York and passed over lower Manhattan with a blackened hellhole where the towers had been. Game 3 presented a chaotic, scary scene. President Bush would be throwing out the first pitch, yet no one really wanted him there. It wasn't personal; we were already terrified, and the additional security just made everything seem scarier. Streets were sealed off, metal detectors were everywhere, and armed police officers guarded the perimeter with German shepherds, the canine symbol of fear. Standing outside the stadium, we watched the president's helicopter entourage approach. There were five or six. One was a hospital chopper, which was so encouraging (what were they expecting?), and the others acted out a sort of three-card monte: they circled one another over and over, trying to confuse a would-be assassin. Which one had the president in it? This one? That one? Guess again?

Finally we were in the ballpark, the atmosphere alive but different. The Yankees were down two games to none and struggling, but they were back home. On everybody's minds was one terrible question: Would there be some kind of attack tonight? We'd never thought like that before, but this was our world now. Janice and I were guests of the Steinbrenners' that night, sitting in a row with Donald Trump, Regis Philbin, and Henry Kissinger, not exactly bleacher creatures. From our vantage point, we could see gunmen with high-powered rifles on the roof of the stadium inching into position as Bob Sheppard, the voice of the Yankees, introduced President Bush. The president walked out there like John Wayne, stood on the mound, and held up the baseball in defiance of the terrorists, as chants of "U.S.A.! U.S.A.!" echoed throughout the Bronx and the rest of the free world. When he threw a perfect strike, it was an electric moment.

Minutes later, the president walked into Steinbrenner's suite, where I was now at the bar, ordering something that might calm me down. "Billy C!" he hollered, sounding as if he were in a musical. "How about my fastball?" I'm thinking, How about finding bin Laden? He boasted that he'd thrown the strike while wearing a bulletproof vest—we were chatting like two fraternity brothers and not the president of the United States, who was about to lead the country into war, and a citizen who thought that was a bad idea. He settled in a few rows behind me and my new pals Donnie, Reeg, and Hank.

In the fourth inning, a video of me appeared on the stadium's big screen. It felt kind of out-of-body to be sitting there watching my image as I talked about what great fans New Yorkers were and I looked down to where my dad and my brothers and I had sat so many years ago, at our first game. This misty reverie was interrupted by "Billy C's on the big scoreboard!" It was W again. At that moment, he seemed more like the president of the Dukes of Hazzard.

He then rose and told us he had to get to a "meetin'" and that there was a lot of work to do. I asked Kissinger if Nixon had had any "meetin's" and he said, "No, only martinis, and then he'd call me something anti-Semitic." Moments after the president left, a crew of men with large electric drills came down the aisles and removed the front wall of the box we were sitting in. It was a sheet of three-quarter-inch bulletproof steel that none of us had realized was there. The men carried it out, following the president and his staff. Trump shook his head, Kissinger kind of smiled, but Regis stood up and screamed, "Where the hell are you going with that? What about us?"

The Yankees won, and the crucial Game 4 was the next day, which was also Halloween. As Janice and I were on our way to the stadium, my brother Joel called and told me that our mom had had a stroke and was in Long Beach Medical Center's emergency room. We turned around and drove out there immediately. The sight of kids wearing their Halloween masks, strolling the neighborhoods, seemed ironic now, as the mask I wore was one of fear and concern.

We spent much of the night there as she labored to make sense of what had happened to her. The next morning, I was told not to spend too much time with her as it was too draining and she needed to rest.

The Yankees had won the game that night in a miracle finish, and now the series was tied. For the only time I can remember, the country was pulling for the Yankees to win. I am not a very religious man, though I love my religion. I am not one who prays in a synagogue when things get overwhelming. After the daytime visit with my mother at the hospital, I found myself needing a place to go, and the only one I could think of was Yankee Stadium. I went to the ballpark late that afternoon and just sat there, alone in the empty stadium. *Dad,* I thought, *if you're anywhere near me, I really need you now. Help her get through this. Give me the strength I need to help her.* That night the Yankees won another miracle game, and as we filed out, George Steinbrenner confronted me. "What's wrong? I can tell something's not right," he said.

I told him about my mom and he said, "Wait here." A few moments later he returned with an autographed ball from the team saying, "Tell her we need her support." When I saw Joe Torre after the game, he also signed a ball to her: "Helen, you are our inspiration. We can't win this without you." The next day I put the balls in her weakened hand, and she couldn't believe it. They were great medicine.

It was so hard to watch her struggle to make sense of things; sometimes she was there and sometimes she wasn't. The worst of those episodes was a Sunday afternoon. The postponed Emmys would air that day, and it was also Game 7 of the World Series. Plus, 61* was up for ten Emmys. We had already won two technical awards—one for Mali Finn for best casting, the other for sound mixing—but these were the big ones, best picture, actor for Barry Pepper, and director among them. I spent the morning with my mom, and she didn't know me as her son. "Billy Crystal, what are you doing here?" she asked me. Heartbroken and dispirited, I went back to my apartment, unable to concentrate on the game or the Emmys; nothing really mattered anymore. During the red carpet coverage, one announcer noted my absence and quipped, "Billy's not here, and we know where he must be: at Game 7 in Phoenix." No, putz, I was in my apartment mourning the loss of my mother's memory and feeling terrified of the days to come. This is the definition of a bad day: we lost all ten nominations, the Yankees lost the World Series, and my mother didn't know me as her son.

She did rally, however, and begin to improve. My brother Rip flew in from Los Angeles to cover for me when I left her for a few days to perform in Seattle at a charity function for children of firemen lost on 9/11. It was sold out, and I couldn't have canceled if I'd wanted to. With the exceptions of the Oscars and Comic Relief, I had not been onstage as a comedian in over sixteen years, and beforehand, I'd been unsure what to do. I didn't have an act anymore. My manager, David Steinberg, had suggested having the comedian David Steinberg interview me. It would be like *Inside the Actors Studio,* which I had just done and really enjoyed. David and I met, and we laid out a plan. We'd talk about my life, my career; we'd show some funny clips from my films and the Oscars and maybe take some questions. It would be entertaining and loose, and I wouldn't have to go out there alone. I hoped we could do an hour or so. Onstage, we settled into our armchairs, and for three thousand people we did well over two hours and never got to the Q & A. I had fun, and the experience got me out of my doldrums and reaffirmed my abilities onstage.

Before returning to Mom's bedside, I flew to Los Angeles for two days, and while there, I bumped into Des McAnuff. He'd directed *Tommy* on Broadway years before, and I'd been so impressed with the show that I'd asked to meet him, at which point we'd talked about me doing a one-man show someday. He brought that up to me in L.A., and I told him what I had just done in Seattle and he said to bring David and do it at his theater, the La Jolla Playhouse.

I was relieved that Mom was doing better and energized by the Seattle performance and Des's offer that afternoon, but then Janice and Rip called me from the hospital to say that Mom seemed more tired than usual and that he was flying back to Los Angeles that afternoon. I called her room, but there was no answer. I figured that either they were taking her for a walk down the hallway or she was in physical therapy. Joel then called to say that Mom had just been hit with another stroke and it looked bad. They were working to save her life as we spoke. I kept picturing the phone ringing and ringing with my call as she struggled. Less than an hour went by before Janice called to tell me she was gone.

Rip's plane had just landed when I reached him. I chartered a plane, and together the two of us flew back that night to help make the arrangements for her funeral. Rip and I had shared a room throughout our childhood, and now, just like we had done for all those years, we slept alongside each other, this time on our way to bury our mother.

At the funeral, her grandchildren spoke, and Berns read an

except from a letter my father had written to him during World War II about how much he loved Helen. Joel spoke, and then I told the packed audience how she was my hero. How after my dad died, my mother had kept us together. She'd made sure that all three of us graduated from college, which had been a dream of both my parents'. We never wanted for anything, except for my father to be with us. She was tough and funny and strong. In a way, my mom was a lot like Muhammad Ali, whom she and I had both admired so much. When she got knocked down, she got right up and continued to fight. I told them about her speech to the draft board and how I'll never forget the tears in her eyes as she read the letter from the draft board with Joel's permanent deferment. Recently I had asked her what would have happened if she had lost. With a twinkle in her eye, she'd said, "I guess you'd be a Toronto Blue Jays fan." Through the dark times, she held up the light so we could see where we were going. She was my champion.

Rip went last. He has a beautiful voice, and Mom had always loved it when he sang. Together with Marc Shaiman on piano, he sang a tune called "You're Nearer," with Joel and me alongside him, just the way we used to perform for her and the family in our living room. We put her to rest next to my father's grave, the two of them together again.

You spend your whole life with someone, and suddenly they're gone. The abruptness of that was very hard to deal with. They say in Judaism that the soul takes thirty days to get to heaven. I believed it. I could feel her around me. Sometimes I'd be sitting alone and I would say out loud, "You're here, aren't you?"

I would be driving in my car and I'd swear she was next to me, wanting to tell me to slow down. A few weeks after the funeral, Rip and I went to play golf. Mom had always encouraged him to play, but he'd say it wasn't for him. One day, he came just to keep me company, and as we walked a fairway together on a cloudless day in Palm Springs, a small rainbow appeared. There was nothing in the blue sky except this rainbow. We both saw it and looked at each other, and when we looked back, it was gone. I didn't feel her presence anymore after that.

One week after my mother died, my godmother, Laurel Shedler, passed away. She was a very funny woman whom I'd been extremely close to. After all, my folks had picked Laurel to take care of me if anything had ever happened to them. She had called me after my mom's funeral and I'd told her, "It's your turn now." Without missing a beat, she'd asked, "What do you like for breakfast?" Two days later, she died.

The final hurt came on December 21, when, after months of being in a coma, Dick Schaap died. Okay, I got it, God: I must have done something to piss you off. My mom, my uncle, my godmother, 9/11, and now one of my best friends?

For a while there were no smiles, no laughs, no jokes. It seemed all I did was give eulogies or lead memorial services for someone I loved. I was reeling from the pain, weighed down in grief.

That February, my niece Faithe had a baby. We happened to be in New York, and everyone gathered at the hospital. The day of Mom's passing, Faithe had visited her in the hospital while seven months pregnant. Mom's left arm had been weakened by the stroke, but when Faithe had walked in she'd freely extended it and touched Faithe's belly. "It's a girl, you know," Mom said. "What makes you so sure?" Faithe asked. Mom then simply said, "God told me last night." A few hours later, Mom would be with God.

Baby girl Holly (named after my mom, Helen) arrived safe and sound. On our way home from the hospital to celebrate at a local Long Beach restaurant, we slowed down as we drove by our beloved house, now sitting sadly empty and alone. At the moment we were all looking at it, the light in the living room went on. It was the timer, of course. Yet it could have gone off at any other moment, even seconds before or after, but no, it was when we all looked at the same time. It was as if Mom was saying she would always be watching out for us.

A year later, my first grandchild, Ella, was born. She couldn't have come at a better time. The joy of watching Jenny pregnant and then, with her husband, Mike, start their family helped lift me from the abyss I had an apartment in.

I did two movies, *America's Sweethearts* with Julia Roberts, and the sequel to *Analyze This,* but my heart was leading me down another path. David Steinberg and I did two performances for Des at the La Jolla Playhouse. We did another charity event in Atlanta, and I was loving being onstage again. I needed it. After that, Des and I had a meeting. He liked what we were doing, he said, then hesitated and added, "I think you should go deeper, and I think you should do it alone." I'd hoped he would say that. I pulled out the four pages of notes I had written in 1998, for something called *700 Sundays.* I had been making more notes on the idea and feeling more confident every time David and I did the show together. I found I was talking to him less and performing more, and I thought I could create a play that would take my life, with its joyous moments and its sad ones, and celebrate them all. At times, the play would be a humorous and poignant look at my grief. Des read intently as I sat across from him, and when he was finished, he raised his head and said, "This is the show. Let's do this." I immediately asked him to direct it. We set aside six weeks to put the show together, heading toward a two-week run and workshop at the famed La Jolla Playhouse.

I asked my friend Alan Zweibel, an exceptional comedy writer, to work with us. We'd started in the clubs together, and there was no one I felt closer to for this project. We rented a small rehearsal space at Pepperdine University, and along with Lurie Horns Pfeffer, our stage manager, we got to work. I brought some jazz recordings and classical pieces to inspire improvisation, and I just started talking, telling Des and Alan the stories of my life— everything from my birth and circumcision ("They cut off the top six to eight inches") to vivid descriptions of what happened the night my father died. We realized as we worked that my story was everyone's story and that this would become part of the show's strength. I just needed to trust that.

New pieces emerged, and older material got a new life. Alan was the perfect addition to the process. He'd ask questions that would lead me to other stories, and on and on. Lurie would transcribe it as best she could. Each new scene was given a large index card, which went up on a board. Before we knew it, the board was full; the show was taking shape. We now had a few days to opening night at the playhouse. In my notes I had said the house I grew up in should be the set and its windows should be screens for my treasure trove of photos and video memorabilia. Using my old photographs, set designer David Weiner cleverly laid out the façade of the house so its windows would be projection screens on which home movies and photos could be seen. In essence, the house became the family album. Next Lindsay and I gathered the photos and edited the home movies into an opening montage. We timed the music to the photos and the film, and then it all went into a computer program. The rehearsals were grueling— over and over again I'd perform the two hours of it for just Des and Alan and Lurie. When we arrived for our first rehearsal onstage, there was my house waiting for me. The opening film montage played in the upstairs windows, and I saw all my relatives in the moments of my most vivid memories. It took my breath away.

Because the show was being created on the fly, I had large notebooks placed in the wings so only I could see the keywords written on them. This way I couldn't get lost. We rehearsed all day, sometimes bringing in students to watch sections of the show. When we announced the fourteen performances at the playhouse, tickets sold out in an hour. The playhouse has been a stepping-stone for many a Broadway play, most recently *Jersey Boys*. Its patrons tend to be sophisticated theatergoers aware that they are seeing something in an infant form. Still, I'm quite sure there has never been an opening night for a play that had no script, just a detailed eight-page outline. The opening night arrived, and from the moment I went out there, through the front door of my "house," I was in heaven. The audiences laughed hard, cried harder, and at the end of each show didn't want to leave the theater. I felt connected to my work and my pain in a way I hadn't before. Like losing weight on some miracle diet, I could feel the grief I'd been wearing like a tailored suit melt away. I knew why I'd stopped doing stand-up so many years ago, and I knew why I was back. I had something to say.

We made changes during the day and implemented them in the evening's performance. I asked my good friend Larry Magid to come out and see the show and produce it with Janice. Larry is one of the top concert producers and was the first nightclub owner to headline me. His Bijou, in Philadelphia, was a tiny treasure of a performance space. Thirty years ago he'd told me that someday I'd do a Broadway show and he'd produce it. The time had come, I told him. After our successful run at La Jolla, we flew to New York to look for a theater; *700 Sundays* was going to Broadway.

I spent that summer getting into shape. Dan Isaacson, who had trained me for every movie, became a constant early morning companion. Janice and I had rented a house on the beach, and before rehearsals, once again at Pepperdine, I would do something I hated to do: run. I love working out, I love to play sports, but running just for running's sake? I'd rather not. Only to handle all that stage time, I needed my legs, wind, and stamina to be top-notch. I was fifty-six years old, and I soon found it second nature to sprint up and down the Malibu beachfront.

When it was announced that the show was coming to New York, we had one of the largest advances in the history of Broadway. We went into previews at the Broadhurst Theatre in November and officially opened on December 5, 2004. Being part of the Broadway community was different from anything I had done. For that whole season, all I could do was eat and breathe the show. Performing it live every night—sometimes twice a day—was tiring, but each audience gave me a special energy, and though it was my own life, I found new ways of telling the same stories. I didn't miss making movies for a second. There was no one to say "Cut, let's do it again"; I didn't have to wait for hours while they lit a set; it was just me and the audience, and I liked the odds.

The backstage visitors, meanwhile, were an eclectic group: from total strangers like Kurt Vonnegut to my cousin Ira, from Mel Brooks and Anne Bancroft to Ahmet Ertegun, from Helen Gurley Brown to Pat Riley and Bobby Knight. Strange combinations like David Letterman and Henry Kissinger, Sandy Koufax and Jimmy Fallon, Bill Clinton and Warren Beatty would step onstage afterward in the empty theater to take a picture with me in the doorway of my "house."

There was only one thing I didn't like about live theater: cell phones. I hated the sound of phones going off during the show, always during the quiet moments. Often they would just ring and ring because the person whose phone was going off didn't want to be pegged as the schmuck. One night a woman in a third row aisle seat was on her phone during the opening moments. I just stared at her as I performed, and soon she whispered into her phone, "I have to go, he's looking at me."

My focus had to be precise every minute of the performance. My preparation each day was the same: eat dinner around 4:30, then get to the theater at six. Answer some e-mails, change into workout clothes, and then go to the gym alongside my dressing room. Stretch and do sets of sit-ups and then walk on the treadmill for a half hour or so. Body now warm, I'd go out onstage in the empty theater and run some lines or walk the stage side to side, sometimes lightly running it as well. Once loose, take "batting practice": stand at center stage and swing at an imaginary ball as crew syncs sound effect of a bat hitting a ball to my swing. Belt them all over the empty theater. (One night I hit the imaginary ball at least five hundred feet, and before I knew it the imaginary commissioner was giving me an imaginary drug test.)

Now relaxed and primed, settle down in my dressing room and play the same CD before every show: *Ella for Lovers*. It's the gorgeous sounds of Ella Fitzgerald singing beautiful, simple love songs. That CD was the first one I played when we started in La

Visitors on the set of *700 Sundays*.

Jolla, and since the run went so well I just kept playing it; the music sets the right mood for me. Seven P.M.: I get dressed, put on my makeup. I don't talk to anyone, I don't see anyone other than the 1950s photos of my family that adorn the walls of my dressing room, taking me back to the time I'm about to reenter.

Eight P.M., they call me to the stage. As I leave the dressing room, I look at the same pictures in the same order, the last one being a smiling three-year-old me, a joyous little boy, and that's how I feel inside. I'm getting another chance to do what I have always loved to do—make people laugh. One last peek in the mirror. "Still foolin' 'em," I say, and then it's time.

My granddaughter Dylan was born to Jenny and Mike in February, and I was torn about being so far away from the joy of our new grandbaby. Her sister, Ella, was now almost three, and I didn't want to miss out on any more precious moments. I knew that when summer came, I would close the show and return to being Grandpa.

It was a fantastic year, the show not only becoming the highest-grossing nonmusical in the history of Broadway but also winning a Tony Award, not only for me but for Janice as a producer as well. Most importantly, I found that you *can* go home again, and for me home was onstage, in front of an audience. I was honored with the Mark Twain Prize at the Kennedy Center in Washington, D.C., the highest award our country gives for humor. Danny DeVito, Rob Reiner, Martin Short, Robin Williams, Robert De Niro, Whoopi Goldberg, Barbara Walters, Jimmy Fallon, Bob Costas, and Joe Torre all made beautiful presentations. Sitting with all my family, Janice by my side, I watched highlights from a career that I'd once doubted I would ever have.

In the fall we took *700 Sundays* on tour. When we were in Phoenix, Lonnie Ali called to tell me that Muhammad was turning sixty-five that day. Would we come over for breakfast and could he see the show that night? Janice and I spent the morning with Ali watching highlights of his career, which were all over television because of his birthday. "Little brother, you looking good. Not as pretty as me, but good," he joked.

That night, he came to the show, but we didn't seat him in the audience. His majestic presence can be a distraction, so we put him in a big easy chair in the wings, out of sight of the audience. Ali was decades past being the wide-eyed genius of the ring; instead, he was now a quiet Buddha whose brilliant statements of the past almost paled in comparison to the eloquence of his silence. I finished the first act, and before we went to intermission, I surprised the audience and brought him out to a three-minute standing ovation. I introduced him as the "greatest senior citizen of all time," and he blew kisses to the crowd as we sang "Happy Birthday."

Afterward, we made our way to the wings, where he was helped into a golf cart that would take him to his car. He was tired. Would I come over tomorrow? he asked in a whisper. "Why, you want to run a golf course or something?" I asked with a sly smile.

He perked up. "We can, little brother. There's lots of Jews here."

Ali is seventy-one now, and every moment I get to spend with him is precious and poignant. In March 2013 I sat with him at Celebrity Fight Night, a fantastic yearly event in Phoenix that raises millions of dollars for Parkinson's research. This year was even more special. Lonnie and Muhammad were aware that Long Beach had been ravaged by Hurricane Sandy. They'd decided that they would divert some of the funds raised that night, which came to $1 million, to help my hometown. I told Lonnie I couldn't believe their generosity, and she simply said, "You are his little brother."

That night, in full view of the one thousand people in the audience, Ali came in late with Lonnie and his small entourage. It's very hard for him to get around now; Parkinson's is winning this fight on all cards. His incredibly animated face is most often a frozen mask. He still has the most recognizable face in the world, but it is no longer filled with the joy and confidence I first saw in 1974. Inside, though, he's still the champ. He sat next to me, and I allowed myself to glance at him and think how so much had happened to us since we first met. He is a fragile man now, and the young man who was feeding his baby when our paths first crossed is a grandfather. I could feel my emotions welling up, but he wouldn't want me to be sad, because he isn't. He believes this is what was chosen for him: to be the great ambassador for peace and understanding.

The fighter who wouldn't fight. I watched him as he scanned the room expressionlessly, though everyone was on their feet greeting him. He looked over and gave me a little smile and a wink. This time he knew who I was.

····

After Christmas and New Year's, I took *700 Sundays* to Australia for five weeks and played Sydney and Melbourne. The show got the same wonderful response Down Under, because, after all, family is family. Janice and I then went to New Zealand for a few weeks of a much-needed vacation. We did some fly-fishing,

Sydney, Australia, 2005. Don't try this at home.

hiking, and jet boating, and we even took a helicopter ride and landed on a glacier and walked on it at nine thousand feet. On my birthday we were staying at a rustic lodge, and I celebrated by herding sheep with a local shepherd and his dogs. I was fifty-nine.

When we returned, I was presented with a most difficult decision. Out of the blue, Peter Chernin and his executives at Fox television, Kevin O'Reilly and Peter Ligouri, asked if I would host a talk show at eleven P.M. It would be my own late-night show, with a half-hour jump on Leno and Letterman. I had been presented with similar talk-show proposals at other times in my career, both on network and in syndication, but obviously never said yes; this time I was interested.

Hosting a talk show is a daunting job, one I thought I could do, but not necessarily one I *wanted* to do. It takes a special talent: keeping things lively, always looking interested, asking the right questions, listening and not competing with your guests, and, most important, delivering fresh comedy meat to the hungry monster that needs to feed every night.

I was pulled in a few directions. On the one hand, I thought it would be an amazing challenge. On the other hand, it would be all I could do. And if I had a third hand, did I want all the scrutiny that would come with the job? They wanted a five-year commitment, so doing this show would pretty much become my life.

I had a few creative meetings with Kevin and Peter, and, confused but tempted, I set up a meeting with Peter Chernin, a man I very much admire as an outstanding executive, a fearless negotiator, and, on top of that, a really intelligent, regular guy.

We sat down at a restaurant in Santa Monica to talk. He is a very persuasive man, and I was feeling uneasy as he made his pitch. He told me that they had done research that showed a very strong favorable reaction to my doing a show like this. (Damn, he's making sense.) With an eleven P.M. start, for the first half hour we would be competing with local news instead of late-night programming. (Gotta be able to beat the weather report and the occasional car chase.) I didn't have to have great ratings. (What?) Solid is all they were looking for—at that hour, a few million people. (I could do that, I have that many cousins.) He also guaranteed the total commitment of the network. Peter stared at me with a look that said, "How could you not do this?" The thought of getting into a late-night war with two old friends who were the kings of the kingdom was scary, but still, I couldn't ignore him.

I pushed forward to my biggest concern.

"How many weeks?" I asked.

"Forty-eight," Peter replied.

Oooh. That hurt. Peter went on to explain that going up against the *Tonight Show* juggernaut and the iconic Letterman, we needed to be on all the time, especially in our first season. Their numbers were starting to go down. When they went on vacation and showed repeats, we would have fresh shows. Forty-eight weeks. I was going to be sixty years old, with a family I wasn't seeing enough of as it was. I would have no personal life, something Janice and I had been able to carve out all these years. Janice and I talked about it over and over again. I wasn't afraid of the work, never have been. But I was afraid that I wouldn't like the work, and I wasn't sure I wanted all that pressure. I had an idea though. What if it were done as a seasonal show, like any other? We'd go on in September and end in May. I'd get the summer off to recharge, spend time with Janice and the family. If they were okay with that, I would do it.

In the end, my plan didn't fly with the affiliates because what would be my replacement during the summer hiatus? Reruns of talk shows don't mean anything. I walked away without any regrets. Yes, they had offered a lot of what we call "Fuck you money," but I had learned over the years that if you're not happy doing what you're doing, then you shouldn't be doing it. In any case, if all had gone perfectly well and the show was able to stay on the air, as I write this I would just be handing it over to whoever they felt could get the eighteen-to-thirty-four-year-old demographic. Oy.

Grandpa

I am a grandpa. I love being a grandparent, and I like being called "Grandpa," even though sometimes when I hear it, I think the kids aren't talking to me. In my mind I'm still the guy from *When Harry Met Sally* . . . , and to them I'm the guy who takes more naps than they do.

Now, it wasn't always "Grandpa." The kids used to call me "Trust Fund," but I stopped that right away.

Grandpa and Gram—that's just fine with Janice and me. We're not the kind of grandparents who hide the fact that we have kids who have kids. You know the types. The ones who have their grandkids call them by their first names because they think that way no one will know how old they are. Who are they fooling? They're driving Rascal scooters, watching reruns of *Matlock,* and their hair is dyed a color only a Russian circus clown would consider using, and people are going to think they're not grandparents just because the little one standing next to them calls them Herb and Sylvia?

You've got to enjoy being a grandparent. You have to embrace it and be happy, because it's a sign from God that you have succeeded as a parent. Plus, your genetic line will continue and if you have a good estate planner, the kids will get your money and the government won't.

If you are a grandparent, you have heard all the jokes: "The great thing about grandparenting is you can hand them back." But to me, it's no joke.

When Jenny first got pregnant, it was a humbling feeling. I was going to be something I wished my dad had had the chance to be. It's at these milestone moments that I think about him most. When we heard the news, Janice and I just held each other for the longest time. We were starting a new phase of our lives. The girl in the bikini and the eighteen-year-old camp counselor who'd followed her down the beach in the summer of 1966 were going to be grandparents. As Jenny's pregnancy developed and her belly blossomed, I kept whispering to it, "I'm waiting for you." So one night I went home and wrote down all the things I was waiting to do, and it became the book *I Already Know I Love You*. Having a grandchild does start another clock ticking. It's the how-old-will-I-be-when-they're-ten-and-then-fifteen-and-twenty-one-and-when-they're-married clock. I couldn't help winding it up, but I don't advise that you do. The numbers get very scary.

When I'm 152, the grandkids will be in their nineties!

Sitting in the waiting room at the hospital awaiting the delivery of my grandchildren was an intense experience. When Janice was delivering our daughters, I was worried, to be sure, but when it's your daughter in there, you worry even more. No parent ever wants their child to suffer any pain. Each time my sons-in-law, Mike and Howie, have come out and announced who just exited our daughter and entered the world and that everything was fine, I felt a relief beyond compare. With all four babies, they chose not to learn the sex beforehand. I loved that. It's one of life's last great surprises.

The joy I had in raising my girls was one thing; seeing them raise their kids is another. Trying to remember what we did in certain situations is not possible. Jumping back into the world of the wee ones is not that easy. Being a grandfather to both sexes has taught me that girls are just different from boys. Not better or worse, mind you, but different. Granddads and grandsons are a great combination because they both think a fart is the funniest thing in the world, and the average grandfather produces more natural gas than the state of Oklahoma. If they'd allow fracking on lower intestines, the average grandpa could produce enough energy to light up Tulsa for a year.

My friends who have granddaughters agree: Don't take everything little girls say to you personally, except for "I love you." They just say whatever they're feeling. When your granddaughters are sweet and loving, there's nothing like it, though it probably means they want you to take them to American Girl—which, of course, you will do.

Today's grandkids are intimidating because they are so smart. When we were younger, we looked at our grandparents like they were the Oracle of Delphi. They were fonts of wisdom: "Billy boy, every time God closes a door, he opens another—that's when the Nazis can see who's hiding in the house. Don't trust anyone." Nowadays, the kids are the brains and we're the idiots. If fifty is the new forty, then three is the new fifteen. My grandson is three, and he has his own Twitter account. "Today I had Cheerios and skipped my nap. Then read Voltaire and shorted Facebook at $25 a share." My seven-year-old granddaughter programmed my TiVo. My ten-year-old does the Sunday *Times* crossword puzzle. Seriously, each age is so different and special.

When they're born, you can't help but stare at them, because that's all you can do. It's a thrill, of course, but they're basically stones. For the first six months, your interactions are restricted to changing diapers and praying for an occasional smile. When I would get one, I'd be elated: "She knows me!" Then the baby would fart and I'd realize it was just gas. Once they start sitting up and recognizing you, it's very obvious what is about to happen. Your kids are going to ask for the grandkids to sleep over at your place. Personally, I love it when my kids look more tired than we do. Sweet revenge. Still, we always say yes.

The first sleepover is a delight for grandmothers and a challenge for grandfathers. The grandmothers can't wait to watch the kids; we can't wait to watch the game. But once they're asleep in our house, life as we know it stops. We tiptoe around like we're the Frank family and the Gestapo is downstairs. The baby monitor is in our room, and the unspoken rule is that when the kids go down, so do we. So at seven P.M., I'm in bed waiting for the sandman to come. I can't watch TV, because the noise may wake up the kids; I can't listen to music with my iPod earbuds, because then I can't hear the monitor; and I can't have sex, because that could wake up Janice.

When they turn one, you can start talking to them. You'll usually sound like a moron, but that won't stop you. You'll talk in that babyspeak that adults use on kids and people from other countries. I have spent entire weekends sounding like the strange guy who delivers for the florist. And once you've been doing it for forty-eight hours, it's impossible to stop. One time we went to the movies after the kids had been with us for the weekend. I sounded a tad demented at the box office: "Can you pweeeze give me two old-people tickies for *Inglourious Basterds,* mister, pweeeeeze?"

At two, they start talking back to you. They learn how to say "NO." It's the "Terrible Twos." Forget the fact that you're in the middle of the Shitty Sixties and that no one else on earth talks to you this way and let it roll off your back. Save up your angst for when they're teenagers. Just change their diaper and cut their meat. It's the same thing they'll do for you when you hit the Hateful Eighties.

Then they go to preschool and it seems that every three weeks or so there's a show, which usually entails the kids standing together onstage and screaming a song or two. The moms are sighing and the grandmas crying and you're thinking, *I'm gonna be late for my meeting.* Make sure you go to every one of these shows. Believe me, you don't want one of your grandchildren asking you why you weren't there.

For me, the next stage has been exciting because my grandkids are starting to understand what I do. The first movie of mine they saw was *Monsters, Inc.,* and for a while I was Grandpa Mike Wazowski. I spent a year and a half talking only like him. Then we'd be out together and someone would stop me for an autograph or to take a picture, and that confused them. But when some of my movies were aired on TV, they started to understand. We showed them *The Princess Bride,* and then I could only talk like Miracle Max for a few months. "Have fun storming the swing set" always got a big laugh. I did a sketch with Miley Cyrus in a special, and I brought them to meet her. "You have a cool grandpa," she told them. That made me a big deal. They watched the Oscars the last time I hosted and saw billboards with my picture on them around L.A. When they came to the premiere of *Parental Guidance,* it was the first time they saw me in a movie as me, and of all things, I was playing a grandpa. People were taking pictures and everyone was making a big fuss. On the drive home, six-year-old Dylan asked Jenny, "Mommy, do people know Grandma is married to Billy Crystal?"

One of the biggest regrets in my life is the fact that I'm not going to be around them forever to enjoy moments like that. Even if everything goes perfectly well, I'll only get so far with them. I know the world they'll be living in will be amazing—after all, just think of the changes the baby boomer generation has seen, from two men landing on the moon to two men on top of a wedding cake. My mind conjures up what the world will be like for them in, say, 2048. It will be a world where America is finally debt-free. And that will be because some of our richest billionaires will finally do the right thing and pay our debt off. They'll just divvy up the check like it's women at lunch.

"Warren, I got defense; you paid for Social Security last time."

"Bill, you had health care and we didn't, so take that."

"Who wants the CIA? It's only twenty-eight billion."

"What tip do you leave on sixteen trillion? The service was so-so."

Thirty-five years from now, the world will be at peace mainly due to the leadership of our new pope, Sol the first. People everywhere will speak the same language, the language of the United States: Spanish. In 2048, the last person who still thought switching to the metric system was a good idea will die. We will make contact with aliens from a new solar system, and during their first visit, Donald Trump's son will ask for their birth certificates. Most comforting, in 2048, the Yankees will win the Intergalactic World Series when seventy-eight-year-old Mariano Rivera records his five thousandth save. . . .

But in my real world, I adore my grandchildren. And I'm getting better in my role every day, so I thought I'd share some rules, some do's and don'ts, about being a successful grandparent.

Learn from your own parenting mistakes. Don't repeat with your grandkids what you did wrong with your own kids. It's time to make all new mistakes. Grandpas sometimes get pushed aside when the baby is born. When the moms are nursing, there's even less you can do. Guys, don't stand back and let the women do all the work; get in there early and help out any way you can. Don't hold the baby like it's a football you're running with. Cradle it gently but confidently. They hear your voice, they feel your tension, they get to know *your* smell. Try to be a part of it right from the start by improving your burping technique. Quick tip: Keep your head turned away from the baby, so it won't smell your beer breath.

As they get around six and older, girls start acting out a little. The shows they watch on TV should be monitored, as some of the "tween" shows can cause some strange behavior. When I was a kid, Annette Funicello of *The Mickey Mouse Club* was kind of sexy, but no one walked around dressed like her—except for my friend Todd, and that got him suspended from school for a week. Today, these tween stars are provocative. Young girls want to be like the older girls, but their bodies don't quite match what they're trying to do. A six- or nine-year-old trying to bump and grind like a twenty-year-old can be challenging. Just smile and say, "Nice shoes." It's times like this when I feel I'm in the middle of a reality show: *Oh, That Stupid Grandpa.*

Try not to overreact when they appear naked in front of you. I'm not sure little boys do this, as only my friends with granddaughters seem to be confronting this problem. For whatever reason, little girls will suddenly strip down, parade around, and flash everyone. You can't get angry and say, "Put your clothes on *now*" or "What the hell are you doing?" You have to act like they *have* clothes on. You can say, "That's not appropriate—we're in a restaurant." Getting naked spontaneously is perfectly normal, I'm told. Yeah, but if my uncle Louie did it, they'd put him in restraints.

It's also hard to remain calm when they start talking about penises and vaginas. Usually it's at the dinner table and they're laughing hysterically. I'd love to join in and be the cool "Lenny Bruce" grandpa—"Dig, took a bath and the water was too hot; I think I blanched the bishop"—but I resist the temptation. When my friend's granddaughter was four, she saw her dad get out of bed naked, and she said, "Daddy, you slept with your penis on." Kids love to talk about poop, penises, and vaginas—oh, and death. Yup, that's a big one, too. You have to check with your kids first about what they tell their children about dying and death and heaven. It all has to be a consistent message. "Grandpa says the maggots eat us!!!" is not something you want your darlings to announce. This is a big one. Kids get scared about dying. You have to present it in the right tone. When I was a kid, my grandfather told me, "You get stiff, they dress you up and put you in a box. Then they bury you in the ground—pass the cookies." That was three years in therapy right there. Kids need to know it isn't the end. They need to feel that heaven is a wonderful, beautiful place where we'll all be together again. On second thought, I guess we all do.

Never threaten them with something you know you're not going to do. Threats don't work with little ones. Just look at the problems we have with the president of Iran. Don't tell them you're going to go away and never see them again. Don't tell them you will take away their food if they don't eat it. They know you won't.

Don't tell them the truth about what you did when you were their age. So how do you handle it when they ask you the hard questions about drugs or sex or alcohol or what life was like in the 1960s? You do the same thing with your grandkids that you did with their parents: you lie your ass off.

Never tell them how much money you're leaving them in the will. That's just an incentive for them to write the words DO NOT RESUSCITATE on your chest when you're napping.

Don't let your fears and worries become theirs. Never forget that you're sixty-five and they're five. Just because we are a bunch of Purell-addicted, rubbing-alcohol-cleaning germaphobes afraid to shake hands doesn't mean our grandkids should be. Pass down money, not phobias. Oh yeah: little ones like to eat their boogers. Just a warning. When you see them do it, don't scream, "Eeech, don't eat that!" If they see that it bothers you, they'll do it again and again; then when you want to go out for lunch, they'll say, "I'm not hungry, I ate."

Please don't do what my grandma did to me when I had something on my face. Never take your napkin and put it in your mouth to get some saliva on it and then rub the "schmutz" off their cheek. Oh, the horror.

Do fun things with them. Take them on one-on-one trips. Let them get to know you in a different way.

Read to them. Show them the joy you can get from a great book. Act it out; make it so that storytime with Grandpa is a joy they will always remember. When they say they want Grandma to read to them instead, make it clear that you understand. Then quietly weep in the bathroom.

Don't think they're your kids. Remember that the whole purpose of life is to raise your kids right so they can raise their kids right. When you see your kids raising your grandkids wrong, just remember these four letters: BTHO. Butt the hell out.

Make a rule that no one can use an iPad or smartphone at the dinner table. Don't be one of those families who don't talk in restaurants because all the kids and parents are using a device of some kind. It's a sad sight. No one is talking, no one is smiling, there is no interaction at all. The kids text Mom what they want to eat so she can e-mail the waiter. Giving your kid a smartphone is just a way to avoid being an interested parent. It's another form of pacifier. We have become a country of Angry Birds–playing zombies who are addicted to this computer-phone-camera-butler in our hands. We walk with it, we drive with it, we take it to the john with us, we text, we Google, we watch movies on it, we— wait I got off the track here; where was I? Oh yes, being a good grandparent. All jokes aside, here's the real deal: there are many moments now when I start thinking that I'm on dessert and the waiter is starting to put the bill together. Every year becomes more precious; every moment, every minute should be enjoyed and valued as they start to dwindle.

Work has always brought me great satisfaction and joy. Those situations are fewer now, and there are more and more people telling me I'm not as important as I once was. The inevitable becomes clearer every day. Sometimes, like a sudden rainstorm, I get that scared, sad feeling that time is getting shorter. The dark part of my imagination overwhelms me, and I picture myself old and feeble, mumbling to my Bahamian aide, whom Janice can't stand but I like 'cause she sneaks me gelato after my sponge bath. I can't stop conjuring the saddest images my mind can muster, and I'm lost—and then I hear the footsteps running toward me and I hear the giggles, and they yell "Grandpa!" and suddenly they're in my arms and I squeeze them and hold on to them for dear life, and that's a very accurate statement. It is a dear life. One that I get to share with them while I watch them grow and help get them ready for what is to come. I am important; I am their star; I am their grandpa.

Celebrate Your Birthdays

Too many people, when they get older, try to ignore their birthdays. "I'm going to let this one go by," I often hear from friends. Why pretend it didn't happen? Embrace it. I love being on the other side of the dirt, and every day that I'm here, I am grateful. I believe birthdays are to be celebrated, especially when you turn sixty-five.

Celebrate the fact that the ancient Mayans were wrong.

Celebrate the fact that you have spent your life in a country where you can be anything you want to be (unless you are a gay illegal immigrant who wants to get married in Utah).

Celebrate the fact that you're alive and that statistically at least one of the people who bullied you in high school is now dead.

Celebrate the fact that you are alive today because you got the proper postnatal nutrients when you were breast-fed from an attachment mom, up until you turned twenty-three.

Celebrate the fact that you now have so many candles on your cake, Al Gore thinks you are the cause of global warming.

And celebrate your mother, just like I celebrate mine.

Sixty-five years ago, that sainted woman screamingly launched me into the world in a thirty-minute procedure she always likened to pooping a pumpkin.

Honestly, my mom always made me feel special on my birthday, March 14. When I was a young boy, she used to wake me up at the exact time I was born: 7:36 A.M. As I grew older and moved out of the house, it became the phone call at 7:36 A.M. Even after I got married and had kids of my own, I always woke up looking forward to her call—it started the day off on the right foot. I put that tradition into *City Slickers,* with Jayne Meadows's voice playing my mom on the other end of the line. Mom's been gone since 2001, but come March 14, I still get up early and look at the alarm clock, and at 7:36, in my mind I hear the phone ring. Her call always ended with her saying, "Do something special." I didn't even mind that she called collect.

The most special thing I ever did on my birthday was when my life's dream came true: I got to play for the New York Yankees.

In 2007, I was in Costa Rica for Christmas vacation and could feel my birthday looming. I was anxious about turning sixty—it felt like a huge number. Derek Jeter happened to be at our hotel. I'd known Derek since his rookie year, and we'd become friends. I told Derek I was going to be sixty and was a little freaked out about it. Jeter asked, "If you could do one thing to make yourself happy, what would it be? You should do something special." Somewhere, my mom was smiling.

....

I knew my answer to Jeter's question right away. When Joe Torre was the Yankees' manager, he had let me work out with the team many times, even before World Series games. Joe and I were very close friends, and he not only knew I could handle myself on the field but thought my presence might even relax the guys. Infield practice was the most fun. I was still a good player, having been an outstanding (if I say so myself) high school second baseman and shortstop, and had played in leagues in New York and Los Angeles into my forties. My skills, though hardly professional, were solid. I still take batting practice regularly in a cage at home, and every morning my gym workout ends with a "catch." Turning double plays with Jeter on the historic infield of old Yankee Stadium was an enormous thrill. I wanted to do it again—this time, for real.

I came up with a plan where I would get one at bat in a spring training game. Whatever happens, happens, and I then announce my retirement and throw the team a party. Jeter *loved* the idea, and a few weeks before my sixtieth birthday, he and George Steinbrenner, Lonn Trost, Randy Levine, Brian Cashman, Bud Selig, and Major League Baseball gave me the greatest birthday gift ever: the Yankees would sign me to a one-day contract, and I would play against the Pittsburgh Pirates in a spring training game in Tampa. The game was on March 13, 2008, the day before my sixtieth birthday.

The official contract was for $4 million! But the nice part was that the Yankees gave me three days to come up with the money. We worked it out so that I would be the DH—designated Hebrew. Even though I wasn't going to be in the field, I needed to prepare. As you get older, there's a fine line between getting a walk and just wandering away from the batter's box. So I went into training.

Reggie Smith, the former great player who'd trained my "Maris and Mantle"—Barry Pepper and Thomas Jane—for *61**, has a baseball academy in Encino, California. He is a great teacher, and a better man. When I told him what was happening, he was almost as excited as I was. We didn't have a lot of time, but every day I worked on my swing with Reggie and his son (also a great teacher), against live pitching. As I left the West Coast for this great moment—accompanied by my good pal Robin Williams and some dear friends from high school—I was hitting eighty-five-mile-per-hour fastballs and felt as ready as a fifty-nine-year-old comedian can feel as he's about to play for the New York Yankees.

....

Trivia freaks will know that I was the oldest person ever to play for the Yankees, and the first player ever to test positive for Maalox. I actually did have to undergo routine testing. When they asked me for blood and urine, I gave them my underwear. The day before the game, I met with Yankee manager Joe Girardi. He wanted me to lead off and play left field. I said that was too far to run. We agreed that I would lead off and DH and have just the one at bat. Joe wanted me to score a run if I could. I wasn't sure (again, that's a long way to run), so we agreed that if I did get on base, Johnny Damon would pinch-run for me. It would be more theatrical, so to speak. I signed my contract with Lonn Trost and Jean Afterman and went and got dressed in the clubhouse. I knew most of the guys in there and had been in the clubhouse many times, but this felt unreal—I was one of them. In a strange way, I was very relaxed about it. It was so natural for me to wait until everyone had left the clubhouse so I could take off my clothes and put on my uniform. Just like high school gym class.

The team was on a road trip, and I spent that day working out with Derek and José Molina, who'd stayed back in Tampa. I took batting practice with Jeter and José while a small crowd and many camera crews looked on. I was on my game, hitting line drive after line drive. I know I shocked everyone, which was a great feeling. But I was in great shape and ready. Tino Martinez was throwing me sixty-mile-per-hour fastballs while Janice videotaped from a distance. Derek saw her and motioned for her to come over by him at the cage. She whispered to him, "How fast is Tino throwing?"

"One-oh-seven," Derek whispered back.

....

I couldn't sleep that night. It was really happening. I arrived at
the park early the next morning. Girardi met me and we hung
out a little, and to this day I can't thank him enough for welcoming me the way he did. This was his first year with the club, and
the last thing he needed was some aging leading man as his leadoff man. Yet he treated me like a ballplayer, which is what I was
that day. I did my pregame stretching and conditioning drills with
the club and, of course, was then ready for a nap. Batting practice
was amazing. I was in the cage with Derek and Damon and
Bobby Abreu and Alex Rodriguez and Jorge Posada. When the
guys nodded to one another that I was okay, I was on cloud nine.
The hard part was that once batting practice was over, we had
about an hour and a half till game time. I could feel my sphincter
tighten, as well as my lower back and hamstrings. Now it wasn't
just fun, it was really on.

I had lunch with Derek and Jorge and tried to be cool, but I
was getting more and more anxious. Jorge and Derek were so
easy with me. We all ate peanut butter and jelly sandwiches: the
same meal I always had before games in high school and all
the league games I'd played in and, actually, before hosting the
Oscars. After lunch I went to put my game uniform on, and that's
when the pranks started. My shoelaces were cut, so when I went
to tie them, they came off in my hands. The toes on my socks
were cut as well, so when I pulled them on, my foot went through.
I took it all in good stride, trying to act like nothing bothered me,
as I knew the guys were watching. I was careful putting on my
cup, as the fear of hot sauce loomed. The pranks continued—my
hat switched with one that didn't fit, my glove missing, a belt with
no holes—until it was time to go to the dugout.

The stands were full as I bounded onto the field with the team
to loosen up. A big roar from the crowd made me feel great, until
I realized that A-Rod and Jeter were standing next to me. The
national anthem was played, and I had a tear in my eye as I

March 13, 2008. Dream come true for Jeter.

looked into the stands to see my brothers, Joel and Rip, and my
daughter Jenny, and of course Janice. Mike Mussina threw a perfect first inning, and then I was up. When the announcer introduced me with "Leading off for the Yankees, the designated
hitter, number 60, Billy Crystal," I just about lost it. Since I'd been
a kid, playing with my dad, brothers, or friends, I'd always dreamed
of this moment, and now it was real. The crowd gave me a tremendous hand as I left the on-deck circle. "Hack," (meaning
swing) said Jeter, patting me on the helmet.

The Pirates' pitcher was Paul Maholm: six foot two, 220 pounds,
from Mississippi. Never been to a Seder. I was nervous, but the
one thing I was not nervous about was getting hit by a pitch. It
never entered my mind. If Maholm hit me, I'd sue. You ever see

a Jew get hit by a pitch? They get plunked in the leg and they grab their neck. Whiplash! Once I'd found out the date of the game, I'd gone to the Pirates' website to see who'd be pitching. I'd then watched Maholm strike out Barry Bonds. A real confidence builder. I studied his motion and his release point and tried to visualize what hitting off him would be like. As I approached the plate, the ump greeted me, as did the Pirates' catcher. I watched Maholm's warm-up pitches, looking for the release point I had seen on the website, and told myself, *I can do this.*

"Play ball!"

I stepped in. Since 1956, from the time I had seen Mickey Mantle play in the first game at the stadium I'd gone to, I had wanted to be a Yankee.

So there I am in the batter's box fifty-two years after that first game, my heart beating into the NY logo on my chest. Maholm is staring in for the sign, and I'm staring back, trying to look like I belong. Here comes the first pitch: ninety-two miles an hour. Ball one. I never see it, but it sounds outside. The ball makes a powerful thud in the catcher's glove. I want to say, "Holy shit," but I act like I see one of those every day. In fact, I do: on TV, not in the FUCKING BATTER'S BOX. The count is 1 and 0. He comes in with a fastball, a little up and away, and I hit a screaming line drive down the first base line, which means I didn't hit it that hard but I'm screaming, "I hit it! I hit it!" Someone yells, "DOUBLE!" Which would be tough because I can't run like I used to and on my way to second base I'd have to stop twice to pee. The last time a Jew my age ran that fast, the caterer was closing down the buffet.

But I'm still thinking double. The ump is thinking, Foul ball. I had made contact with a major league fastball. Okay, 1 and 1. Ball inside, 2 and 1, and another ball and it's 3 and 1. I'm this close to getting to first base, just like at my prom. I look over, and Derek Jeter is in the on-deck circle yelling, "Swing, swing!"

The windup, the pitch. It's a cutter. The nastiest cutter I've seen since my bris. But I swing and miss. The first time I've swung and missed in two days at Tampa. Now it's 3 and 2. The crowd stands up. This is my only shot, my only at bat. Ever. Maholm winds, I look to the release point, and there it is: eighty-nine miles per hour, a cut fastball, the same pitch he threw to that obstructer of justice Barry Bonds. I swing over it. Strike three. I'm out of there.

I head back to the bench, but before I do, I check with the ump: "Strike?" He shakes his head no: low and inside. I'm so mad I missed it, and also mad I didn't take the pitch, that I almost don't hear the crowd standing and cheering. The guys are giving me high fives. Girardi hugs me, then Kevin Long, the great hitting coach, and then Jorge. Then, for the first time in baseball history, they stop the game and give the batter a ball for striking out. A-Rod hands it to me, saying, "Great at bat!" My teammates greet me as if I've just hit a home run. Mariano Rivera hugs me, and others keep saying the same thing:

"Six pitches, man, you saw six pitches!"

I sit with Yogi Berra and Ron Guidry for a few innings, and if that isn't cool enough, I'm asked to come up to Mr. Steinbrenner's office. In full uniform I walk into the boss's lair. He gives me a big hug and then says with a straight face that I've been traded for Jerry Seinfeld. I thank him over and over again for a chance to be a Yankee, and he says he loved it and, most importantly, the fans loved it. That's what it's really all about.

••••

Once the game is over and I've done my press, the clubhouse attendants hand me my uniform as a gift. Before I leave, I ask who was pulling those locker room pranks on me before the game.

"LaTroy Hawkins," I'm told.

"What can I do to get back at him?"

"You want me to shit in his shoes?" someone asks.

"No, but thanks—maybe something more clever," I suggest. One of the attendants then says he has an idea. LaTroy has just gotten a pair of new dress shoes, so let's screw them to the wall of his locker. How he thinks of that so quickly, I have no idea. He

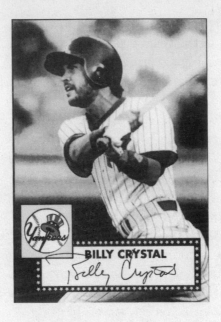

BILLY CRYSTAL

returns with a drill, and we take LaTroy's brand-new $700 shoes and screw them to the back wall of his locker. Janice made fun baseball cards of me as a present, and I put one in each shoe, with a note saying, "Don't fuck with my stuff." I leave wishing I were coming back the next day.

I've had some great moments in my career, but nothing compares to the fact that I can say, "I was the leadoff man for the New York Yankees." I realize, of course, that this was a once-in-a-lifetime event. But I say to all of you, as my mom said to me: Do something special on your birthday. Whatever you do, celebrate the fact that you're here, and that people love you and you love them. We only do this once.

Let Him Go

My first memory is of being in a cemetery. I guess I was three years old, not aware of where I was, because I was playing leapfrog on various headstones as my family and the rest of the mourners were saying the Jewish prayer for the dead for my aunt Rose. Rose was a tiny wrinkled Russian woman with one arm several inches longer than the other. My dad claimed it was because she played trombone. She was so Russian-looking that you had the feeling you could twist her head off and another, smaller version of her would be inside. Anyway, I was just jumping away, carefree, on the flat chiseled granite markers when my father gently grabbed me by the back of the neck and said, "Don't do that." Thus began my relationship with my dad and death.

Growing up, I was always around the old, the sick, and the complaining. My relatives were very matter-of-fact about death: That's it, and that's all. "When I go, you can have my sweaters for half price." Although my relatives were a joyous group, a low-hanging fog always seemed to surround them, and one by one they disappeared into it. My father led the parade by dying suddenly when I was just fifteen years old.

I missed him terribly for most of my life, always regretting never having had the chance to be face-to-face again, so I could say I was sorry about our last heated encounter. When I became a father and then a grandfather, there was always an empty pocket in my soul. Every time I've had a personal moment of joy—like my wedding, or the births of my daughters, their weddings, the births of my four grandchildren, or successes in my career—I've wished I could have shared it with him. This search for my father always becomes tangled with the vines of my own aging. We never had a chance to grow older together.

After my father's death, his brother Berns, my uncle, took on an important role in my life. He always knew how to talk to me. Maybe it was the artist in him that understood that my jokes were my sketches, and my monologues were my paintings. He knew how to praise and how to form a criticism (which is more difficult). As time went on, life started to catch up to him—or, more accurately, death started to. It became clear that this giant was getting shorter every day. Normal functions were being robbed from him, yet he never complained, except to say, "The golden years are brass."

After he collapsed at Jenny's wedding brunch, he made me his medical proxy, which meant that at some point in his inevitable demise I would be the one to say, "No more, that's enough." Somehow, I never thought that day would come. But in August 2008, I got an urgent phone call from his doctor in New York, who told me that Berns had had what appeared to be a stroke, and death was imminent.

"What do you want to do if we get into that area where a decision is needed whether to resuscitate him or not?" he asked me.

I suddenly felt angry at my uncle. I knew he'd given me this power because he loved and trusted me, but I really didn't want it. "It's tough playing God," his doctor said.

"It's tougher playing nephew," I responded weakly.

Berns was in a semicomatose state for weeks, a humbling and insulting journey for this vibrant warrior. I felt a strong urge to say to him, "Uncle, maybe it's time to stop fighting," but then I would get scared and mad at myself. Some days, there were flickers of hope, which I clung to, the way a little child hangs on to the first dime he is given. You squeeze it as hard as you can, so no one can take it away. But I was now sixty years old, so far from the carefree child in a cemetery jumping on headstones—stones that now bore the names of all my uncles and aunts, grandparents, my dad, and now my mother, as well.

Growing older with Berns was one of the great gifts in my life. I wasn't ready to say, "No more, that's enough."

One night, alone and exhausted by the consuming worry about Berns, I fell asleep early. Janice was visiting her parents, who were nervously preparing for a most delicate surgery on my father-in-law. It seemed that impending doom was everywhere. I awoke startled, in the dark, feeling scared and suddenly very cold, which was strange, because it was August and I don't use the air-conditioning. I felt someone next to me, standing alongside the bed. I was frozen with fear, and as cold as I was, I was also sweating profusely. I turned slowly and fearfully, thinking it was some sort of home invader. In the dark, I saw a shadowy figure that appeared to be wearing a long black coat, with a cowl covering its head. I didn't have the courage to look at its face, though I could sense that it had one. It didn't speak, but I felt a message being transmitted into my head: "Let him go. . . . It's time." These words were repeated several times before I sensed that the presence had left. The room was warm again. I looked at the clock; it was three-ten in the morning.

My heart was beating through my soaked T-shirt. I flipped on the light and walked around the house, splashed some water on my face, toweled off. I gazed out the window at the night and its stars, and I knew what had happened. My father had come to me, to tell me it was okay to let Berns go. I had seen those shows where people swear they've been visited from the "other side," and I'd never believed them. Now I did.

Performing *700 Sundays* had given me some sense of peace and closure. The last scene in the show has me meeting my father in heaven, and he forgives me. After each performance, I would feel so enriched, so grateful for the chance to act this out. But that was a play; this was so real. It sounds crazy, but I really believed he had come. I stayed up until Janice returned the next day.

"It was the air conditioner," she said, looking at me as if I had three heads.

"No, I didn't have it on." I felt like Richard Dreyfuss in *Close Encounters*. I also told a few friends what had happened. Some nodded and listened patiently; others, I got the feeling, thought I had imagined it or simply made it up, considering the circumstances. I must have sounded like those people in the trailer park who swear that a spaceship landed and a little green man emerged and asked them for change for a twenty. But I never questioned the experience.

Unnerved by the encounter, to say the least, I received a call just as I landed in New York. I was there to attend the final game at old Yankee Stadium. ESPN had requested that I commentate for an inning during this final broadcast. Since Dad had introduced me to it in 1956, the park had become a sanctuary for me. If ballparks can be called cathedrals, then this was my synagogue. The phone call was from the doctor, who told me Berns might not last the night. One of those evil "hospital infections" had found an easy target. I entered his hospital room with terrible fear.

I wasn't there when either of my parents died, and I'd been angry at them for not waiting for me. But God doesn't have to wait for anyone, does he? I held Berns's hand and whispered the punch line of a dirty joke he had told me when I was a kid; it was our way of saying hello. "An eagle swallows a mouse whole and is flying up to the clouds when the mouse crawls out of the eagle's asshole and says, 'Eagle, how high are we?' The eagle says, 'Five thousand feet.' A few minutes later, the mouse again asks, 'Eagle, how high are we?' 'Ten thousand feet,' says the eagle. One last time the mouse pops his head out and asks, 'Eagle, how high are we?' The eagle says, 'Twenty thousand feet,' and the mouse says, 'You ain't shitting me, are you?'" So that's what I whispered in his ear: "You ain't shitting me, are you?"

He moved his head slightly, sensing where I was, and a huge diamond of a tear rolled down his exhausted face and onto his gown, the stain spreading. "Don't cry, Uncle, you're going to get better," I said. I think he wasn't crying for himself; he was crying for me. I left hours later, sure I wouldn't see him again.

I slept in my clothes, alongside the phone. It rang at nine the next morning. "Come, Billy," his aide told me. "The fever broke and he's very alert."

I raced over. "You ain't shitting me, are you?" He opened both eyes, something he hadn't been able to do for weeks, and smiled. I held his hand, and he immediately started to fail. The nurse rushed in and told me to keep talking to him, for he was passing away. I was still holding his hand, and if God was going to take him, it would be one hell of a tug-of-war. I began panicking. The nurse calmed me down and told me to talk him through it.

"It's okay to go. . . . I love you," I said.

"He waited for you," the nurse whispered, listening to his failing heart.

Miraculously, Berns held on, and the episode ended. I was terrified and exhausted. It was like being on a raft in the ocean and a shark takes a bite out of it and swims off, but it's only a matter of time before he returns for more. My brother Joel arrived, and we sat by the foot of our beloved uncle's bed. Berns was alert, though his agonal breathing sounded ominous, and we could hear the dreaded rattle. He did manage to get a huge laugh out of everyone when a young resident asked him how he was feeling. Uncle Berns never said a word; he opened both eyes—again, something he hadn't done for a month—and, in a perfect Oliver Hardy moment, stared at the resident as if to say, "You are a moron."

His daughter, Dorothy, arrived, and my daughter Lindsay and her fiancé, Howie, as well. Berns labored again, and then it happened so quickly. The doctor told us once again that he was failing. We gathered around Berns, I held his right hand, and we all told him good-bye and encouraged him to go. He loved to sing "I Got Shoes," an old spiritual that ends with "When I get to heaven, gonna put on my shoes, and walk all over God's heaven." I saw him trying so hard to stay alive, but his body was making the transition, and I found myself saying into his ear, "Put on your shoes."

He made a slight motion of his head to me, there was a hint of resignation, a glimmer of a smile, and he stopped breathing. He was gone.

No one had ever died in front of me. It's not pleasant, but it was what I'd always wanted in my thoughts of my parents' deaths. They were there when I came into this world; I should have been there when they left it. I had been through the experience now with the last link to my father. It was fitting, I thought, that on the day Yankee Stadium expired, my uncle, the brother of my father, who taught me to love that place, would also expire. Also, as was revealed that night, the new stadium would open on April 16, my father's one hundredth birthday. The next day, I had one last good-bye at the funeral home before Berns was sent on his way to be cremated, per his wishes. He hadn't wanted a funeral—to be laid out, as he said, looking "like the last pastry on the cart."

I walked into the viewing room to do the legal identification. I just started sobbing and saying thank you: Thank you for your love, your inspiration, your support, your guidance, your laughter. When I ran out of thank-yous, I finally said good-bye. What you learn when you witness a death is that once the life is out of someone, the body is just the container of it. His spirit was gone, freed of his illness and frailty. The remains seemed like a costume and a mask, like all the ones he had worn entertaining us when we were kids. "Hocus pocus, chimnio smokus, halaballoo, halaballa" were his magic words as the "Great Bernardo" would make something disappear. Now he had made himself vanish. That afternoon, I went over to his apartment to spend some time with his widow, Deborah. Berns's devoted aide Alma was there. She had taken care of him for two years. A vibrant Jamaican woman, she had grown to be his close friend. He'd trusted her with his physical problems, and they'd laughed and enjoyed each other's company. She sat, now; the emptiness in the apartment was huge. In her beautiful Jamaican accent, Alma asked, "Billy, did Berns tell you about your father coming to him?"

"What do you mean?" I said.

"Before he got real bad, Berns said your father come to him, in the middle of the night, wearing a long black coat with a hood, and told him, 'It's time, let go, you'll be all right.'"

I was stunned. Her face lit up. "He said it was as clear as could be. So I said to Berns, Tell your brother not to come around here no more."

Can't Take It with You

I tend to keep things.

I've had the same car for eleven years, I wear three-year-old Nikes, and my cell phone is from the Reformation.

This isn't because I'm OCD or superstitious, afraid that something horrible will happen if I get rid of things—knock on wood three times while standing on my left foot—it's because of what happened with my high school letter sweater. At Long Beach High, a white sweater with blue trim meant you had earned one sports letter. That was totally cool, but I had the Holy Grail, a blue sweater with white trim, signifying two things: that I had earned four letters (three for baseball, one for basketball) and that, as the possessor of said sweater, I was a superior male specimen and therefore ripe for mating with the high school's nubile young women. (If I had actually done that, I would have knitted myself a sweater.) I earned the coveted sweater in 1965 and, of course, held on to it because there are two words no young man has ever uttered: spring cleaning.

Fast-forward to July 1976. Janice and I were packing to leave New York for good. "Do you really need this sweater?" she asked.

"Need" as in "Is it essential to keep me from freezing to death in balmy Los Angeles, our new home?" No.

Need emotionally? Of course! I had a deep spiritual connection to it, just like every guy has to his letter sweater, his favorite hat, or his penis.

But the practicality of Janice's look when she asked the question somehow won the day, and I threw it out.

A few days later, we were pulling away from the curb, leaving the only life we had ever known, when I saw a homeless guy going through our trash, picking through the remains of twenty-eight years of my life . . . while wearing my letter sweater.

"Janice, that's my sweater," I said.

"Don't look back," she countered. "Just drive." To this day, I regret not stopping. The vision of that guy wearing my sweater is what has kept me from giving away anything with any possible significance ever again.

Hey, I have no problem giving away things that don't have a memory attached. Old suits and clothes go to Goodwill or the Salvation Army. There are at least three people living on the beach in Santa Monica wearing Armani tuxedos topped off with a hat that says OSCAR HOST. I give old suits away to the UCLA theater department in hopes that one day the male lead in the student production of *The Book of Mormon* will look really good, as long as he is a 40 regular.

But it doesn't matter who you are or what you do; by sixty-five, all of us have accumulated what Janice calls *crap*. *Crap* we don't know where we got it from, *crap* we know where we got it from but don't remember why. We're all one Hummel figurine away from being on *Hoarders*.

When my kids and their husbands come over and walk into

my office, where the walls are lined with things that scream, "Me me me," I know that they are looking at the treasures of my life and thinking, *We're going to have to get rid of all this crap one day.* I've been in that position. When my mother and my uncle died, it took years to dispose of all the *crap* they had.

It's so much harder when it comes to your own things. What do you do? You have friends who hit sixty-five and start simplifying and giving things away, then bragging about living a life without clutter. But can you do it?

Now some of my *crap* can go because there are other people to think about. My kids don't want to be stuck with a mess.

I can get rid of the things that are just objects, that I'm not emotionally attached to. Like what 70 percent of guys in show business do with their first wife.

However, there are things that to everyone else must seem like mere objects (a.k.a. *crap*) but to me are precious mementos with layers and layers of emotional context. Like the tassel from my high school graduation cap, which hangs ten feet away from my work desk, where I can see it every day; it's staying. I know what you're thinking: Why does he need that? If I had two, I could spin them from my nipples the next time I play Fifty Shades of Grey: The Home Game, but one? The answer is, I need it. It's not just a tassel; it's something that reminds me of high school and all the friends I had then, some of whom remain good buddies today.

Right next to it is the bedroom door from my house in Long Beach, which Joel and Rip took off its hinges and gave me as my fiftieth birthday present. It's a plain old door covered with decals of Ted Williams and other great ballplayers of the fifties. To me it's a work of art.

Do you know how many guys have come over to my house, seen that door, and said, "I wish I had the bedroom door from when I was growing up"? Sometimes when I look at it, I wish I could open that door and walk back into my bedroom. There I'd be, sixteen years old, in bed, under the covers, then suddenly turning and saying, "Next time fucking knock—I'm reading!" Let's just say not one guy wants the mattress from his bed when he was sixteen.

Keeping things like this also happens to be a way to collect something really valuable and not so easily come by these days: smiles. But there's another use for them: when you hit a certain age, you need something to prompt memories.

So I'm not giving them away. Is that what we're supposed to do, give away our memories? The idea seems to be: "I'm gonna die tomorrow, so I better not have anything around that reminds me of the good times."

As my aunts and uncles got older, every purchase was tinged with sadness. "This is it, the last sofa we'll buy." "Enjoy it, it's the last winter coat you'll need." "Buy only half a dozen eggs—you never know."

Some of my relatives not only refused to buy, they started to give everything away. Psychologists tell you to be on the lookout for seniors who give too many things away: it's a sign that they're shutting down, that they're getting ready for the next move in their life, which is about twenty miles to the left and six feet down. Like my uncle Louie. The day he turned his three score and ten, he started unloading everything. "Here, Billy, take this, it's my favorite gramophone. What do you mean, you don't have any 78s?" He sensed the end was near. Seventy was old for his generation, so within weeks he was down to a chair, a bed, one suit, one pair of socks, one pair of shoes, one fork, a knife, a plate, and a coffee cup. He lived to be 107.

Me? I have a different plan. I want to keep those things that remind me of where I've been, because I know where I'm going.

But even though I know where I'm going eventually, one question remains: Where do I live till I get there? That's right—what about the house?

I love this house. Almost everything important and meaningful in my life has happened in this house. And that's what really matters to me. I'm not a hoarder of things, I'm a hoarder of memories (some of which I guess I am giving away—no, sharing—in this book), and every room of this house holds a memory of our kids or of Janice and me.

I can't tell you what's right for you. Friends of mine have sold their houses and are perfectly happy in apartments or smaller homes.

Recently people started saying to me, "The kids have their own families—why do the two of you need such a big house?" And you know something? They were 100 percent right.

So we made it bigger.

Is there any more sure sign that you aren't giving up? Is there any more sure signal that you intend to cling to your memories like a fifteen-year-old grasping her iPhone? When you decide at age sixty-five to do a total renovation and expansion of your house, that's your way of spitting in the eye of the term life salesman and saying, "I may be sixty-five, but I plan to live and work another thirty years so I can pay off this home equity loan."

So we did construction, and by construction I mean that afterward they're going to have to adjust every image on Google Earth.

The idea to make the house bigger was hatched when my grandson Hudson was born. The kids and the grandkids don't live nearby, so we figured, "If we build it, they will come."

And that's because we wanted them to have the memories of going to Grandma and Grandpa's house, like we did.

When I was a kid, I loved going to my grandparents' house . . . until they started to smell stale. What is that smell? It's some sweet-and-sour combination of cookies, plastic slipcovers, urine-soaked wool, and old books. I wonder if one day our kids will think we smell like Kindles.

Going over was always fun because it was like a visit with the aristocracy. Every time I left their house, I better understood my lineage and where I stood in the world. It was my responsibility to take everything they taught me and, when the time came, pass it on to my kids and make them as petrified and neurotic as my grandparents had made me. I also thought, *They have money, and when they die maybe I'll get some.*

I want my grandkids to have that same feeling—about the connection and the lineage, not the money part—and to have that generational understanding of our family tree, which keeps growing and reaching for the sky.

And to foster that you need a house, because families need centers, and we wanted our house to be the center, the place where people gathered. Especially for Thanksgiving. Thanksgiving at your own house is the best; Thanksgiving at someone else's house is like being a Chicago Cub at the World Series—in other words, you don't belong. It's someone else's tradition, someone else's turkey, and, even worse, a strange toilet.

So we wanted our house to be the family center, and we wanted the grandkids to come over more and spend the night, to create more family memories, and to do that we needed more room.

When we bought our house, in 1979, it had three small bedrooms, one of which we turned into a closet. In 2010, Janice decided that it would be perfect if she added an airline terminal to the house.

Think of renovating a house like operating the federal government. You start with a budget and the revenue to finance it. Then the special interests keep adding items to the list; you have to end the war between the interior decorator and the electrician, so you pump in more money to buy peace; and by the time you're done, you're $16 trillion in debt and having to borrow money from the Chinese.

Once we got the plans finalized, in late 2012, we started work. Based on the lead contractor's estimate—and he's been very accurate on this so far—they should wrap everything up in the year 2037.

I'm not here to tell you how to run your life, but let me say this: You know that swimming with a great white shark while holding a bloody halibut in your mouth is dumb. You know that invading Iraq is dumber. Living in your house while it's being renovated is even dumber than that. You can't tell if the house has been blown up or is being put back together. There are people constantly in and out, talking and hammering and working.

They finished the Empire State Building in less time than it's taking us to redo this house, and that has 102 stories with a basement.

We only have two stories: the story the contractor told us when he started and the story he tells me every day when I ask when he is going to finish.

And every day is the same. The workers get there promptly at seven and, after a brisk forty-five minutes of work, go on a two-hour break.

Back to work at nine forty-five, and then at ten the lunch wagon comes, music blasting out of the speakers, and trust me, that's something you want in a nice neighborhood, a food truck with a big mural of Cantinflas on the side.

And the guy who owns the truck is clever—he plays the appropriate music for the special of the day.

Godfather theme: spaghetti and meatballs.

"Tequila": tacos.

And he plays the Mets theme song when the food he has that day stinks.

Some days all the workers cook their own lunch—it must be casual Fridays. They bring their own little grills and hot plates and set up tents and build little fires in the empty lot next to my house. It looks like a Civil War battlefield.

Once they got in the swing of things, there was progress. Until the day the construction chief told me my house had termites. We had no idea until they started to swarm. They flew out of the living room floor and ceiling with their little wings, like the confetti that's shot out at the end of the Super Bowl.

We first knew something was up when the construction chief pulled out a stethoscope and started listening to the wall. He then took a hammer and opened up the wall, and it was like one of those old-fashioned nightclubs. The termites were in tuxedos and evening gowns, the band was playing, they had on bibs and they were eating prime rib, which in this case was the back of my house.

Termites only do two things: eat wood and make baby termites. We replaced the windows, we knocked down walls, and we even had to install steel beams. We then put in new wood, and they ate that. Our house was a twenty-four-hour termite buffet.

Later on I found out that termites don't eat redwood. I found that out after we had fed them two more walls and the supervisor of the work crew came over one morning and said, Why didn't you get redwood? Termites are redwood intolerant; it gives them gas. They're the Jews of the insect world.

So we rebuilt the entire house out of redwood, and now whenever I go to a meeting the first thing people tell me is that I smell like a picnic table.

As the workers were digging out the hillside to build a retaining wall about twelve feet down, they found bones—a hip and a femur and a few ribs. When they saw the bones, they backed off. It was like a Tarzan movie from the 1930s when the natives get scared and say, "Bad booloo, bad booloo."

Everything stopped because the health department put up crime tape and it looked like a murder scene; before work could proceed, they had to find out if those were human bones. So they tried to call in a forensic pathologist, but it was hard to find one because they're all working on television shows. Three days later, the results came back—they think it was an elk or a deer, or some other strange creature like a blogger. We were kind of disappointed because this used to be Indian land, and if they had been Indian bones, I could have turned my house into a casino and lived tax-free.

So the house is now 99 percent done and our idea is working out. The grandkids come here and sleep over, and I can wake up to the sound of them playing. As I listen to them giggling, I get a little misty and think that one day after I'm gone, these beautiful kids, all grown up, will come over here and they'll have one of their friends or maybe even their intended along and they'll proudly take them into my office and say, "This was Grandpa Billy's office. It's where he had everything that meant so much to him . . . and once I got rid of all his *crap*, I turned it into a dance studio."

Buying the Plot

This is the hard one. The chapter I was dreading. The one
that took the longest to write because it's about . . . death.
My death. Our biggest fear. Wait—your biggest fear is
not my death. Our own death is our biggest fear. It weighs on us
so much that we, as humans, have developed all kinds of psycho-
logical ways to deal with it. Elizabeth Kübler-Ross wrote about the
five stages as she saw them: denial, anger, bargaining, depression,
and acceptance. She was a genius. And now she's dead.

She was *the* expert on death, and now she's just . . . dead.

I look at the stages of death differently. To me they are retirement village, assisted living, nursing home, hospice, and burial
plot.

I know what you're thinking: *Billy, you're such an optimist,
and now you're going dark on us.* No, I'm just being realistic. I do
see a silver lining; it's the satin in my coffin.

The actuarial tables tell us that once we hit sixty-five, we can expect to live into our nineties. And then . . . bye-bye. And you know how in the back of your mind you're thinking that you're going to be the one that gets away with it, that you're going to be the one that God, like a bouncer at a nightclub, lets slip by? It doesn't work that way. For anyone. In fact, you know who else thought they might slip by? Every single person now in a cemetery.

So we have to plan ahead for what happens when we go.

Personally, I do not like planning a huge party I won't be attending. And as with our federal debt, I may just decide to stick my grandchildren with the bill.

You also don't know how you are going to go. Everyone has the same fantasy: that you are lying in bed, it's serene and quiet, everyone you love is gathered around you to say good-bye, there is no pain, and you leave this earth with a smile on your face. Except that's not how people go.

We're eaten by a giant shark.

Crash into a building while parasailing with a fly-by-night company run by a Mexican drug cartel.

Crushed beyond recognition by a falling boulder.

Burned to a crisp when your car rear-ends a fuel truck.

You eat something bad and get poisoned by *E. coli.*

Flesh-eating bacteria eat you.

Shopping at a farmers' market, you're run over by a fellow senior citizen who shouldn't have a license because he's legally blind.

Reading this book in the bathtub, you doze off and drown.

And those are some of the more pleasant things that can happen.

So although you have no control over how or when you are going to go (though some sadly do), you do have a say about where you spend eternity. I don't mean in the deeper sense of where the soul will go to rest and whether you should call ahead and get a good table.

This is about what my uncle Danny used to say after every Thanksgiving meal: WHAT DO WE DO WITH THE CARCASS?

My favorite philosopher, Yogi Berra, when asked by his wife, Carmen, where he'd like to be buried, simply said, "Surprise me."

Janice and I have had lengthy discussions about this because we don't want to burden the kids with the decision. And judging by the presents they get me for Father's Day and my birthday, I can't trust them. So Janice and I keep talking.

"What do you want?"

"What should we do?"

"Where do you want to be?"

We sound like we're in a scene from that great movie *Marty*.

"Where you wanna be when you're dead, Janice?"

"I dunno, Billy, where you wanna be?"

We've talked about getting cremated. I can't do that because I know my luck. The day after they cremate me, they'll find a cure for what I had. Once you're burned up, you have no hope of being put back together again. I've lived too long a life to be turned into Tang.

The big question then becomes what to do with the ashes. People are usually scattered in a special place they love. This won't work for me because that would be in front of the TV in my favorite chair. Then I know what would happen. Janice would come home one day and find our housekeeper, vacuuming.

"¿Dónde está Señor Crystal?"

"OH NO!"

The other problem with cremation is that if you are scattered around, there is no place for the kids to go to feel guilty. Of course you can be cremated and kept in an urn in the living room so you're still in the middle of the action. The only problem there is that you are in a FUCKING URN.

But I have heard some lovely things about cremation. A good friend of mine, seventy-two years old, lost his wife a few years ago. What she loved more than anything in the world was tending to her roses. After she was cremated, he sprinkled her ashes on her flower bed. The next spring, when the roses bloomed, they were the most beautiful roses he had ever seen—although he swears that late at night he can hear her whisper, "Do you have a sweater? It's cold out here—would it have killed you to put a blanket over me?"

I explored other options. I researched getting laminated. Seriously. Put me in Plexiglas, lean me against the bar in the rec room with the Yankee game on, and I'll be very happy. And since the company also does trophy fish and game, why not put a smile on my face and hang me on the wall?

There is also a process where they use heated water and potassium hydroxide to liquefy the body, leaving only bones behind. Coincidentally, this is the way my grandmother made chicken soup. That's actually kind of comforting. Drop my bones in a big pot of boiling water, add a matzoh ball and an onion, and have me for the Seder. If there are any leftovers, freeze me, because if anyone gets a cold, what's better than a bowl of me?

That's a little creepy but no creepier than giving the bones to the family, which is what they recommend. This scares me because Jenny and Mike have a two-hundred-pound English mastiff. If I'm going to be buried, I want to be in a cemetery, not in the backyard.

In Georgia, they have something called Eternal Reefs. They mix your cremated body with concrete and throw you in the ocean, where you become a reef for fish. Didn't they do this to Jimmy Hoffa? Leave the dead guy, take the cannoli. (And by "they," I didn't mean the Mafia.)

Then there's freezing. The children of Ted Williams arranged to turn him into a "Pop"sicle. They hired a cryonics company that cut off Ted's head and froze it. What's the point of that? The amazing thing is, Ted's frozen head still hit .315!

Related to this is an alternative called Promession, which involves freeze-drying. You are immersed in liquid nitrogen, which makes you really brittle, and then vibrations shake your body. It sounds like a waiter with a severe haircut in a New Age restaurant telling you how you will be prepared: "Chef takes you and immerses you in a liquid nitrogen reduction, then he shakes you

apart. The meat falls right off the bone." But that's better than
what they really do. After they shake you apart, they suck all the
fluids out of you, and not in a fun way (could there be a fun way
for this to be accomplished?), then turn you into compost. I don't
want to spend the next millennium smelling like doody.

Space burial is the new thing. They shot Scotty from *Star Trek*
into outer space. But because of the high cost of space flight, they
can't send all 165 pounds of you. So they cremate you and send
three grams of your "cremains" into space. Wait a second—the
soul is supposed to weigh twenty-one grams and they're only
sending one-seventh of it into space? That means I'll have eighteen grams of soul still here on earth. Just about as much as John
Boehner.

The Neptune Society will bury you at sea. You know that
organization by another name. SEAL Team 6.

None of these options appealed to me or Janice, so we decided
to go old dead school: a plot. In a way, it's a family tradition.
Years ago, during World War II, my grandparents bought a family
plot for themselves and all of their children and their husbands
and wives, so everyone could spend eternity together in New
Jersey. Which sounds redundant. I actually like going to the cemetery, as painful as it is. The plot is on a gentle hillside, under
beautiful trees. My parents are there and all my aunts and uncles,
and it's very comforting to see everyone in the same position they
sat in at the dining room table. The plot is full now. One big happy
dead family. So, with that thought in my mind, I went shopping
for a plot.

Have you ever spent time with a burial plot salesman? I guess
we're all selling something, but how bad did you fuck up on your
SATs so that this is the job your guidance counselor recommends?
"You know something, son? Your aptitude tests show you'd be
great at selling graves." Explain that one to your folks. "Mom, Dad,
I'm going into real estate. Kinda."

This burial salesman was far too cheerful.

"Well, somebody looks mahvelous! . . . And will forever!" He shook my hand a little too hard and laughed way too loud. Then he abruptly changed tones: "How many plots do you need?"

"Just two for now—I still haven't discussed this with the kids. They may want to be on their own. We're really just looking."

"You know, we have a special this year: six plots for the price of five," he told me, producing a lovely brochure. "They make a lovely Hanukkah gift," he added.

That will go over well. "Hey, everyone, instead of taking you to Hawaii this year, I bought burial plots."

The salesman tried to convince me that now was the time to get in.

"You know, Billy, you can buy the plots for yourself and Janice and then give your family what we call 'eternity gift certificates.'"

He was starting to press me, so I tried to back him off. I'm not good when I'm pressured by a salesman. I have a John Deere tractor, two hip replacements, and a llama farm I didn't need.

"You know, I'm not dying tomorrow," I joked, starting to sweat.

"You don't know that, now, do you, Mr. C?" Mr. C? Suddenly he was a maître d' in a club I didn't want to belong to.

At this point I had to get out of the office, so I asked him to take me to see some plots. The first place he brought me to was what he called "Headliners' Haven."

"Jack Benny has a plot right there, and you're only a tombstone's throw away from Jolson," he said.

I told him I wasn't interested. Being around famous people would bring tourists, and who needs that? Isn't there a quieter place? Maybe where the opening acts are?

He said, "If you can wait a little, we have a brand-new section opening up in 2015. I could be"—he looked me in the eye—"convinced"—*wink wink*—"to hold some plots for you. It's right by our lake, wonderful view."

"WHO GIVES A FUCK ABOUT THE VIEW? I'M DEAD!"

"The view isn't for you, it's for the mourners—they like the lake."

"Yeah, well, lakes mean ducks, and ducks mean duck shit,

and I don't want mourners to have duck shit on their shoes when they come to visit. I'll smell it and start to gag."

The more I thought about it, the less I wanted to be in the ground. "The worms crawl in, the worms crawl out . . ." I asked about a mausoleum.

At this, his face brightened up.

"I've got the perfect one. White marble, very distinguished, above ground, no mold."

Now, that sounded like me. But it had to be private. When people come to visit, I don't want the paparazzi taking pictures of them at my grave. I also told him I didn't want a vault in a wall, like Marilyn Monroe. I won't like it; I can't even sleep on a plane.

He explained that the mausoleum (which looked like a marble doghouse) was "very private and very tasteful, with its own garden area."

"How much?"

"Two hundred thousand dollars . . . each. . . . More complicated, we build a vault for you both. George and Gracie are in a vault together. It's lovely."

I couldn't breathe. Before I knew it, I was running away from him through the cemetery. I ran to the lake and ripped off my clothes and dove in. As I swam, I could see a small group of mourners at a lakeside service. I emerged from the water stark naked, and a woman in black lifted her veil. "Billeee, Billeee . . . kiss me twice." Sophia Loren and I were about to make love on Jolson's tombstone when I heard, "Mr. C? Are you okay?"

"Huh? Yeah," I said meekly, distracted by my daydream. "I want to think about all this. Where do you do the service?"

"You'll love it," he said. "We have a beautiful theater—it seats two hundred."

"We'll need more room," I said.

"You can do two shows. Plus, we valet for those we recognize."

My demise started to feel too real as I imagined everyone at the service. A tidal wave of sweat moved across me.

I excused myself to wash my face. While I was in the men's

room, I realized that all I really wanted was a simple service. That and not to die. All I want is for it to be funny, for Janice to be stunning and charming, as she always is, for my friends to tell great stories. I want my kids to be strong and make people laugh, I want my grandkids not to kick the chair in front of them, for Derek Jeter to say, "He could really play," and for the service to end with an Asian girl on a unicycle who uses her feet to flip soup bowls onto her head. She does halftimes at Clipper games, and she performed at my fiftieth birthday party. It's a real crowd-pleaser. Google her—she's amazing.

While the salesman was in the office, I scooted out the back door, like a criminal on the lam in a detective movie. I got in my car and drove home. I started to think maybe I should have bought the plot. And I will someday, but not now; I'm not ready.

How can I handle my own death when I still have trouble with everyone else's? I have lost so many people I cared about. Life is like a big game of musical chairs. One by one we get eliminated, except there's no winner at the end; it's just an empty chair, a covered mirror, and a lot of leftover sponge cake.

So what does death mean to me? Death just means . . . no more. No more laughs with my brothers and friends, no more watching my kids grow older. It means no more seeing what amazing things are ahead for my grandchildren, and it means . . . no more Janice and me.

That's the hardest part. As I sit here writing and look across the room at Janice, I keep thinking of the most heartbreaking question: Which one of us will go first? It could happen that we go together; we could be like all those white-haired couples in Iowa: he's ninety-seven, she's ninety-six, they met at the state fair in 1926, he dies in bed, and an hour later she just slips away so she can be with him for eternity. But chances are, one of us will go and the other will live on.

So that's what it comes to. I can't bear to think of life without Janice. I want to go first, because I don't want to miss her. That would be a pain far worse than any death. I don't want to miss the way she makes me laugh. I don't want to miss waking up and realizing she's holding my hand while she quietly sleeps. I don't want to miss hugging her when nothing else in the world makes sense. I don't want to miss her finishing my sentences because we're thinking the same thing. I would rather be gone than have to miss her. I won't buy the plot right now, because I can't. I'm going to just go on and keep living and laughing and loving. I'd like to think there is a heaven and it starts from the happiest day in your life. I'll be eighteen and Janice Goldfinger will walk by me in a bikini, and I will follow her and it will start all over again. I'd really like to think that.

Epilogue

March 14, 2013, the evening of my sixty-fifth birthday. We were having a small dinner party in the dining room at my daughter Lindsay's house while she was in her bedroom having big labor pains.

A few hours later my fourth grandchild and second grandson, Griffin, was born.

I had told Lindsay no gifts, but you know kids, they never listen. "Do something special" my mom always said about my birthday. It doesn't get any more special than this.

The day that started with angst ended with me holding the greatest treasure one can ever receive: a healthy, beautiful baby. This little guy and I will be forever united by our birthday.

Once we got home from the hospital, I got into bed just after two A.M., and I did something I don't usually do in the dark—I smiled.

It is a great life with plenty more to go, I hope. Time to see

how my little ones fare in the world we turn over to them. That
is our task after all. Get them ready for the rain. Teach them all
we know and help them try to be better than us. That is my job
as I begin my sixty-sixth trip around the sun. And yours . . . fly
safe . . . wait a second . . .

HOLY SHIT! I found my keys!

"Happy Birthday to Us, Happy Birthday to Us . . ."
3-14-1948 meets 3-14-2013,
the greatest gift of all.

Acknowledgments

After I retired from the Yankees, I didn't know what to do with myself. As I approached my sixty-fifth birthday, I thought it would be great fun to go out on tour and do stand-up again. I'd talk about all the things that were going on in my head and to my body as I neared the milestone. Inspired, I started writing, and after I had sixty funny pages or so, I read them aloud as if it were a performance. Instead it felt like a book. Here are the people who agreed with me:

Simon Green at CAA was a pleasure to deal with, and his knowledge of the book world was essential. Thanks to Steve Rubin at Henry Holt, who believed in the material and his wardrobe, and to Gillian Blake—so smart, so easy to work with, who pushed me to be better. To the production team at Holt for their talents and for being so open to ideas. To my managers, David Steinberg and Larry Brezner, for their expertise, friendship, and unwavering support all these thirty-nine years. To those named in the book throughout the chapters of my life: each one of you is an important part of my ongoing tour de chance. For those not named—or named but Gillian cut you out or wouldn't let me wax on—I'll name you now. John Goodman, John Lassiter, and all the genius folks at Pixar; the backstage crew at the Oscars and my writing team all stars, Jon Macks, Dave Boone, Ed Driscoll, and Billy Martin. Thanks to Troy Miller, Dan Butz, and the talented group at Dakota Films for magically putting me in all those nominated films, and to Mike Seligman for always finding the dough. To Barry, Wanda, and maestro Giorgio Armani's beautiful designs and his ability to make me look taller. To Manny Kladitis and my Broadhurst Theatre family; it was an honor to walk that stage.

Al and Michael Shedler, Steve Tenenbaum, Cindi Berger, Heidi Schaeffer, and Sol Rosenthal for doing things the right way. To Richard Lovett and Jimmy Darmody for their guidance as we keep moving forward. To the Los Angeles Clippers for giving me something to cheer about. To Jimmy Walker and Lonnie Ali and the support of my friends at Fight Night in Phoenix, Arizona.

To Sid Caesar, Mel Brooks, Carl Reiner, Neil Simon, and the late Larry Gelbart for their genius, inspiration, and friendship. To my entire family, especially my brothers Joel and Rip, who are the only ones to witness all of my sixty-five years, much love to you all. To my fans: your support during my career is everything, and I'll try and tweet more often. Finally, to my grandchildren, Ella, Dylan, Hudson, and Griffin: if I forget to tell you some of these stories, you'll always have this book.

About the Author

BILLY CRYSTAL is a comedian, actor, producer, director, author, and nine-time Oscars host. He has starred in many hit films, among them *When Harry Met Sally . . .*, *City Slickers*, and *Analyze This*. He is the author of two children's books and the Tony Award–winning play *700 Sundays*, about his relationship with his late father, which was later adapted into a book. A former cast member of *Saturday Night Live*, Crystal is a six-time Emmy winner and a recipient of the Mark Twain Prize for American Humor. He lives in Los Angeles with his wife, Janice.